The
LANGUAGE
of
CLOTHES

ALISON LURIE

with illustrations assembled
by Doris Palca

Vintage Books
A Division Of Random House
New York

The
LANGUAGE
of
CLOTHES

First Vintage Books Edition, November 1983
Published in the United States by Random House, Inc., New York, and
simultaneously in Canada by Random House of Canada Limited, Toronto. Originally
published by Random House, Inc. in 1981.

Grateful acknowledgment is made to the following for permission
to reprint previously published material:
Harcourt Brace Jovanovich, Inc. and Faber & Faber Limited: Two lines
from "The Love Song of J. Alfred Prufrock" in Collected Poems 1909–1962 by T. S.
Eliot, copyright 1936 by Harcourt Brace Jovanovich, Inc.; copyright © 1963,
1964 by T. S. Eliot. Reprinted by permissions of Harcourt Brace Jovanovich,
Inc. and Faber & Faber Limited.
University of Pennsylvania Press: Excerpt from "Honky-Tonk Bud," from
The Life: The Lore and Folk Poetry of the Black Hustler by Dennis Wepman et al., 1976.
Reprinted by permission of University of Pennsylvania Press.

Library of Congress Cataloging in Publication Data
Lurie, Alison.
The language of clothes.
Bibliography: p.
1. Clothing and dress—Social aspects.
2. Fashion—Social aspects.
I. Title.
GT525.L87 1983   391   83-47804
ISBN 0-394-71713-9

Manufactured in the United States of America

BOOK DESIGN BY LILLY LANGOTSKY

For Ted,
and for Alfred

PREFACE

To write a comprehensive history of the language of clothes would take immense learning and far more than one volume. All I can do here is to suggest some of the sorts of information that can be conveyed by dress, and some of the rules that seem to be operating. Books and articles on the psychological and sociological aspects of clothing often contain perceptive comments, some of which are reported or quoted here. Among the many excellent writers on these subjects, the best seem to me to be Quentin Bell, Prudence Glynn, Anne Hollander, the late James Laver and Geoffrey Squire. Their works, which are a pleasure to read as well as highly original and often brilliant, are listed in the bibliography.

As an amateur in the history of costume I have had to rely for my facts on the work of professionals. I am especially indebted to Ernestine Carter's *The Changing World of Fashion*, Rachel H. Kemper's *Costume*, James Laver's *The Concise History of Costume and Fashion*, Geoffrey Squire's *Dress and Society* and Doreen Yarwood's *The Encyclopaedia of World Costume*, all of which also contain interesting and often profound insights into the meaning of clothes.

When it came to finding examples of specific garments and styles that indicated their wearers' age, class, origin, opinions and moods, the histories of costume could not be consulted. Luckily, however, there was already on record an immense amount of data, recorded over several hundred years by men and women of unusual perception and expressive skill: British and American novelists and playwrights. Everyone recalls the classic cases—Miss Havisham in her ancient wedding gown, Gatsby displaying his collection of luxurious shirts—but in fact most of the great novels and plays are full of such material. In some cases, unfortunately, their authors assumed that everyone would know what was conveyed by a certain style or garment, and their insights are now lost; often, however, the meaning remains clear. I have let these experts speak for me whenever possible in the chapters that follow.

Once they begin to think about it, everyone knows that clothes mean something, and many of the best observations in this book have come from people with whom I discussed the project. I should especially like to thank Joshua Bishop, Alexander Cockburn, Betsy and Ronald Dworkin, Barbara Epstein, David Jackson, Melanie Jackson, Diane Johnson, Louis Lapham, Diana Melly, James Merrill, Lady Antonia Pinter, Hilary Rubinstein, Dan Schwartz and John Stallworthy. Joe Fox of Random House and Roland Gant and Nigel Hollis of Heinemann not only provided much fascinating information but showed remarkable patience when my finished manuscript kept getting longer and longer and therefore later and later. I am also most grateful to my gifted copy editor, Jean McNutt, whose care and expertise prevented many errors.

Finding the illustrations for a book like this and getting all the facts right is a complicated and sometimes tiresome job that makes demands on the tolerance of both friends and strangers. On behalf of Doris Palca as well as myself I should like to thank all those who helped us locate pictures, check references, find books and type manuscripts and letters, especially Arthur and Audrey Abeles, Pat Ballou, Phil Blumberg, Martin Bondell, Tania Butler, Kit Callahan, Susan Ebersole, Sally Fisher, May FitzGerald, Jane Freeman, Julie Galant, Susan Kramarsky, Zachary Leader, Jim Mairs, Fred McDarrah, Anne Munroe, Julia Palca, Marcia Panama,

Naomi Pascal, Mary Pettman, Michael Peyser, Naomi Rosenblum, Polly and Stephen Rubin, Wendy Shadwell, Gordon Stone, Hope Smith, Sheila Smith, Jerry L. Thompson, René Tweitmann, Ira Tulipan, Roberta Valente, Anne Wallach, Wendy Warnken and Marjorie Welish. Above all we are grateful for the existence of the library of the Fashion Institute of Technology in New York: its kind and knowledgeable staff, fine collection, agreeable working conditions and generous hours.

Our special thanks go to those who lent us their family photographs and gave permission for them to be used in this book, among them Barbara Deming, Roland Gant, Lynn Hoffman, Diane Johnson, Mary Mills, Lady Antonia Pinter, Alison Shank and Dee Wells.

CONTENTS

The
LANGUAGE
of
CLOTHES

CLOTHING AS A
SIGN SYSTEM

Clothes are inevitable. They are nothing less than the furniture of the mind made visible.

—James Laver, *Style in Costume*

For thousands of years human beings have communicated with one another first in the language of dress. Long before I am near enough to talk to you on the street, in a meeting, or at a party, you announce your sex, age and class to me through what you are wearing—and very possibly give me important information (or misinformation) as to your occupation, origin, personality, opinions, tastes, sexual desires and current mood. I may not be able to put what I observe into words, but I register the information unconsciously; and you simultaneously do the same for me. By the time we meet and converse we have already spoken to each other in an older and more universal tongue.

The statement that clothing is a language, though occasionally made with the air of a man finding a flying saucer in his backyard, is not new. Balzac, in *Daughter of Eve* (1839), observed that for a woman dress is "a continual manifestation of intimate thoughts, a language, a symbol." Today, as semiotics becomes fashionable, sociologists tell us that fashion too is a language of signs, a nonverbal system of communication. The French structuralist Roland Barthes, for instance, in "The Diseases of Costume," speaks of theatrical dress as a kind of writing, of which the basic element is the sign.

None of these theorists, however, have gone on to remark what seems obvious: that if clothing is a language, it must have a vocabulary and a grammar like other languages. Of course, as with human speech, there is not a single language of dress, but many: some (like Dutch and German) closely related and others (like Basque) almost unique. And within every language of clothes there are many different dialects and accents, some almost unintelligible to members of the mainstream culture. Moreover, as with speech, each individual has his own stock of words and employs personal variations of tone and meaning.

"It's a look I believe in."

In the language of dress, as with speech, each individual has his own stock of "words" and employs personal variations of tone and meaning. Cartoon by Koren. Copyright © 1978, The New Yorker Magazine, Inc.

THE VOCABULARY OF FASHION

The vocabulary of dress includes not only items of clothing, but also hair styles, accessories, jewelry, make-up and body decoration. Theoretically at least this vocabulary is as large as or larger than that of any spoken tongue, since it includes every garment, hair style, and type of body decoration ever invented. In practice, of course, the sartorial resources of an individual may be very restricted. Those of a sharecropper, for instance, may be limited to five or ten "words" from which it is possible to create only a few "sentences" almost bare of decoration and expressing only the most basic concepts. A so-called fashion leader, on the other hand, may have several hundred "words" at his or her disposal, and thus be able to form thousands of different "sentences" that will express a wide range of meanings. Just as the average English-speaking person knows many more words than he or she will ever use in conversation, so all of us are able to understand the meaning of styles we will never wear.

To choose clothes, either in a store or at home, is to define and describe ourselves. Occasionally, of course, practical considerations enter into these choices: considerations of comfort, durability, availability and price. Especially in the case of persons of limited wardrobe, an article may be worn because it is warm or rainproof or handy to cover up a wet bathing suit—in the same way that persons of limited vocabulary use the phrase "you know" or adjectives such as "great" or "fantastic." Yet, just as with spoken language, such choices usually give us some information, even if it is only equivalent to the statement "I don't give a damn what I look like today." And there are limits even here. In this

The sartorial vocabulary of some people is very limited. A sharecropper, for instance, may be limited to five or ten "words," or garments, from which it is possible to create only a few "sentences," or costumes, expressing only the most basic concepts. An Ozark mountain family in 1940. Photograph by John Vachon.

culture, like many others, certain garments are taboo for certain persons. Most men, however cold or wet they might be, would not put on a woman's dress, just as they would not use words and phrases such as "simply marvelous," which in this culture are considered specifically feminine.

ARCHAIC WORDS

Besides containing "words" that are taboo, the language of clothes, like speech, also includes modern and ancient words, words of native and foreign origin, dialect words, colloquialisms, slang and vulgarities. Genuine articles of clothing from the past (or skillful imitations) are used in the same way a writer or speaker might use archaisms: to give an air of culture, erudition or wit. Just as in educated discourse, such "words" are usually employed sparingly, most often one at a time—a single Victorian cameo or a pair of 1940s platform shoes or an Edwardian velvet waistcoat, never a complete costume. A whole outfit composed of archaic items from a single period, rather than projecting elegance and sophistication, will imply that one is on one's way to a masquerade, acting in a play or film or putting oneself on display for advertising purposes. Mixing garments from several different periods of the past, on the other hand, suggests a confused but intriguingly "original" theatrical personality. It is therefore often fashionable in those sections of the art and entertainment industry in which instant celebrities are manufactured and sold.

When using archaic words, it is essential to choose ones that are decently old. The sight of a white plastic Courrèges miniraincoat and boots (in 1963 the height of fashion) at a gallery opening or theater today would produce the same shiver of ridicule and revulsion as the use of words such as "groovy," "Negro," or "self-actualizing."

In Taste and Fashion, one of the best books ever written on costume, the late James Laver proposed a timetable to explain such reactions; this has come to be known as Laver's Law. According to him, the same costume will be

Indecent	10 years before its time
Shameless	5 years before its time
Daring	1 year before its time
Smart	
Dowdy	1 year after its time
Hideous	10 years after its time
Ridiculous	20 years after its time
Amusing	30 years after its time
Quaint	50 years after its time
Charming	70 years after its time
Romantic	100 years after its time
Beautiful	150 years after its time

A mixture of modern, archaic, native and foreign garments can suggest either creative originality or mental confusion. Note the man's Indian (or possibly Greek) shawl and the woman's contemporary white ankle socks. Members of the audience at an outdoor music festival, 1969. Photograph by Ken Heyman.

Laver possibly overemphasizes the shock value of incoming fashion, which today may be seen merely as weird or ugly. And of course he is speaking of the complete outfit, or "sentence." The speed with which a single "word" passes in and out of fashion can vary, just as in spoken and written languages.

FOREIGN WORDS

The appearance of foreign garments in an otherwise indigenous costume is similar in function to the use of foreign words or phrases in standard English speech. This phenomenon, which is common in certain circles, may have several different meanings.

First, of course, it can be a deliberate sign of national origin in someone who otherwise, sartorially or linguistically speaking, has no accent. Often this message is expressed through headgear. The Japanese-American lady in Western dress but with an elaborate Oriental hairdo, or the Oxford-educated Arab who tops his Savile Row suit with a turban, are telling us graphically that they have not been psychologically assimilated; that their ideas and opinions remain those of an Asian. As a result we tend to see the non-European in Western dress with native headgear or hairdo as dignified, even formidable; while the reverse outfit

—the Oriental lady in a kimono and a plastic rain hat, or the sheik in native robes and a black bowler—appears comic. Such costumes seem to announce that their wearers, though not physically at ease in our country, have their heads full of half-baked Western ideas. It would perhaps be well for Anglo-American tourists to keep this principle in mind when traveling to exotic places. Very possibly the members of a package tour in Mexican sombreros or Russian bearskin hats look equally ridiculous and weak-minded to the natives of the countries they are visiting.

More often the wearing of a single foreign garment, like the dropping of a foreign word or phrase in conversation, is meant not to advertise foreign origin or allegiance but to indicate sophistication. It can also be a means of advertising wealth. When we see a fancy Swiss watch, we know that its owner either bought it at home for three times the price of a good English or American watch, or else he or she spent even more money traveling to Switzerland.

SLANG AND VULGAR WORDS

Casual dress, like casual speech, tends to be loose, relaxed and colorful. It often contains what might be called "slang words": blue jeans, sneakers, baseball caps, aprons, flowered cotton housedresses and the like. These garments could not be worn on a formal occasion without causing disapproval, but in ordinary circumstances they pass without remark. "Vulgar words" in dress, on the other hand, give emphasis and get immediate attention in almost any circumstances, just as they do in speech. Only the skillful can employ them without some loss of face, and even then they must be used in the right way. A torn, unbuttoned shirt, or wildly un-combed hair, can signify strong emotions: passion, grief, rage, despair. They are most effective if people already think of you as being neatly dressed, just as the curses of well-spoken persons count for more than those of the customarily foul-mouthed.

Items of dress that are the sartorial equivalent of forbidden words have more impact when they appear seldom and

Though in a casual situation worn or untidy clothing, like casual dress, may seem appropriate, in a formal urban setting it instantly marks its wearer as a person of low status. Green Park, London, just outside the Ritz Hotel. Photograph by Ernst Haas.

as if by accident. The Edwardian lady, lifting her heavy floor-length skirt to board a tram, appeared unaware that she was revealing a froth of lacy petticoats and embroidered black stockings. Similarly, today's braless executive woman, leaning over her desk at a conference, may affect not to know that her nipples show through her silk blouse. Perhaps she does not know it consciously; we are here in the ambiguous region of intention vs. interpretation which has given so much trouble to linguists.

In speech, slang terms and vulgarities may eventually become respectable dictionary words; the same thing is true of colloquial and vulgar fashions. Garments or styles that enter the fashionable vocabulary from a colloquial source usually have a longer life span than those that begin as vulgarities. Thigh-high patent leather boots, first worn by the most obvious variety of rentable female as a sign that she was willing to help act out certain male fantasies, shot with relative speed into and out of high fashion; while blue jeans made their way upward much more gradually from work clothes to casual to business and formal wear, and are still engaged in a slow descent.

ADJECTIVES AND ADVERBS:
THE DECORATED STYLE OF DRESS

Though the idea is attractive, it does not seem possible to equate different articles of clothing with the different parts of speech. A case can be made, however, for considering trimmings and accessories as adjectives or adverbs—modifiers in the sentence that is the total outfit—but it must be remembered that one era's trimmings and accessories are another's essential parts of the costume. At one time shoes were actually fastened with buckles, and the buttons on the sleeves of a suit jacket were used to secure turned-up cuffs. Today such buttons, or the linked brass rods on a pair of Gucci shoes, are purely vestigial and have no useful function. If they are missing, however, the jacket or the shoes are felt to be damaged and unfit for wear.

Accessories, too, may be considered essential to an outfit. In the 1940s and 1950s, for instance, a woman was not properly dressed unless she wore gloves. Emily Post, among many others, made this clear:

> Always wear gloves, of course, in church, and also on the street. A really smart woman wears them outdoors always, even in the country. Always wear gloves in a restaurant, in a theatre, when you go to lunch, or to a formal dinner, or to a dance. . . . A lady never takes off her gloves to shake hands, no matter when or where. . . . On formal occasions she should *put gloves on* to shake hands with a hostess or with her own guests.

If we consider only those accessories and trimmings that are currently optional, however, we may reasonably speak of them as modifiers. It then becomes possible to distinguish an elaborately decorated style of dress from a simple and plain one, whatever the period. As in speech, it is harder to communicate well in a highly decorated style, though when this is done successfully the result may be very impressive. A costume loaded with accessories and trimmings can easily appear cluttered, pretentious or confusing. Very rarely the whole becomes greater than its many parts, and the total effect is luxurious, elegant and often highly sensual.

THE CHANGING VOCABULARY OF FASHION

As writers on costume have often pointed out, the average individual above the poverty line has many more clothes than he needs to cover his body, even allowing for washing and changes of weather. Moreover, we often discard garments that show little or no wear and purchase new ones. What is the reason for this? Some have claimed that it is all the result of brainwashing by commercial interests. But the conspiracy theory of fashion change—the idea that the adoption of new styles is simply the result of a plot by greedy designers and manufacturers and fashion editors—has, I think, less foundation than is generally believed. Certainly the fashion industry might like us to throw away all our clothes each year and buy a whole new wardrobe, but it has never been able to achieve this goal. For one thing, it is not true that the public will wear anything suggested to it, nor has it ever been true. Ever since fashion became big business, designers have proposed a bewildering array of styles every season. A few of these have been selected or adapted by manufacturers for mass production, but only a certain proportion of them have caught on.

As James Laver has remarked, modes are but the reflection of the manners of the time; they are the mirror, not the original. Within the limits imposed by economics, clothes are acquired, used and discarded just as words are, because they meet our needs and express our ideas and emotions. All the exhortations of experts on language cannot save outmoded terms of speech or persuade people to use new ones "correctly." In the same way, those garments that reflect what we are or want to be at the moment will be purchased and worn, and those that do not will not, however frantically they may be ballyhooed.

In the past, gifted artists of fashion from Worth to Mary Quant have been able to make inspired guesses about what people will want their clothes to say each year. Today a few designers seem to have retained this ability, but many others have proved to be as hopelessly out of touch as designers in the American auto industry. The classic case is that of the maxiskirt, a style which made women look older and heavier and impeded their movements at a time (1969) when youth, slimness and energy were at the height of their vogue. The maxiskirt was introduced with tremendous fanfare and not a little deception. Magazines and newspapers printed (sometimes perhaps unknowingly) photos of New York and London street scenes populated with hired models in long skirts disguised as passers-by, to give readers in Podunk and Lesser Puddleton the impression that the capitals had capitulated. But these strenuous efforts were in vain: the maxiskirt failed miserably, producing well-deserved financial disaster for its backers.

The fashion industry is no more able to preserve a style that men and women have decided to abandon than to introduce one they do not choose to accept. In America, for instance, huge advertising budgets and the wholehearted cooperation of magazines such as *Vogue* and *Esquire* have not been able to save the hat, which for centuries was an essential part of everyone's outdoor (and often of their indoor) costume. It survives now mainly as a utilitarian protection against weather, as part of ritual dress (at formal weddings, for example) or as a sign of age or individual eccentricity.

PERSONAL FASHION: SITUATION AND SELF

As with speech, the meaning of any costume depends on circumstances. It is not "spoken" in a vacuum, but at a specific place and time, any change in which may alter its meaning. Like the remark "Let's get on with this damn business," the two-piece tan business suit and boldly striped shirt and tie that signify energy and determination in the office will have quite another resonance at a funeral or picnic.

According to Irving Goffman, the concept of "proper dress" is totally dependent on situation. To wear the costume considered "proper" for a situation acts as a sign of involvement in it, and the person whose clothes do not conform to these standards is likely to be more or less subtly excluded from participation. When other signs of deep involvement are present, rules about proper dress may be waived. Persons who have just escaped from a fire or flood are not censured for wearing pajamas or having uncombed hair; someone bursting into a formal social occasion to announce important news is excused for being in jeans and T-shirt.

In language we distinguish between someone who speaks a sentence well—clearly, and with confidence and dignity—and someone who speaks it badly. In dress too, manner is as important as matter, and in judging the meaning of any garment we will automatically consider whether it fits well or is too large or too small; whether it is old or new; and especially whether it is in good condition, slightly rumpled and soiled or crushed and filthy. Cleanliness may not always be next to godliness, but it is usually regarded as a sign of respectability or at least of self-respect. It is also a sign of status, since to be clean and neat always involves the expense of time and money.

In a few circles, of course, disregard for cleanliness has been considered a virtue. Saint Jerome's remark that "the purity of the body and its garments means the impurity of the soul" inspired generations of unwashed and smelly hermits. In the sixties some hippies and mystics scorned overly clean and tidy dress as a sign of compromise with the Establishment and too great an attachment to the things of this world. There is also a more widespread rural and small-town dislike of the person whose clothes are too clean, slick and smooth. He—or, less often, she—is suspected of being untrustworthy, a smoothie or a city slicker.

As with speech, the meaning of any costume depends on who "says" it and the circumstances in which it appears. When ordinary clothes are worn in disreputable surroundings, the effect is to mock, shock or offend establishment values. James Dean, 1954. Photograph by Dennis Stock.

In general, however, to wear dirty, rumpled or torn clothing is to invite scorn and condescension. This reaction is ancient; indeed it goes back beyond the dawn of humanity. In most species, a strange animal in poor condition—mangy, or with matted and muddy fur—is more likely to be attacked by other animals. In the same way, shabbily dressed people are more apt to be treated shabbily. A man in a clean, well-pressed suit who falls down in a central London or Manhattan street is likely to be helped up sooner than one in filthy tatters.

At certain times and places—a dark night, a deserted alley—dirt and rags, like mumbled or growled speech, may be alarming. In Dickens's *Great Expectations* they are part of the terror the boy Pip feels when he first sees the convict Magwitch in the graveyard: "A fearful man, all in coarse grey, with a great iron on his leg. A man with no hat, and with broken shoes, and with an old rag tied round his head."

A costume not only appears at a specific place and time, it must be "spoken"—that is, worn—by a specific person. Even a simple statement like "I want a drink," or a simple costume—shorts and T-shirt, for example—will have a very different aspect in association with a sixty-year-old man, a sixteen-year-old girl and a six-year-old child. But age and sex are not the only variables to be considered. In judging a costume we will also take into account the physical attributes of the person who is wearing it, assessing him or her in terms of height, weight, posture, racial or ethnic type and facial features and expression. The same outfit will look different on a person whose face and body we consider attractive and on one whom we think ugly. Of course, the idea of "attractiveness" itself is not only subjective, but subject to the historical and geographical vagaries of fashion, as Sir Kenneth Clark has demonstrated in *The Nude.* In twentieth-century Britain and America, for instance, weight above the norm has been considered unattractive and felt to detract from dignity and status; as Emily Post put it in 1922, "The tendency of fat is to take away from one's gentility; therefore, any one inclined to be fat must be ultra conservative—in order to counteract the effect." The overweight person who does not follow this rule is in danger of appearing vulgar or even revolting. In Conrad's *Lord Jim* the shame of the corrupt Dutch captain is underlined by the fact that, though grossly fat, he wears orange-and-green-striped pajamas in public.

ECCENTRIC AND CONVENTIONAL SPEECH

In dress as in language there is a possible range of expression from the most eccentric statement to the most conventional. At one end of the spectrum is the outfit of which the individual parts or "words" are highly incongruent, marking its wearer (if not on stage or involved in some natural disaster) as very peculiar or possibly deranged. Imagine for instance

Certain costumes are the equivalent of a conventional statement or a cliché. Such an outfit follows some established style in every particular, and identifies its wearer as a member of some recognized social group. Advertisement for British Rail, 1978.

BUSINESS TRAVELLERS
Standard tickets and Executive packages.

WEEKENDERS
Weekend Returns and mini-holiday packages.

HOLIDAYMAKERS AND FAMILIES
Monthly and Economy Returns. Golden Rail Holidays. Children's fares.

STUDENTS
Railcards.

DAYTRIPPERS
Awaydays and other local off-peak fares.

SENIOR CITIZENS
Railcards.

REGULAR TRAVELLERS
Season tickets – Weekly, Monthly, Quarterly and Annual.

a transparent sequined evening blouse over a dirty Victorian cotton petticoat and black rubber galoshes. (I have observed this getup in real life; it was worn to a lunch party at a famous Irish country house.) If the same costume were worn by a man, or if the usual grammatical order of the sentence were altered—one of the galoshes placed upside down on the head, for example—the effect of insanity would be even greater.

At the opposite end of the spectrum is the costume that is the equivalent of a cliché; it follows some established style in every particular and instantly establishes its wearer as a doctor, a debutante, a hippie or a whore. Such outfits are not uncommon, for as two British sociologists have remarked, "Identification with and active participation in a social group always involves the human body and its adornment and clothing." The more significant any social role is for an individual, the more likely he or she is to dress for it. When two roles conflict, the costume will either reflect the more important one or it will combine them, sometimes with incongruous effects, as in the case of the secretary whose sober, efficient-looking dark suit only partly conceals a tight, bright, low-cut blouse.

Teenagers in blue jeans are almost identical below the waist, but above it they may wear anything from a T-shirt to an embroidered blouse. Grammatically, this costume seems to be a sign that in their lower or physical natures they are alike, however dissimiliar they may be socially or culturally.

The cliché outfit may in some cases become so standardized that it is spoken of as a "uniform": the pin-striped suit, bowler and black umbrella of the London City man, for instance, or the blue jeans and T-shirts of high-school students. Usually, however, these costumes only look like uniforms to outsiders; peers will be aware of significant differences. The London businessman's tie will tell his associates where he went to school; the cut and fabric of his suit will allow them to guess at his income. High-school students, in a single glance, can distinguish new jeans from those that are fashionably worn, functionally or decoratively patched or carelessly ragged; they grasp the fine distinctions of meaning conveyed by straight-leg, flared, boot-cut and peg-top. When two pairs of jeans are identical to the naked eye a label handily affixed to the back pocket gives useful information, identifying the garment as expensive (so-called designer jeans) or discount-department-store. And even within the latter category there are distinctions: in our local junior high school, according to a native informant, "freaks always wear Lees, greasers wear Wranglers, and everyone else wears Levis."

Of course, to the careful observer all these students are only identical below the waist; above it they may wear anything from a lumberjack shirt to a lace blouse. Grammatically, this costume seems to be a sign that in their lower or physical natures these persons are alike, however dissimilar they may be socially, intellectually or aesthetically. If this is so, the opposite statement can be imagined—and was actually made by my own college classmates thirty years ago. During the daytime we wore identical baggy sweaters over a wide variety of slacks, plaid kilts, full cotton or straight tweed or slinky jersey skirts, ski pants and Bermuda shorts. "We're all nice coeds from the waist up; we think and talk alike," this costume proclaimed, "but as women we are infinitely various."

THE UNIFORM

The extreme form of conventional dress is the costume totally determined by others: the uniform. No matter what sort of uniform it is—military, civil or religious; the outfit of a general, a postman, a nun, a butler, a football player or a waitress—to put on such livery is to give up one's right to act as an individual—in terms of speech, to be partially or wholly censored. What one does, as well as what one wears, will be determined by external authorities—to a greater or lesser degree, depending upon whether one is, for example, a Trappist monk or a boy scout. The uniform acts as a sign that we should not or need not treat someone as a human being, and that they need not and should not treat us as one. It is no accident that people in uniform, rather than speaking to us honestly and straightforwardly, often repeat mechanical lies. "It was a pleasure having you on board," they say; "I cannot give you that information"; or "The doctor will see you shortly."

Constant wearing of official costume can so transform someone that it becomes difficult or impossible for him or her to react normally. Dr. Grantly, the archdeacon in Anthony Trollope's *The Warden* (1855), is pious and solemn even when alone with his wife: " 'Tis only when he has exchanged that ever-new shovel hat for a tasselled nightcap, and those shining black habiliments for his accustomed *robe de nuit,* that Dr. Grantly talks, and looks, and thinks like an ordinary man."

Though the uniform is supposed to transform individuals into homogeneous members of a group, it can never do so completely—especially when there is a conflict between the requirements of the organization and those of fashion. Sea Scouts, S. S. Endeavor *Post 601, California, in the era of the miniskirt. Photograph by Bill Owens, 1968.*

To take off a uniform is usually a relief, just as it is a relief to abandon official speech; sometimes it is also a sign of defiance. When the schoolgirls in Flannery O'Connor's story "A Temple of the Holy Ghost" come home on holiday, she writes that "They came in the brown convent uniforms they had to wear at Mount St. Scholastica but as soon as they opened their suitcases, they took off the uniforms and put on red skirts and loud blouses. They put on lipstick and their Sunday shoes and walked around in the high heels all over the house."

In certain circumstances, however, putting on a uniform may be a relief, or even an agreeable experience. It can ease the transition from one role to another, as Anthony Powell points out in *Faces in My Time* when he describes joining the British Army in 1939:

> Complete forgetfulness was needed of all that had constituted one's life only a few weeks before. This condition of mind was helped by the anonymity of uniform, something which has to be experienced to be appreciated; in one sense more noticeable off duty in such environments as railway carriages or bars.

It is also true that both physical and psychological disadvantage can be concealed by a uniform, or even canceled out; the robes of a judge or a surgeon may successfully hide a scrawny physique or fears of incompetence, giving him or her both dignity and confidence.

Unlike most civilian clothing, the uniform is often consciously and deliberately symbolic. It identifies its wearer as a member of some group and often locates him or her within a hierarchy; sometimes it gives information about his or her achievements, as do the merit badges of a scout and the battle ribbons of a general. Even when some details of an official costume are not dictated from above, they may by custom come to have a definite meaning. James Laver remarks that in Britain

> until quite recently it was still possible to deduce a clergyman's religious opinions from his neckwear. If you wore an ordinary collar with a white tie you were probably Low Church and Evangelical. If you wore any version of the Roman collar you displayed your sympathy with the . . . Oxford Movement.

It is likely that when they were first designed all uniforms made symbolic sense and were as easy to "read" as the outfit of a *Playboy* Bunny today. But official costume tends to freeze the styles of the time in which it was invented, and today the sixteenth-century uniforms of the guards at the Tower of London or the late-Edwardian morning dress of the butler may merely seem old-fashioned to us. Military uniforms, as James Laver points out, were originally intended "to impress and even to terrify the enemy" in hand-to-hand combat (just like the war whoops and battle cries that accompanied them), and warriors accordingly disguised themselves as devils, skeletons and wild beasts. Even after gunpowder made this style of fighting rare, the desire to terrify "survived into modern times in such vestigial forms as the death's head on the hussar's headgear and the bare ribs of the skeleton originally painted on the warrior's body and later transformed into the froggings of his tunic."

To wear a uniform is to give up your right to free speech in the language of clothes; instead you are forced to repeat dialogue composed by someone else. In the extreme case you become part of a mass of identical persons, all of whom are, as it were, shouting the same words at the same time. Photograph by Ken Heyman, 1956.

The wearing of a uniform by people who are obviously not carrying out the duties it involves has often suggested personal laxity—as in the case of drunken soldiers carousing in the streets. In this century, however, it has been adopted as a form of political protest, and both men and women have appeared at rallies and marches in their Army, Navy, or police uniforms, the implied statement being "I'm a soldier, but I support disarmament/open housing/gay rights,'' etc. A related development in the 1960s was the American hippie custom of wearing parts of old Army uniforms—Civil War, World War I and World War II. This military garb puzzled many observers, especially when it appeared in anti-Vietnam demonstrations. Others understood the implicit message, which was that the longhaired kid in the Confederate tunic or the Eisenhower jacket was not some kind of coward or sissy; that he was not against all wars—just against the cruel and unnecessary one he was in danger of being drafted into.

ELOQUENCE AND BAD TASTE

Between cliché and madness in the language of dress are all the known varieties of speech: eloquence, wit, information, irony, propaganda, humor, pathos and even (though rarely) true poetry. Just as a gifted writer combines unexpected words and images, risking (and sometimes briefly gaining) the reputation of being deranged, so certain gifted persons have been able to combine odd items of clothing, old and new, native and foreign, into a brilliant eloquence of personal statement. While other people merely follow the style of the age in which they live, these men and women transform contemporary fashion into individual expression. Some of their achievements are celebrated in the history of costume, but here, as in all the arts, there must be many unknown geniuses.

Unfortunately, just as there are more no-talent artists than there are genuises, there are also many persons who do not dress very well, not because of lack of money but because of innate lack of taste. In some cases their clothes are merely monotonous, suggesting an uninteresting but consistent personality. Others seem to have a knack for combining colors, patterns and styles in a way that—rightly or wrongly—suggests personal awkwardness and disharmony. In Henry James's *The Bostonians* (1886), the bad taste in clothes of the heroine, Verena Tarrant, foreshadows her moral confusion and her bad taste in men. Verena, who has bright-red hair, makes her first public appearance wearing "a light-brown dress, of a shape that struck [Basil Ransom] as fantastic, a yellow petticoat, and a large crimson sash fastened at the side; while round her neck, and falling low upon her flat young chest, she had a double chain of amber beads." And, as if this were not enough, Verena also carried "a large red fan, which she kept constantly in movement."

Like any elaborate nonverbal language, costume is sometimes more eloquent than the native speech of its wearers. Indeed, the more inarticulate someone is verbally, the more important are the statements made by his or her clothes. People who are skilled in verbal discourse, on the other hand, can afford to be somewhat careless or dull in their dress, as in the case of certain teachers and politicians. Even they, of course, are telling us something, but they may not be telling us very much.

OTHER PEOPLE'S CLOTHES

Men and women in uniform are not the only ones who wear clothes they have not selected themselves. All of us were first dressed in such garments, and often our late childhood and early adolescence were made stormy by our struggles to choose our own wardrobe—in verbal terms, to speak for ourselves. A few of us did not win this battle, or won only temporarily, and became those men (or, more rarely, women) most of whose clothes are selected by their wives, husbands or mothers.

All of us, however, even as adults, have at some time been the grateful or ungrateful recipients of garments bought by relatives or friends. Such a gift is a mixed blessing, for to wear clothes chosen by someone else is to accept and project their donor's image of you; in a sense, to become a ventriloquist's doll. Sometimes, of course, the gift may be welcome or flattering: the Christmas tie that is just right, the low-cut lace nightgown that encourages a woman of only moderate attractions to think of herself as a glamourpuss. Often, however, the gift is felt as a demand, and one harder to refuse because it comes disguised as a favor. When I was first married I dressed in a style that might be described as Radcliffe Beatnik (black jerseys and bright cotton-print skirts). My mother-in-law, hoping to remodel me into a nice country-club young matron, frequently presented me with tiny-collared, classically styled silk blouses and cashmere sweaters in white, beige or pale green which I never wore and could not give away because they were monogrammed.

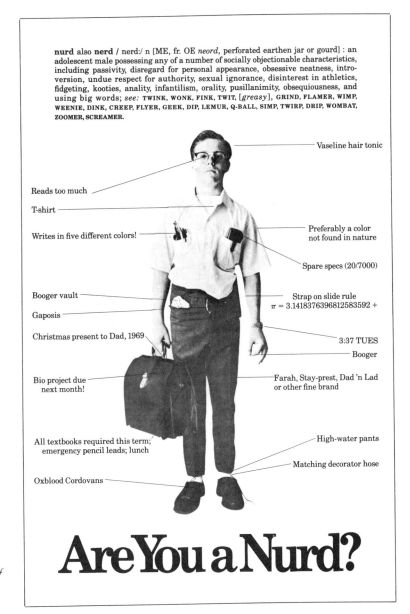

nurd also **nerd** / nerd:/ n [ME, fr. OE *neord*, perforated earthen jar or gourd] : an adolescent male possessing any of a number of socially objectionable characteristics, including passivity, disregard for personal appearance, obsessive neatness, introversion, undue respect for authority, sexual ignorance, disinterest in athletics, fidgeting, kooties, anality, infantilism, orality, pusillanimity, obsequiousness, and using big words; *see:* TWINK, WONK, FINK, TWIT, [*greasy*], GRIND, FLAMER, WIMP, WEENIE, DINK, CREEP, FLYER, GEEK, DIP, LEMUR, Q-BALL, SIMP, TWIRP, DRIP, WOMBAT, ZOOMER, SCREAMER.

Vaseline hair tonic

Reads too much

T-shirt

Writes in five different colors!

Preferably a color not found in nature

Spare specs (20/7000)

Booger vault

Gaposis

Strap on slide rule
$\pi = 3.1418376396812583592 +$

Christmas present to Dad, 1969

3:37 TUES

Booger

Bio project due next month!

Farah, Stay-prest, Dad 'n Lad or other fine brand

All textbooks required this term; emergency pencil leads; lunch

High-water pants

Matching decorator hose

Oxblood Cordovans

Are You a Nurd?

Just as some people speak awkwardly and haltingly, so some inform us by every detail of their costume that they are one of life's losers or dullards. The Nurd as a college student.

To put on someone else's clothes is symbolically to take on their personality. This is true even when one's motives are hostile. In Dickens's *Our Mutual Friend* (1864–65), the teacher Bradley Headstone disguises himself in "rough waterside second-hand clothing" and a "red neckerchief stained black . . . by wear" which are identical with those worn by Rogue Riderhood, so that Riderhood shall be blamed for the murder Headstone is planning to commit. In assuming this costume Headstone literally becomes just such a low, vicious and guilty man as Riderhood.

In this culture the innocent exchange of clothing is most common among teenage girls, who in this way confirm not only their friendship but their identity, just as they do by using the same slang and expressing the same ideas. The custom may persist into adult life, and also occurs between lovers and between husband and wife, though in the latter case the borrowing is usually one-way. The sharing of clothes is always a strong indication of shared tastes, opinions and even personality. Next time you are at a large party, meeting or public event, look around the room and ask yourself if there is anyone present whose clothes you would be willing to wear yourself on that occasion. If so, he or she is apt to be a soul mate.

LIES AND DISGUISES

Perhaps the most difficult aspect of sartorial communication is the fact that any language that is able to convey information can also be used to convey misinformation. You can lie in the language of dress just as you can in English, French or Latin, and this sort of deception has the advantage that one cannot usually be accused of doing it deliberately. The costume that suggests youth or wealth, unlike the statement that one is twenty-nine years old and has a six-figure income, cannot be directly challenged or disproved.

A sartorial lie may be white, like Cinderella's ball gowns; it may be various shades of gray, or it may be downright black, as in the case of the radical-hippie disguise of the FBI informant or the stolen military uniform of the spy. The lie may be voluntary, or it may be involuntary, as when a tomboy is forced into a velvet party dress by her parents.

It may even be unconscious, as with the man who innocently wears a leather vest and boots to a bar patronized by homosexuals, or the American lady touring Scotland in a plaid she thought looked awfully pretty in the shop, but to which she has no hereditary right. If a complete grammar of clothing is ever written it will have to deal not only with these forms of dishonesty, but with many others that face linguists and semioticians: ambiguity, error, self-deception, misinterpretation, irony and framing.

Theatrical dress, or costume in the colloquial sense, is a special case of sartorial deception, one in which the audience willingly cooperates, recognizing that the clothes the actor wears, like the words he speaks, are not his own. Sometimes, however, what is only a temporary disguise for an actor becomes part of the everyday wardrobe of some members of the public. Popular culture, which has done so much to homogenize our life, has at the same time, almost paradoxically, helped to preserve and even to invent distinctive dress through a kind of feedback process. It is convenient for producers of films, TV programs and commercials that clothes should instantly and clearly indicate age, class, regional origin and if possible occupation and personality. Imagine that a certain costume is assigned to an actor representing a tough, handsome young auto mechanic, by a costume designer who has seen something like it in a local bar. Actual auto mechanics, viewing the program and others like it, unconsciously accept this outfit as characteristic; they are imitated by others who have not even seen the program. Finally the outfit becomes standard, and thus genuine.

Somewhere between theatrical costume and the uniform is ritual dress, the special clothing we adopt for the important ceremonies of our life: birth (the christening robe), college graduation, weddings, funerals and other portentous occasions that also tend to involve ritual speech.

DRESSING FOR "SUCCESS"

A more ambiguous sort of disguise is the costume that is deliberately chosen on the advice of others in order to deceive the beholder. For over a hundred years books and magazines have been busy translating the correct language

Dress, like other languages, can be both eloquent and original. A modern dandy: Tom Wolfe, American writer. Photograph copyright © 1981 by Thomas Victor.

of fashion, telling men and women what they should wear to seem genteel, rich, sophisticated and attractive to the other sex. Journals addressed to what used to be called "the career girl" advised her how to dress to attract "the right kind of man"—successful, marriage-minded. Regardless of the current fashion, a discreet femininity was always recommended: soft fabrics and colors, flowers and ruffles in modest profusion, hair slightly longer and curlier than that of the other girls in the office. The costume must be neither too stylish (suggesting expense to the future husband) nor dowdy (suggesting boredom). Above all, a delicate balance must be struck between the prim and the seductive, one tending not to attract men and the other to attract the wrong kind. Times have changed somewhat, and the fashion pages of magazines such as *Cosmopolitan* now seem to specialize in telling the career girl what to wear to charm the particular wrong type of man who reads *Playboy,* while the editorial pages tell her how to cope with the resulting psychic damage.

Two recent paperbacks, *Dress for Success* and *The Woman's Dress for Success Book,* by John T. Molloy, instruct businessmen and women on how to select their clothes so that they will look efficient, authoritative and reliable even when they are incompetent, weak and shifty. Molloy, who is by no means unintelligent, claims that his "wardrobe engineering" is based on scientific research and opinion polls. Also, in a departure from tradition, he is interested in telling women how to get promoted, not how to get married. The secret, apparently, is to wear an expensive but conventional "skirted suit" in medium gray or navy wool with a modestly cut blouse. No sweaters, no pants, no very bright colors, no cleavage, no long or excessively curly hair.

Anyone interested in scenic variety must hope that Molloy is mistaken; but my own opinion-polling, unfortunately, backs him up. A fast-rising lady executive in a local bank reports to me—reluctantly—that "Suits do help separate the women from the girls—provided the women can tolerate the separation, which is another question altogether."

WHY WE WEAR CLOTHES:
UTILITY, STATUS AND SEX

We put on clothing for some of the same reasons that we speak: to make living and working easier and more comfortable, to proclaim (or disguise) our identities and to attract erotic attention. James Laver has designated these motives as the Utility Principle, the Hierarchical Principle and the Seduction Principle. Anyone who has recently been to a large party or professional meeting will recall that most of the conversation that was not directed to practical ends ("Where are the drinks?" "Here is the agenda for this afternoon") was principally motivated by the Hierarchical or the Seduction Principle. In the same way, the clothes worn on that occasion, as well as more or less sheltering the nakedness of those present, were chosen to indicate their wearer's place in the world and/or to make him or her look more attractive.

The earliest utilitarian clothing was probably makeshift. Faced with extremes of climate—icy winters, drench-

Clothes designed for strenuous physical work are often transformed into fashionable playclothes. The more dangerous and specialized the occupation, the higher the status of the resulting fashions. Advertisement from The New York Times. *Photograph by D. James Dee, 1980.*

ing rainstorms or the baking heat of the sun—men and women slung or tied the skins of animals around themselves; they fastened broad leaves to their heads as simple rain hats and made crude sandals from strips of hide or bark, as primitive tribes do today. Such protective clothing has a long history, but it has never acquired much prestige. The garment with a purely practical function is the glamourless equivalent of the flat, declarative sentence: "It's raining." "I'm working in the garden." But it is difficult, in costume as in speech, to make a truly simple statement. The pair of plain black rubbers which states that it is raining may also remark, "The streets are wet, and I can't afford to damage my shoes." If the streets are not in fact very wet, the rubbers may also declare silently, "This is a dull, timid, fussy person."

Sometimes, regardless of the weather, utility in itself is a minus quality. The more water-repellent a raincoat is, ordinarily, the more it repels admiration—unless it is also fashionably colored or cut, or in some other way evidently expensive. Boots of molded synthetic leather that keep your feet warm and dry are thought to be less aesthetically pleasing than decorated leather ones which soon leak, and thus imply ownership of a car or familiarity with taxis.

Practical clothing usually seems most attractive when it is worn by persons who do not need it and probably never will need it. The spotless starched pinafore that covers a child's party dress or the striped overalls favored by some of today's college students look much more charming than they would on the housemaids and farmers for whom they were first intended.

This transformation of protective clothing into fashionable costume has a long history. As Rachel Kemper points out, the sort of garments that become fashionable most rapidly and most completely are those which were originally designed for warfare, dangerous work or strenuous sports:

> Garments intended to deflect the point of a lance, flying arrows, or solar radiation possess a strange kind of instant chic and are sure to be modified into fashions for both men and women. Contemporary examples abound: the ubiquitous avi-

ator glasses that line the rails of fashionable singles bars, perforated racing gloves that grip the wheels of sedate family cars, impressively complicated scuba divers' watches that will never be immersed in any body of water more challenging than the country-club pool.

MAGICAL CLOTHING

Common sense and most historians of costume have assumed that the demands of either utility, status or sex must have been responsible for the invention of clothing. However, as sometimes happens in human affairs, both common sense and the historians were apparently wrong: scholars have recently informed us that the original purpose of clothing was magical. Archaeologists digging up past civilizations and anthropologists studying primitive tribes have come to the conclusion that, as Rachel Kemper puts it, "Paint, ornament, and rudimentary clothing were first employed to attract good animistic powers and to ward off evil." When Charles Darwin visited Tierra del Fuego, a cold, wet, disagreeable land plagued by constant winds, he found the natives naked except for feathers in their hair and symbolic designs painted on their bodies. Modern Australian bushmen, who may spend hours decorating themselves and their relatives with patterns in colored clay, often wear nothing else but an amulet or two.

However skimpy it may be, primitive dress almost everywhere, like primitive speech, is full of magic. A necklace of shark's teeth or a girdle of cowrie shells or feathers serves the same purpose as a prayer or spell, and may magically replace—or more often supplement—a spoken charm. In the first instance a form of *contagious* magic is at work: the shark's teeth are believed to endow their wearer with the qualities of a fierce and successful fisherman. The cowrie shells, on the other hand, work through *sympathetic* magic: since they resemble the female sexual parts, they are thought to increase or preserve fertility.

In civilized society today belief in the supernatural powers of clothing—like belief in prayers, spells and charms —remains widespread, though we denigrate it with the name "superstition." Advertisements announce that im-

Supernatural garments are still seen today, even in highly civilized society. A wedding dress by Jean Muir printed with ancient magical symbols, including the four-pointed star and the crescent moon, worn in London by Antonia Fraser in 1980.

probable and romantic events will follow the application of a particular sort of grease to our faces, hair or bodies; they claim that members of the opposite (or our own) sex will be drawn to us by the smell of a particular soap. Nobody believes those ads, you may say. Maybe not, but we behave as though we did: look in your bathroom cabinet.

The supernatural garments of European folk tales—the seven-league boots, the cloaks of invisibility and the magic rings—are not forgotten, merely transformed, so that today we have the track star who can only win a race in a particular hat or shoes, the plain-clothes cop who feels no one can see him in his raincoat and the wife who takes off her wedding ring before going to a motel with her lover. Amulets also remain very popular: circlets of elephant hair for strength and long life, copper bracelets as a charm against arthritis. In both cases what is operating is a form of magical thinking like that of the Australian aborigine: Elephants are strong and long-lived; if we constantly rub ourselves with their hair we may acquire these qualities. Copper conducts electricity, therefore it will conduct nerve impulses to cramped and unresponsive muscles, either by primitive contagious magic as with the elephant-hair bracelet, or by the modern contagious magic of pseudoscience: the copper "attracting and concentrating free-floating electrons," as a believer explained it to me.

Sympathetic or symbolic magic is also often employed, as when we hang crosses, stars or one of the current symbols of female power and solidarity around our necks, thus silently involving the protection of Jesus, Jehovah or Astarte. Such amulets, of course, may be worn to announce our allegiance to some faith or cause rather than as a charm. Or they may serve both purposes simultaneously—or sequentially. The crucifix concealed below the parochial-school uniform speaks only to God until some devilish human force persuades its wearer to remove his or her clothes; then it acts —or fails to act—as a warning against sin as well as a protective talisman.

Articles of clothing, too, may be treated as if they had mana, the impersonal supernatural force that tends to concentrate itself in objects. When I was in college it was common to wear a particular "lucky" sweater, shirt or hat to final

Even today garments may be endowed with magical properties by their wearers. Dave Wottle, international track star and Olympic gold medalist, in the cap that, he believed, brought him victory—and without which he refused to run; 1972.

examinations, and this practice continues today. Here it is usually contagious magic that is at work: the chosen garment has become lucky by being worn on the occasion of some earlier success, or has been given to its owner by some favored person. The wearing of such magical garments is especially common in sports, where they are often publicly credited with bringing their owners luck. Their loss or abandonment is thought to cause injury as well as defeat. Actors also believe ardently in the magic of clothes, possibly because they are so familiar with the near-magical transforming power of theatrical costume.

Sometimes the lucky garment is believed to be even more fortunate when it is put on backwards or inside out. There may be different explanations of this belief. A student of my acquaintance, whose faded lucky sweat shirt bears the name of her high-school swimming team, suggests that reversing the garment places the printed side against her body, thus allowing the mana to work on her more directly.

Ordinarily, nonmagical clothes may also be worn inside out or reversed for magical reasons. The custom of turning your apron to change your luck after a series of household mishaps is widely known in both Britain and America; I have seen it done myself in upstate New York. Gamblers today sometimes turn their clothes before commencing play, and the practice was even more common in the past. The eighteenth-century British statesman Charles James Fox often sat at the gaming tables all night long with his coat turned inside out and his face blackened to propitiate the goddess of chance. Or perhaps to disguise himself from her; according to folk tradition, the usual explanation for the turning of garments is that it confuses demons. In blackface and with the elegant trimmings of his dress coat hidden, Fox was invisible to Lady Luck; the evil spirits that haunt housewives fail to recognize their intended victims and fly on to torment someone else.

MALEVOLENT CLOTHING

At the other extreme from clothing which brings good luck and success is the garment of ill-omen. The most common and harmless version of this is the dress, suit or shirt which (like some children) seems to attract or even to seek out dirt, grease, protruding nails, falling ketchup and other hazards. Enid Nemy, who has written perceptively about such clothes for *The New York Times,* suggests that they may be lazy: "they'd just as soon rest on a hanger, or in a box—and they revolt when they're hauled into action." Or, she adds, they may be snobs, unwilling to associate with ordinary people. Whatever the cause, such accident-prone garments rarely if ever reform, and once one has been identified it is best to break off relations with it immediately. Otherwise, like accident-prone persons, it is apt to involve you in much inconvenience and possibly actual disaster, turning some important interview or romantic tryst into a scene of farce or humiliation. More sinister, and fortunately more rare, is the garment which seems to attract disasters to you rather than to itself. Ms. Nemy mentions an orange linen dress that apparently took a dislike to its owner, one Margaret Turner of Dover Publications. Orange clothes, as it happens, are likely to arouse hostility in our culture, but this dress seems to have been a special case. "Women friends seemed cattier, men seemed more aloof, and I'd get into bad situations with my boss," Ms. Turner reported. "And that wasn't all. I'd spill coffee, miss train connections, and the car would break down."

Even when our clothes are not invested with this sort of supernatural power, they may have symbolic meanings that tend to increase with age. The man who comes home from work to discover that his wife has thrown out his shabby, stained tweed jacket or his old army pants is often much angrier than the situation seems to call for, and his anger may be mixed with depression and even fear. Not only has he lost a magical garment, he has been forced to see his spouse as in some real sense his enemy—as a person who wishes to deprive him of comfort and protection.

A pleasanter sort of magic occurs in the exchange of garments common among lovers. In the Middle Ages a lady would often give her kerchief or glove to a chosen knight. When he went into battle or fought in a tournament he would place it against his heart or pin it to his helmet. Today, probably because of the taboo against the wearing of

The symbolic meaning of some clothes increases with age even if they are seldom or never worn. Anyone who proposes to destroy them is in effect proposing to destroy our connection with our own, often more heroic or romantic, past self. Cartoon by Helen E. Hokinson. Copyright © 1936, 1964, The New Yorker Magazine, Inc.

"You aren't going to need this Yale crew sweater again, are you, Osgood?"

female garments by men, the traffic is all one-way. The teenage girl wears her boyfriend's basketball jacket to school; the secretary who has spent the night impulsively and successfully at a friend's apartment goes home next morning with his London Fog raincoat over her disco outfit; and the wife, in a playful and affectionate mood, puts on her husband's red flannel pajama top. Often the woman feels so good and looks so well in the magical borrowed garment that it is never returned.

If the relationship sours, though, the exchange alters its meaning; the good spell becomes a curse. The magical article may be returned, often in poor condition: soiled or wrinkled, or with "accidental" cigarette burns. Or it may be deliberately destroyed: thrown in the trash, or even vindictively cut to shreds. An especially refined form of black magic is to give the garment away to the Salvation Army, in the hope that it will soon be worn by a drunken and incontinent bum —ideally, someplace where your former lover will see and recognize it.

NEUROTIC CLOTHING AND FREE SPEECH

As with the spoken language, communication through dress is easiest and least problematical when only one purpose is being served; when we wear a garment solely to keep warm, to attend a graduation ceremony, to announce our political views, to look sexy or to protect ourselves from bad luck. Unfortunately, just as with speech, our motives in making any statement are apt to be double or multiple. The man who goes to buy a winter coat may simultaneously want it to shelter him from bad weather, look expensive and fashionable, announce that he is sophisticated and rugged, attract a certain sort of sexual partner and magically infect him with the qualities of Robert Redford.

Naturally it is often impossible to satisfy all these requirements and make all these statements at once. Even if they do not contradict one another, the ideal garment of our fantasy may not be available in any of the stores we can get to, and if it is we may not be able to afford it. Therefore, just as with speech, it often happens that we cannot say what we really mean because we don't have the right "words." The woman who complains formulaically that she hasn't got anything to wear is in just this situation. Like a tourist abroad, she may be able to manage all right in shops and on trains, but she cannot go out to dinner, because her vocabulary is so limited that she would misrepresent herself and perhaps attract ridicule.

At present all these difficulties are compounded by contradictory messages about the value of dress in general. The Protestant ethic stressed modesty and simplicity of dress.

Cleanliness was next to godliness, but finery and display were of the Devil, and the serious man or woman had no time for such folly. Even today to declare that one never pays much attention to what he or she is wearing is to claim virtue, and usually to receive respect. At the same time, however, we are told by advertisers and fashion experts that we must dress well and use cosmetics to, as they put it, liberate the "natural" beauty within. If we do not "take care of our looks" and "make the best of ourselves," we are scolded by our relatives and pitied by our friends. To juggle these conflicting demands is difficult and often exhausting.

When two or more wishes or demands conflict, a common psychological result is some disorder of expression. Indeed, one of the earliest theorists of dress, the psychologist J. C. Flügel, saw all human clothing as a neurotic symptom. In his view, the irreconcilable emotions are modesty and the desire for attention:

> . . . our attitude towards clothes is *ab initio* "ambivalent," to use the invaluable term which has been introduced into psychology by the psychoanalysts; we are trying to satisfy two contradictory tendencies. . . . In this respect the discovery, or at any rate the use, of clothes, seems, in its psychological aspects, to resemble the process whereby a neurotic symptom is developed.

Flügel is considering only a single opposition; he does not even contemplate the neurotic confusion that can result when three or more motives are in conflict—as they often are. Given this state of things, we should not be surprised to find in the language of clothing the equivalent of many of the psychological disorders of speech. We will hear, or rather see, the repetitive stammer of the man who always wears the same jacket or pair of shoes whatever the climate or occasion; the childish lisp of the woman who clings to the frills and ribbons of her early youth; and those embarrassing lapses of the tongue—or rather of the garment—of which the classical examples are the unzipped fly and the slip that becomes a social error. We will also notice the signs of more temporary inner distress: the too-loud or harsh "voice" that exhausts our eye rather than our ear with glaring colors and clashing patterns, and the drab, colorless equivalent of the inability to speak above a whisper.

Dress is an aspect of human life that arouses strong feelings, some intensely pleasant and others very disagreeable. It is no accident that many of our daydreams involve fine raiment; nor that one of the most common and disturbing human nightmares is of finding ourselves in public inappropriately and/or incompletely clothed.

For some people the daily task of choosing a costume is tedious, oppressive or even frightening. Occasionally such people tell us that fashion is unnecessary; that in the ideal world of the future we will all wear some sort of identical jump suit—washable, waterproof, stretchable, temperature-controlled; timeless, ageless and sexless. What a convenience, what a relief it will be, they say, never to worry about how to dress for a job interview, a romantic tryst or a funeral!

Convenient perhaps, but not exactly a relief. Such a utopia would give most of us the same kind of chill we feel when a stadium full of Communist-bloc athletes in identical sports outfits, shouting slogans in unison, appears on TV. Most people do not want to be told what to wear any more than they want to be told what to say. In Belfast recently four hundred Irish Republican prisoners "refused to wear any clothes at all, draping themselves day and night in blankets," rather than put on prison uniforms. Even the offer of civilian-style dress did not satisfy them; they insisted on wearing their own clothes brought from home, or nothing. Fashion is free speech, and one of the privileges, if not always one of the pleasures, of a free world.

II
YOUTH
AND AGE

I grow old . . . I grow old . . .
I shall wear the bottoms of my trousers rolled.

—T.S. Eliot, "The Love Song of J. Alfred
Prufrock"

Almost since its invention clothing has been used to differentiate youth and age. In primitive tribes, initiation into manhood or womanhood was marked by the gift of new and adult garments or ornaments; the same custom has often been followed in so-called civilized societies. When a boy came of age in ancient Rome he put off his short tunic and assumed the toga virilis. In America, up to about fifty years ago, he exchanged his short pants for long ones in a ritual of equal significance.

During the Middle Ages and for several centuries thereafter childhood ended at about the age of seven, often earlier. Very young children wore long gowns or dresses, and there was little difference between the clothing of boys and that of girls. Between three and six the boy became a little man and the girl a little woman; they then wore scaled-down versions of adult modes. Little or no concession was made to what we now consider the obvious need of children for free physical activity. Medieval and Renaissance portraits show small children dressed in all the extravagant inconveniences of grownup fashion: ruffs, farthingales, padded breeches, trailing sleeves, dragging skirts, high-heeled shoes and hats top-heavy with feathers and flowers.

Before the late eighteenth century, well-to-do children were dressed as miniature adults, in all the extravagant inconveniences of grown-up fashion. Prince James Francis Edward Stuart with His Sister, *by Largillière, 1695.*

THE INVENTION OF JUVENILE COSTUME

In the later half of the eighteenth century, Jean-Jacques Rousseau and his followers put forward a new view of childhood as a separate and natural state, and the child as a being valuable in him or herself rather than an imperfect undersized adult. They called for a change, not only in the education of children, but in their dress. Rousseau advised in his *Émile* that

> . . . the limbs of a growing child should be free to move easily in his clothing; nothing should cramp their growth or movement; . . . The best plan is to keep children in frocks as long as possible and then to provide them with loose clothing, without trying to define the shape which is only another way of deforming it. Their defects of body and mind may all be traced to the same source, the desire to make men of them before their time.

The early Romantics were the first to see childhood as valuable in itself. They believed that boys and girls should not be forced into adult fashions, but instead dressed in simple, loose clothes that would give them freedom to play and grow. These aristocratic late-eighteenth-century children wear styles that have been associated with youth for nearly two hundred years and can still be seen today. The Sackville Children, *by John Hoppner, 1797.*

Before long these views had begun to manifest them-selves in a new look for children. Little girls, instead of being put into hoops and stays, now continued to wear the simple, comfortable, low-necked muslin frocks of their infancy. Gradually this privilege was extended to older and older children, and by the 1780s such frocks were often worn well into the teens. At the same time, boys were relieved of the long coat, tight waistcoat, high-collared shirt and knee breeches of their fathers. Instead they were dressed in a short jacket, a shirt with a soft turnover collar and trousers. In the 1790s the trousers began to be buttoned onto the jacket, producing what was rather ominously called the skeleton suit. It was worn for the next forty years by most boys between three and seven. Flat slippers and simple hair-cuts for both sexes replaced the wigs and powder that con-tinued to be fashionable for adults.

OLD-FASHIONED QUAINTNESS:
THE KATE GREENAWAY LOOK

The children's fashions introduced in the late eighteenth century are still familiar to us from the illustrations of the English artist Kate Greenaway. Though her books appeared in the 1880s and 1890s, the children in them are dressed in the costume of a hundred years earlier, which she considered more picturesque and beautiful than that of her own time. Her work was so popular that it soon began to have an influence on actual children's clothes. Mothers of the late nineteenth and early twentieth centuries often put their tots into Greenaway-style frocks; and the so-called "aesthetic dress" of the period owes almost as much to her drawings as it does to Pre-Raphaelite notions of the medieval. Even today, well-to-do little girls go to parties in outfits which descend from the Greenaway tradition; and so, occasionally, do their mothers. Now, however, this costume (currently known in Britain as the "Laura Ashley" Look after the designer who reintroduced it) does not necessarily signify aesthetic leanings.

The authentic Kate Greenaway little girl, whatever her period, wears a floor-length or ankle-length dress. Girls' skirts did not begin to grow shorter until the 1820s, and what they revealed at first were long white lace-edged underdrawers or pantalettes. Though these too became briefer with time, the Victorian sensitivity to the sexual implications of what were called "the female limbs" remained. In an age when "leg" was so suggestive a concept that the well-turned limbs of pianos might be modestly shrouded in fringed brocade, the length of a girl's skirt was carefully regulated. An article in *Harper's Bazar* for 1868 contains a diagram indicating the proper height for different ages from four (just below the knee) to sixteen (just above the tops of the high-button boots). The grown woman of the time, it should be noted, wore a crinoline that swept the floor.

For boys, the Kate Greenaway look did not last beyond the 1830s. Charles Dickens, who had worn a skeleton suit himself, describes it in *Sketches by Boz* (1838–39):

The late-nineteenth-century artist Kate Greenaway dressed the children in her books in the simple costumes of the 1790s in preference to the more elaborate ones of her own time. This classic Kate Greenaway dress, however, shows the influence of the late-Victorian bustle.

. . . one of those straight blue cloth cases in which small boys used to be confined before belts and tunics had come in . . . an ingenious contrivance for displaying the symmetry of a boy's figure by fastening him into a very tight jacket, with an ornamental row of buttons over each shoulder and then buttoning his trousers over it so as to give his legs the appearance of being hooked on just under the armpits.

ALL AT SEA: THE SAILOR SUIT

The tunics Dickens refers to, which look to us like full-skirted short dresses, continued to be worn by boys between the ages of three and seven until the 1860s, when they began to be replaced by various combinations of jacket and pants—and also, increasingly, by the sailor suit. This costume, first introduced at the end of the eighteenth century in schools that trained boys for the Navy, soon began to be seen on children of all ages and both sexes. (The girls' version, of course, was made with a skirt instead of shorts or knickers.)

Although sailor suits were soon common wear for children in both America and continental Europe, their greatest vogue was in Britain. Though most popular on holidays and at the seaside, they were by no means limited to such scenes. Indeed, in the early twentieth century, the sailor suit or sailor blouse and skirt was almost the standard everyday costume for middle-class boys and girls—as can be seen in the illustrations to the books of contemporary juvenile authors. In city and country, at home and abroad, in navy blue for warmth and wear or in white for summer and parties, the children of Britain proclaimed that she ruled the waves. It was not until after World War II, when Britannia had waived the rule and naval strength counted for less on the international scene, that the sailor suit began to lose its popularity. At a summer camp for girls I attended in 1940–41, our Sunday dress-up uniform was a white middy blouse and skirt with a red-silk neckerchief. In this costume, every weekend, we sat on the porch of the main building and sang patriotic songs, often with a seagoing theme: "Anchors Aweigh" and "Sailing, Sailing" were favorites. As Paul Goodman asks after a description of similar ceremonies at

The sailor suit as the costume of adolescent eroticism: Tadzio from the film version of Thomas Mann's Death in Venice, *1971.*

The sailor suit as a camp uniform. These little girls, photographed in upstate New York in 1930, are over a hundred miles from the ocean.

his summer camp, "Where were we all going to, sitting down?"

When worn by children who had reached adolescence, nautical costume had additional, sometimes contradictory meanings. It could convey a rugged heartiness, as in Arthur Ransome's stories about juvenile sailors; or it could suggest a pampered, overcivilized beauty such as that of fourteen-year-old Tadzio in Thomas Mann's *Death in Venice,* whose "English sailor suit" gave him "a spoilt, exquisite air."

MOTHER'S DARLING: THE FAUNTLEROY SUIT

During their heyday, sailor outfits found favor with both adults and children. Another juvenile style introduced in the late nineteenth century, though admired by parents, was detested by nearly all the little boys who were forced into it. This, of course, was the Fauntleroy suit, popularized (but not invented) by Frances Hodgson Burnett and pictured by Reginald Birch in the early editions of her *Little Lord Fauntleroy* (1886). In its original form, it consisted of a black or sapphire-blue velvet jacket and knickers worn over a white blouse with a large lace Vandyke collar. It was completed by a colored silk sash, silk stockings, buckled pumps, an oversize velvet beret and long curls. The original inspiration of the costume seems to have been Gainsborough's portrait of Master Jonathan Buttall, known familiarly as *The Blue Boy;* its meaning for fond parents was romantic and aristocratic, recalling pictures of Charles II as a child and Dumas's *Three Musketeers.* It is perhaps no coincidence that this costume appeared at a time when the dress-up clothes of adult men were uniformly drab, formal and solemn.

Cedric, the eponymous hero of *Little Lord Fauntleroy,* is by no means a "mollycoddle"—the contemporary phrase for a boy too well coddled by mollies, or women. He can hold his own or better against other boys his age, and excels at sports.

Little Lord Fauntleroy in the original Fauntleroy suit, as portrayed by Reginald Birch in 1886.

His outfit, however, soon became the quintessential sign of the sissy. Generations of boys in both England and America grew up with awful memories of having been forced to wear it, and authors of children's books used it as a sign that a character was at best a weak nincompoop and at worst a sniveling sneak.

The ill repute of the Fauntleroy suit may in part have been due to its resemblance to contemporary aesthetic dress for men. This costume, which differed from Cedric's by including a flowing tie, was adopted most prominently by Oscar Wilde. In 1882, he toured America in black velvet knickerbockers and curls, speaking about poetry to large and

Oscar Wilde in aesthetic dress of the type worn by Little Lord Fauntleroy: black velvet jacket, vest and knee breeches; silk stockings; bowed pumps; flowing curls. This caricature by Thomas Nast shows Wilde lecturing in New York in 1882 on the beauty of the wide-brimmed hats and high boots of the Rocky Mountain miners, whom he considered the only well-dressed men in America.

adoring audiences—and possibly influencing Mrs. Burnett's choice of outfit both for her own two sons and for Cedric. Wilde's subsequent trial and imprisonment cast a shadow not only over the role of the aesthete, but also over the costume he had worn, which was henceforth obscurely contaminated. Among the final results of his disgrace, therefore, we should perhaps count not only a generation of tiresomely manly and aesthetically timid writers, but also the release of thousands of little boys from their scratchy lace collars and tight velvet suits.

SHORTS AND KNICKERS

Even after they had escaped from the Fauntleroy costume boys continued for many years to wear short pants, both for everyday and for special occasions. Until about the age of seven or eight they would probably be dressed in shorts; later they were more apt to wear knickerbockers much like those their fathers put on for golf or bicycling. This is an early example of the rule still in force today that the sports clothes of the adult are the everyday clothes of the child. This principle has now been extended to spectator sports, and kids of both sexes (especially boys) go to school in tiny imitation football jerseys, baseball shirts and track shoes, often emblazoned with the insignia of their favorite team.

In America long trousers for small boys began to be available in the 1920s, but they were uncommon. Gradually the age at which one assumed one's first long pants was lowered, until by 1940 even three- and four-year-olds might wear them, especially for play. Today in America short pants are strictly warm-weather wear, and knickers are unknown.

In Britain the change from short to long pants was more gradual. Even now, many school uniforms are short-legged. On dark, cold winter days, elementary playgrounds are spotted with knobby, raw, scarred red knees that glow painfully between the gray or navy shorts and the long gray socks. Common sense would suggest that they be covered; but common sense counts for little in the history of dress.

Besides, historically, bare knees have always suggested manly toughness: they are associated with the warlike costumes of the ancient Britons, the ancient and modern kilted Scots, empire-building explorers and heroic footballers. To cover them would be a sign of national weakness.

THE DECLINE OF JUVENILE COSTUME

Apart from a few survivals, the concept of special styles for older children is in abeyance today. We have in effect returned to the medieval system that recognizes infancy as a separate state but dresses children like their elders—or at least like their elders at play. This is perhaps appropriate, since physically as well as socially children grow up faster than they used to. In the 1860s, for example, the average age of first menstruation in America was 16.5, and girls who had not yet reached that age were, appropriately enough, dressed as children: in tight bodices and short full skirts, with pantalettes or long white stockings below.

Today the average age of menarche is eleven or less. Even ten-year-olds wear what are called "training bras" in sizes AA and AAA, completely nonfunctional except as a sign that the child will eventually become a woman. Girls' outer clothes, too, even those of three- and four-year-olds, are often designed so as to suggest (or perhaps magically encourage) the development of secondary sex characteristics. Nonexistent hips are suggested by excess fullness and breasts are outlined on the tiny flat chest and filled in with ruffles.

The sports clothes of the adult are the everyday clothes of the child; today both boys and girls wear imitation football, baseball and track uniforms. New York, 1980.

FASHION AND AGE

The passage from maturity to what are now called the golden years has often been marked by a change of costume. Occasionally the change is deliberate and abrupt. Thus Léa in Colette's *La Fin de Chéri* transforms herself from a beautiful and voluptuous courtesan into "A healthy old woman, . . . with heavy jowls and a double chin," whose plain skirt and jacket "proclaimed the abdication, the retraction of

The lowering of the age of menarche has been exploited and even anticipated by manufacturers, and today ten- and eleven-year-olds are encouraged to wear imitations of adult lingerie. My First Bra by Teenform, 1981.

femininity, and a sort of sexless dignity." Often the shift in appearance is more gradual and more unconscious. Over a period of several years, impelled not by any exterior force but rather as if under some slow-working spell, senior citizens put on those clothes which in their society are the customary signs of age.

Various factors seem to determine these signs. Some are practical: for instance, older persons tend to have poor circulation, and the garments they wear to protect themselves from chill often become signifiers for old age. In classical Rome, where stockings as such were unknown, lengths of cloth called fascia were sometimes wrapped around the legs for warmth. They were regarded, however, as proper only for old men and women—on anyone else they were a sign of weakness or effeminacy. In more recent times, mufflers, nightcaps and bedsocks have had a similar meaning. The wearing of heavy wraps on a warm day also suggests age—though it may also signify illness or eccentricity.

In other cases, some garment which is not in itself any warmer than similar garments has come to stand for old age. The white or gray crocheted shawl now associated with the concept "grandmother" is no better at keeping out drafts than a red or green shawl of the same construction; the man's tan or gray cardigan sweater associated with retirement and often also with infirmity gives less protection than a pullover of the same weight. Why these styles should signify advancing years is hard to explain. Of course, they have been around for quite a while, and there may be a tendency, other things being equal, for the clothes that our grandparents wore when we were young to become fixed in our minds as the characteristic garb of old age. This process, however, is not invariable: anyone who was a child in the 1960s, for instance, probably saw his or her grandmother in miniskirts.

THE LONG ROBE

One persistent indicator of advancing years in men has been the long robe or gown. It is also often a sign of eminence, and of temporal or spiritual power. In its classical form, the robe appears as the floor-length chiton and toga of Greece and Rome; it is familiar to us from the statues of gods and emperors, and can be seen on Greek vases. The long robe also appears in Byzantine mosaics, and in the sculpture and manuscript illuminations of the Middle Ages. It was worn by men of age or prominence through the Renaissance and well into the eighteenth century, taking different forms as modes changed, but retaining its meanings. In the theater it became the recognized costume for old men, and is still traditionally assigned to Polonius, Lear and other senior citizens, while Hamlet, Edgar and Prince Hal are dressed in

Elderly persons are easily subject to chill, and the wearing of heavy wraps on a warm day has therefore become a signifier of old age, as has the carrying of a walking stick. Imogen Cunningham and a friend in 1977. Photograph by Donna Deitch.

doublet and hose. (Falstaff, to whose age and station a long robe would be appropriate, also usually wears tights, as a sign to the audience that he has not given up youthful follies.)

During the eighteenth century the full-length robe was gradually abandoned for public wear even by the old. It has survived, however, in the ritual dress of certain professions —most notably medicine, religion and the law. The vestments of priests and the robes of many American and all British judges descend from this tradition. So of course does the academic gown of university scholars; and also that of semiliterate high-school graduates, who however—perhaps out of a collective sense of unworthiness, perhaps out of economy—tend to wear their robes considerably shorter.

Though the long gown ceased to be worn by laymen in public, in private it could be seen for at least another hundred years in the form of the long nightshirt. Pajamas are a comparatively recent addition to Western civilization, though in the East they have been known for centuries. Before 1900 most men in Europe and America wore loose nightshirts to bed: long-sleeved, full-cut and almost always white, like the costume of a ghost; they might be of any length from midthigh to the floor.

When a new style is tried, the older generation is usually the last to lay the old aside. Even after pajamas were widely available and had been popularized by such Hollywood films as *It Happened One Night* (1934), long nightshirts of white cotton or red flannel continued to be worn by conservative elderly men, especially in rural areas. (Until very recently they could be ordered from the Sears catalogue.) The wearing of somewhat outmoded daytime fashions is another a recognized sign of age—and of the possession of aged opinions and beliefs, as we shall see later.

It also seems to be a general principle that if a garment is available in different lengths, the longer version will be worn by older persons. If we look at contemporary prints and paintings we can see that when the nightshirt was standard wear, older men wore them longer. A very young man's was likely to be quite brief—or he might simply go to bed in his shirt. The same rule applies to women's clothes. Cur-

The snooker player on the left wears the type of cardigan sweater traditionally associated with age and retirement, together with a casual knit shirt and neckerchief; his friend is still dressed for business. Yorkshire, 1975. Photograph by John Myers.

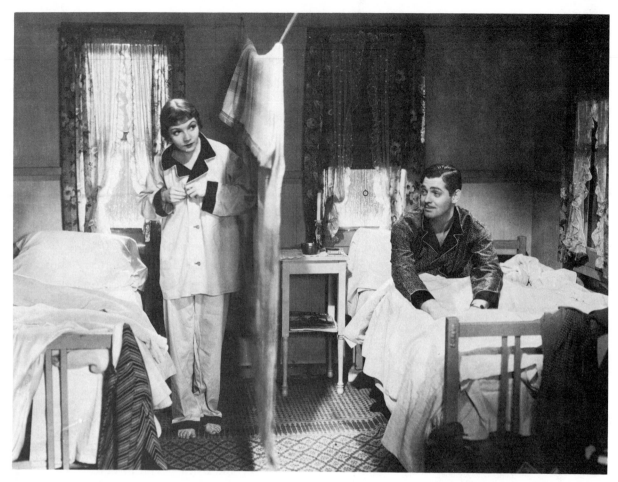

The film It Happened One Night *(1934) made man-tailored pajamas popular for both men and women. Claudette Colbert in Clark Gable's pajamas in the pivotal scene.*

rently, more baby-doll and shorty nightgowns (and those unattractive inventions, shorty pajamas) are sold to teenagers, and more floor-length or waltz-length nightgowns to older women. Older women also tend to wear relatively longer skirts, whatever the current styles. Indeed, they are instructed to do so. At the height of the miniskirt boom, for instance, an American women's magazine published a guide to the proper hem length for women of different ages. A photograph showed three generations of smiling middle-class housewives in identical dresses. Grandmother's skirt clears her knees; Mother's is about four inches shorter; and Daughter's four inches above that. Today, of course, all three of them look to us like the unfortunate old woman in the nursery rhyme who fell asleep by the King's highway, had her petticoats cut off, and suffered an identity crisis:

She began to shiver, and she began to shake;
She began to laugh, and she began to cry—
"Lawkamercy on me, this is none of I!"

In the history of costume there are only a few exceptions to the rule "Longer Equals Older." One is the infant's gown or christening robe. Customarily it is at least twice the length of the baby who wears it, and very grand infants may have gowns up to six feet long. It is as if the skirts (though not the bodice and sleeves) of the christening gown have been cut to fit the man or woman the child will become. The garment is thus the sartorial equivalent of a magical spell, one more necessary in previous centuries when so many children did not live to grow up. It also has other symbolic qualities, indicated by its traditional whiteness (in our culture, the color of purity and innocence) and the fineness of its materials.

HAIR AS AN AGE INDICATOR

With increasing years, human hair tends to lose its pigmentation and become first gray and then white. Gray hair has therefore always been a sign of age, though sometimes a deceptive one. In the eighteenth century, when both men and women powdered their hair or wore wigs, a white-haired beauty might be sixteen. White curls were believed to be becoming to the complexion, and to have a softening, youthful influence. During most other periods, however, the reverse notion has prevailed, and naturally white or gray hair has been dyed back to its original or some other hue to disguise the look of aging. In the past, the substances used were harsh and often actually dangerous; the result usually fooled very few people, and lowered the wearer's reputation in the eyes of the undeceived. Today the art of hair coloring has been developed to the point where it is often impossible to detect, and causes only the mildest disapproval or none at all. The fact that President Reagan probably dyes his hair is taken for granted, and endears him to millions of Americans who do the same.

For men, throughout history, one important sign of advancing years has been the full beard, especially one that is gray or white. In classical times, when most males were clean-shaven, beards were worn by old men and old gods: Jupiter, Vulcan, Neptune. Like the long robe, they suggested temporal power. They were also an attribute of moral authority and of wisdom, or at least of learning: Socrates and many other Greek philosophers were bearded. In the Christian era, too, abundant facial hair has often been associated with age, power and wisdom. The Biblical patriarchs and prophets, the hermits and fathers of the Church—Moses, Solomon and Noah; Isaiah and Ezekiel; Saint Anthony and Saint Jerome—are usually portrayed with full, and often with flowing, beards. Younger characters such as Jacob and David normally appear clean-shaven. God the Father is always heavily whiskered; Jesus, on the other hand, usually wears a neatly trimmed, often rather skimpy beard of the kind most fashionable at the time the artist depicted him.

DRESSING ONE'S AGE

Human beings do not always act their age verbally. Persons in middle life or beyond occasionally use "with-it" slang, though sometimes of an outmoded sort; young men and women attempt to impress one another or their elders with judiciously formal pronouncements and long words. The same kind of thing occurs in the language of clothes. At any large social gathering it is possible to see people dressed younger or older than current mores prescribe. Whether conscious or not, their clothes are a message, and one which everyone else present instinctively understands. We can thus watch out for—in either the positive or the negative sense, according to our own preferences—those people who wish to be thought of as spontaneous, fun-loving and impulsive; who want us to play with them and indulge them and take care of them and forgive their childish errors. We can also watch out for those persons who may be willing to assume our responsibilities, solve our problems, forgive our mistakes, take care of us and tell us what to think and order

The traditional infant's gown or christening robe is at least twice as long as the baby. It anticipates, or perhaps magically ensures, that he or she will outlive the years of high mortality. Mary Meigs and Sarah Meigs Brown, Washington, D.C., 1919.

us around. The items of dress that give us such information may be very subtle: a slightly brighter hue of shirt or tie, a flyaway bow or an inch or two less of skirt.

Occasionally a more obvious deviation from both the verbal and the sartorial code occurs. Grown men and women speak baby talk, often to one another; wise or wise-ass children confound and/or shock their elders by using words they are "not supposed to know." The same kind of thing occurs in the language of clothes, where it tends to meet with the same, largely critical, response. People are expected to dress their age, and most societies have imposed sanctions against wearing the costume of another generation. These sanctions vary, according to the rigidity of the society and the severity of the offense, from affectionate ridicule to ostracism.

LAMB DRESSED AS MUTTON

Dressing older than one really is has generally been treated more leniently than the reverse. The seven-year-old who puts on her mother's dress and experiments with her mother's cosmetics is often considered cute, as long as she does so only occasionally and in the privacy of her own or a friend's house. Everyone recognizes that she is only playing. But if she habitually goes to school wearing red nail polish and lipstick, carrying a miniature handbag, strangers observing her getup will frown, other children will make fun of her and her teacher may complain to her parents. The parents will also be held responsible if a little boy comes to school in a suit too old for his age or (which is currently the same thing) too formal for everyday wear.

A few years later, sanctions against dressing beyond one's years are usually applied by children's peers. If the difference is not too great, however, the offender may rather be admired. The boy who wears a suit to the junior high school dance may draw glances of envy as well as scorn; the girl who manages to leave the house without being told to go back upstairs and wipe that stuff off her face may be treated by her friends as a kind of heroine.

Or, of course, she may get into serious trouble. A classic instance occurs in Carson McCullers's *A Member of the Wedding,* whose twelve-year-old heroine Frankie is in unhappy transition from child to woman. During the summer of 1943 in which the book takes place, she is in what anthropologists call a liminal (or threshold) position—as McCullers puts it, she is "an unjoined person who hung around in doorways." Her mother is dead and her father remote and uninterested, so there is nobody to stop Frankie from going downtown one morning in her best pink organdy dress, wearing "lipstick and Sweet Serenade." In this culture, as in many others, children put on more adult clothes for formal occasions, and Frankie's dress would no doubt have been perfectly appropriate for a twelve-year-old at a party or in church. But in an everyday setting, even without the lipstick, it is too old for her, as the remark of the black fortuneteller Big Mama suggests: "That's a sweet dress you got on. And them silver shoes! And silk stockings! You look like a regular grown girl." Unwisely, Frankie wears this outfit to the Blue Moon Café, which she knows is "a forbidden place to children." There she meets a callow and drunken soldier to whom she looks like "a cute dish" and old enough for a bit of fun. Frankie, who does not realize what is going on, narrowly escapes being raped.

Unless they are clearly a form of play-acting, grownup party clothes on a child younger than Frankie can be very disturbing, since they suggest a precocious sexuality. It is for this reason, perhaps, that adult circus midgets, with their aged baby faces, satin gowns and miniature tuxedos, make us so uneasy. The child who dresses—or is dressed—in workaday adult clothes troubles us less. Often we assume that he or she has adult cares and responsibilities: Victorian literature is full of these "little men" and "little women."

After adolescence, dressing older today simply involves dressing more formally or more conservatively than one's peers. It may convey information about one's political opinions, social background or cultural tastes, as with the outfits worn by Young Republican supporters and certain civil engineers. Or such a costume may be assumed for pragmatic reasons. The young executive or teacher who wants to look

Theatrical midgets, with their small stature, aged baby faces and elaborate clothes, may make us uneasy because they seem to be both children and adults. A midget orchestra from the 1920s.

older or more authoritative may wear a dark suit and heavy rimmed spectacles. If he is male, he may grow a mustache —which, like a beard, tends to suggest age, though less dramatically; even a large mustache seldom adds more than a few years. And of course the effort may backfire: a very bushy or elaborate mustache, on a young face, can look as if it had been bought at the toy counter of Woolworth's.

It is also possible to dress beyond one's years for a specific occasion: to gain admission to a bar or get a job in a restricted occupation—or, in the case of women, to attract older men or avoid looking like jailbait. Such deliberate and temporary deception, however, is most often limited to teenagers.

MUTTON DRESSED AS LAMB

Dressing younger than one's actual age seems always to have been more common than its opposite, if only because adults have more control over what they wear than children do, and for a longer period of time. In moderation it is well rewarded in contemporary Western society, where "young" is a plus adjective when applied to any garment or hair style

—or indeed to any dish, automobile or packaged smell. We are encouraged to think young, feel young, act young and speak young—spicing our tired middle-aged discourse with up-to-date phrases and catchwords. Above all, we are encouraged to dress young, and the most disparate styles for both men and women are praised in advertising copy as "young" or at least "youthful."

Overdoing the act, however, has always been treated harshly. Ridicule and scorn are heaped upon the man or woman over forty who uses adolescent slang or tries unsuccessfully to disguise the natural signs of aging: advancing waistline, retreating hairline, fading complexion or graying curls. Since classical times, literature has been full of elderly and not-so-elderly comic characters who affect the costume and manners of youth. The older woman who makes this error is especially apt to be castigated as "mutton dressed as lamb"; but men are by no means immune. Cousin Feenix, the elderly beau in *Dombey and Son,* "so juvenile in figure and in manner, and so well got up," is just as much a figure of fun as his relative the Hon. Mrs. Skewton, though he does not inspire the same horror—perhaps because it is only she that we are allowed to see in private at her toilet:

> The painted object shrivelled under her hand; the form collapsed, the hair dropped off, the arched dark eyebrows changed to scanty tufts of grey; the lips shrunk, the skin became cadaverous and loose; an old, worn, yellow nodding woman, with red eyes, alone remained in Cleopatra's place, huddled up, like a slovenly bundle, in a greasy flannel gown.

The crime of dressing too young is ranked according to the degree of the offense. A borderline case is judged merely as folly: the slightly too-youthful dress or suit, like slightly naïve language, suggests that you are a little immature, eager to be accepted by younger people or clinging a bit pathetically to youth. When the age gap between costume and wearer is greater, the offender is considered not only silly or pathetic, but a walking social embarrassment—the sartorial equivalent of someone who lies blatantly about his or her age. In this case, however, the shame is worse, since clothes never shut up.

Extreme disparity of age and costume, as with Mrs. Skewton, is seen as disgusting or even frightening. Why this should be so is unclear. There is no logical reason that a woman of sixty in a girlish dress should make us ill or terrify us, when we would be unaffected by the dress and the woman separately. Evidently some strong taboo is being broken by their juxtaposition; something forbidden is being said in the language of clothes. Possibly the forbidden message has to do with the persistence of sexuality into age, a phenomenon that until recently was often overlooked or denied. The past few years, however, have seen some improvement in the situation, and current rules about what an elderly man or woman can properly wear are also more relaxed. The sheep in lamb's clothing has also more or less vanished from serious fiction, at least as an object of teror.

The adult of any age who dresses as a child rather than as a younger adult is a special case. Occasionally the message of such a costume is sexual; it is a conscious appeal to pedophilia. In other cases the childlike outfit announces that a physically mature man or woman is mentally or emotionally

Childish dress on adults suggests emotional immaturity. The Alice-in-Wonderland hairdo worn by Julie Haydon in Tennessee Williams's The Glass Menagerie *(1945) canceled out the effect of her chiffon gown, and was especially striking in an era when almost all grown women had naturally curly or permanent-waved hair.*

still a little boy or girl. Photographs of retarded adults often show them in shorts or little-girl dresses, and in literature, too, childish dress is an accepted sign of permanent immaturity. Tennessee Williams uses it in this way both for Laura in *The Glass Menagerie* (1945) with her Alice-in-Wonderland hairdo, and for the child-bride in the film *Baby Doll* (1956), which gave its name to a style of feminine nightwear.

TEMPORARY LAMBS

For normal persons there is a taboo against wearing children's clothes, but it is one that operates only in the workaday world. When at play, and especially on holiday, the rules are relaxed. Indeed, resort wear everywhere bears a striking similarity to the everyday costume of children— often indeed of very small children.

The southern resort where I am writing this chapter (Key West, Florida) is full of adults dressed as toddlers or even as infants. They wear styles identical with those sold in the baby departments of stores: elastic-waistband skirts and shorts and slacks, polo and T-shirts with easy-off open necks and snap closings, and rompers or crawlers (now called "jump suits"). These simple garments are constructed of the traditional materials of infant wear—cotton jersey, seersucker and polyester—and come in the traditional colors: pale pink, pale yellow, baby blue, lime green and white. Often they are printed or appliquéd with whimsical images of birds and beasts, the penguin and the alligator being current favorites. Others of these temporary children wear loose shirts or frocks patterned with cheerful nursery designs of flowers, fish or sailboats.

Such clothes, which at home or in an office would be considered shocking or ridiculous, are perfectly designed for their purpose. They announce to the world that their adult or even elderly wearers are now honorary toddlers, licensed to play in the sand, dabble in the warm waves, eat soft, sweet, sticky, ordinarily forbidden foods and ride around on a miniature sightseeing train which is very much like the toy trains provided at amusement parks for the enjoyment of small children.

Among these happy infants one may see a few tourists who have not been able, or willing, to drink fully from the fountain of youth. They wear the dark or drab conservatively cut apparel of their everyday life, often supplemented by impatient or disapproving expressions. Others, more numerous, are clothed like children only from the waist up; below this point they wear city skirts or slacks and city shoes instead of the toddler's sandals or sneakers. Occasionally one sees a vacationer who is a baby down to the ankles but retains the lace-up shoes and socks or dark closed pumps of the business world, thus broadcasting the aesthetically unpleasing but unmistakable message that his or her feet are still on the ground.

Tourists who take their holidays in the mountains rather than at the seaside also dress as children, but as somewhat older children. Semiotically, this is quite appropriate, since their pleasures are those most often enjoyed between the ages of, say, seven and twelve: climbing up snowy hills and sliding down them, exploring the woods, sleeping and cooking outdoors and playing easy competitive games with a ball. For these simple but physically strenuous activities they wear the sort of sturdy, warm, brightly colored clothing usually seen on privileged grade-school children: jeans and sweaters and windbreakers and parkas and ski pants, all in the simple primary colors of an elementary school art-room chart: fire-engine red, grass-green, sunshine yellow, sky blue. Decoration and pattern are eschewed except for the simplest of stripes and checks. And, like boys and girls of the age they are announcing themselves to be for the duration of the holiday, they are rather boastful about their equipment, though now the scout knife with five blades and the two-color flashlight have been replaced by the more refined and far more expensive ourdoor paraphernalia available from L. L. Bean, Kelty and Grumman.

III
FASHION
AND TIME

Know, first, who you are; and then
adorn yourself accordingly.

—Epictetus, *Discourses,* 3.1

Although individuals have often been censured for
dressing too young or too old, fashion itself has sometimes
committed the same crime. At certain periods in history a
whole generation of sheep—not to mention some wolves—
has put on lamb's clothing; at other times the prevailing
styles for men and women have suggested advanced maturity, giving even the young a middle-aged air. These shifts
in fashion are not arbitrary and whimsical, as some writers
on costume have claimed, but the outward and visible sign
of profound social and cultural alterations. As two American
sociologists put it, "changes in fundamental modes of dress
indicate changes in the social roles and self-concepts of
members of that society."

The adoption of juvenile styles has attracted greater
attention from historians of costume, perhaps because it
usually happens more suddenly. Such a change, however,
never involves costume alone: rather, the whole existing
order of things begins to seem flat, stale and repressive.
Invention, experiment, novelty and above all, youth, come
into fashion; fashions themselves begin to imitate the costumes of children. Sometimes the modes copied are contemporary, but more often they are those which the latest
generation of adults wore when they themselves were

Eighteenth-century fashions were formal and complex. Hair, especially, often took strange and elaborate forms. Two examples of the "Macaroni" style followed by British dandies in the 1770s, and imitated in America by Yankee Doodle.

young. In putting on such styles they announce graphically that they refuse to step into their parents' shoes or to resemble them in any way. Instead they prefer to become, or to remain, children.

THE ROMANTIC REVOLUTION IN FASHION

In the late eighteenth century, clothes were—and for a long time had been—extremely formal, stiff and elaborate. The well-to-do of both sexes wore heavily padded, boned, laced and gilded and embroidered garments that made them resemble walking birthday cakes. Their feet were squeezed into high-heeled pointed shoes. Men's heads were burdened with curled and powdered wigs; women's with complicated constructions of real and false hair that might take hours to arrange and sometimes reached amazing heights; they can be seen in portraits of Marie Antoinette and the ladies of her court. Some fashionable men went almost as far: the "macaroni" style, originated about 1770 by young English dandies who had traveled in Italy, included an exaggerated pompadour topped with whimsical headgear. When Yankee Doodle "stuck a feather in his hat and called it Macaroni" he was imitating these gallants—not, as I once thought, pretending to have decorated his tricorn with pasta.

Although a shift to simpler and more childlike styles took place at the time of the American and French Revolutions, it was not the result of these upheavals, but rather another manifestation of widespread political, social and cultural change. Even before 1776 the Romantic movement, with its emphasis on the simple and the natural, had begun to be reflected in costume. It was especially evident in England, where lace ruffles for men and immense hoops for women began to disappear in the early 1770s. American fashions followed the English, though at some distance, as is usual in the provinces. The American Revolution did little to revolutionize dress, and many of the Founding Fathers wore gold-laced coats and powdered hair.

In France extravagance and overdecoration continued up to the eve of the Revolution, when the Third Estate abolished class distinctions in dress and terrified aristocrats gave up their hoops and jewels. In a crisis, however, few people have time to buy or design new outfits; and Citizen Robespierre, when ordering noblemen to the guillotine, wore garments cut much like theirs, though without elaborate decoration. Once the crisis had passed, simpler styles came in, first imitating those already worn in England, and then carrying them to extremes.

By 1800, women and men on both sides of the Channel were wearing the sort of clothes they might have worn as children: low-cut, high-waisted white muslin dresses for women; simple untrimmed jackets and white or buff-colored trousers for men. The elaborate wigs and coiffures had given way to shorter, more natural-looking hair. Skirts had risen from the ground to reveal ankles clad in childish white stockings, and flat-heeled slippers were favored by both sexes. Just as the poems of Blake and Wordsworth proclaimed the natural virtue and nobility of childhood, so these outfits announced the childlike energy, spontaneity and romantic sensibility of their wearers.

EARLY VICTORIANS: THE SILLY LITTLE GIRL AND THE DROOPING ADOLESCENT

As the Romantic movement entered its second generation, producing the rich and highly colored poetry of Keats, Byron and Shelley, modes began to alter. Female dress, though retaining its basic high-waisted, tubular shape, became more richly decorated and colorful. Gradually, skirts and sleeves grew fuller; ruffles, trimmings and bows appeared; and young women began to look like walking boudoir lamps. Men's clothes, though they did not change as much, also became bulkier and more colorful. This was the period of the dandy, with his high stock, pouter-pigeon chest, striped waistcoat and tight yellow buckskin trousers. By 1820, the early Victorian pattern was established: the elegant, inflated male and the elaborately trimmed childish female, immature in both mind and body.

The next thirty years saw variations on this theme

which have been well described by historians of fashion. First came the silly-little-girl look of the 1820s, all ribbons and puffs and curls, ballooning sleeves and oversize, flyaway hats. To be small and slight was now an advantage: tiny hands, feet and waists were made the most of, and the bosom was suppressed or concealed by flat shawl collars. As these clothes suggest, frivolity and even inanity had become desirable feminine characteristics. Ignorance, which implied innocence, was preferred to wit and sense, which suggested familiarity with—if not experience of—impurity. Dora Spenlow in *David Copperfield,* with her sighs and pouts and childish fears, is a fine example of the type, portrayed twenty years later when its disadvantages had become more apparent.

Geoffrey Squire, in his brilliant study *Dress and Society,* has pointed out that during the course of the nineteenth century the feminine ideal as revealed by fashion gradually aged. Women's clothes evolved from the simple white muslin frocks of 1800 (which, though he does not say so, might well be compared to baby dresses) to the heavy, matronly "tailor-mades" of the nineties. In 1810, the ideal woman was a toddler; in 1820 she had grown into a child; and by the mid-1830s she had become a sensitive adolescent, modest and retiring rather than naïvely pert. The good girls in

By the early 1800s adults as well as children had abandoned the elaborate, uncomfortable fashions of the eighteenth century and were wearing simple clothes and hair styles of the sort that had earlier been recommended for the young by Rousseau and his followers. The Hope Family, *by Benjamin West, 1802.*

the early novels of Dickens are often of this type, from Rose Maylie and Florence Dombey ("both child and woman seemed at once expressed in her fair face and fragile delicacy of shape") to Little Dorrit. Jane Eyre, too, whatever her internal turmoil, presents this aspect to the world.

The early Victorian beauty as portrayed in contemporary illustrations and fashion plates was small and slender in build like the young Queen Victoria herself. She had girlish breasts and a narrow waist, large liquid dark eyes, no nose or chin to speak of and a tiny rosebud mouth. Rather than looking as if she were about to bounce away like a hot-air balloon, she seemed hardly strong enough to stand upright without the support of her clothes. Her head drooped helplessly if gracefully on her slender neck above sloping shoulders—the more sloping the better. Between 1830 and 1870 "the more closely a woman's shoulders resembled the top of a champagne bottle the more she was admired."

Clothes metamorphosed to suit this new ideal. Skirts dropped to the floor again, and the huge puffed sleeves sank weakly toward the wrists and then deflated entirely; neat tucks and braid replaced the flyaway bows and frills of the early 1830s. The look of childish high spirits vanished; instead dresses were cut to accentuate the submissive slope of the dropped shoulders. In these clothes women walked and moved less vigorously. The longer corsets and heavier skirts weighed them down, while deep collars, tight lace fichus and bulky fringed shawls made it difficult or even impossible for the fashionable female to raise her arms very far, emphasizing her charming helplessness. Her hair, too, lost its curl and bounce; now it was parted in the middle and drawn back in two smooth, drooping wings. The sides of her hat descended and closed in on her face, becoming a poke bonnet that shut out the view on both sides like a horse's blinkers. This inconvenient form of headdress graphically announced that its wearer was too delicate and sensitive to bear the gaze of the multitude. At the same time, it perfectly expressed the idea that a nice woman would naturally have a limited and narrow view of the world; that her glance would not stray aside as she passed through life.

It should be pointed out, of course, that the early Victo-

THE QUEEN & PRINCE ALBERT'S POLKA.

Queen Victoria as a girl conformed to the early-Victorian ideal of beauty: she was small and slender, with large dark eyes and a rosebud mouth. The Queen dancing with her husband, Prince Albert, in 1840, the year of her wedding.

rian woman was an ideal, not an actuality. Women whose personality and physical attributes fit the prevailing mode adopted it gladly, just as they do today. Others were less fortunate:

> For the first fifty years of the nineteenth century, while the whole aim of fashionable dress was to create an idealized youthful fragile prettiness, those women who were large, brisk, and middle-aged often had no alternative but to appear comic or tragic, should they be inclined to comply with the mode.

Those who did not want to look girlish and helpless, or were physically ill-equipped for the part, might prefer to be out of fashion, at least for the time being.

THE VICTORIAN MAN AND HIS BEARD

As the years passed, styles for both sexes gradually became more mature, with men at first holding a considerable lead. Already by mid-century they had begun to give up their colorful cravats, elegant figure-fitting coats, tight trousers and flat pumps. The ideal man was no longer a slim, romantic youth; he was now large, even solid. During the latter part of the century it was no disgrace to be portly, and the phrase "a fine figure of a man" implied dimensions that today would suggest self-indulgence and imminent heart attack.

Men's clothes emphasized this outsize look. Looser coats and fuller trousers suggested or accommodated excess weight; apparent height was increased by boots with substantial heels and a tall, shiny top hat. Darker colors also began to dominate, and by mid-century black was the only respectable color for a respectable evening suit. When in public the fashionable male usually carried a cane or a rolled umbrella as a sign of his masculine power and authority. In cold weather he wore a heavy overcoat often made even heavier by the addition of one or more capes; sometimes this garment was so long and full as to suggest the robe traditionally associated with age and authority.

The full beards and mustaches that became fashionable during the second half of the nineteenth century added to the look of maturity. To a social historian the phenomenon is extremely striking, since for the previous hundred and fifty years most men in England and America had been clean-shaven; whiskers were so rare that in 1794 a lady in Philadelphia was equally astonished to see an elephant and two bearded men on the streets of that city. The full, untrimmed beard, especially, was a sign of extreme old age and/or of negligence and eccentricity—possibly even of madness, as with the thick white beard worn by King George III in his final years. In Washington Irving's story, Rip Van Winkle's foot-long gray beard is the first thing that strikes his former neighbors when he returns from his long sleep:

> They all stared at him with equal marks of surprise, and whenever they cast their eyes upon him, invariably stroked their chins.

And when he reenters the village,

> A troop of strange children ran at his heels, hooting after him, and pointing at his grey beard. The dogs, too, . . . barked at him as he passed.

Ostracism or even worse was likely to be the fate of anyone who consistently refused to shave. In 1830, for example, when a bearded man named Joseph Palmer moved to Fitchburg, Massachusetts, no one in town would speak to him. His windows were broken, and children threw stones at him when he went out. He was publicly admonished by the minister and when he stubbornly continued to wear his beard was refused communion. Finally Palmer was attacked in the street by four men. They threw him to the ground, injuring his back, and tried to shave him forcibly; Palmer drew a knife and fought them off. As a result he (not his assailants) was arrested for assault and sent to prison for a year.

But while Joseph Palmer languished (still stubbornly bearded) in jail, there were signs that the climate was changing. As early as the 1800s a few men had grown modest side whiskers, and by the 1820s and 30s some of these whiskers, like those of the English novelist Edward Bulwer-Lytton and his friend Count Alfred d'Orsay, had begun stealthily to creep toward each other under the chin. In 1852 *Tait's Edinburgh Magazine* prophesied the return of beards; and during the next few years they began to be recommended in both British and American periodicals, which pointed out that not only the Bible but "Nature" and "Health" favored them.

Then suddenly, on both sides of the Atlantic, men of all ages and professions began to let their facial hair grow; by 1860 every public gathering could show a flourishing crop of beards, mustaches and side whiskers (later known as *sideburns* after General Ambrose Burnside, the Civil War hero, who had a flourishing set). This remarkable vegetative phenomenon has never been fully explained. Some writers have attributed it to the influence of the Crimean and/or the American Civil War, when soldiers in the field found it hard to shave regularly. Though this may have helped to encourage the new fashion, it must be pointed out that beards did not become popular during earlier wars, when shaving must have been just as difficult. It has also been suggested that American men were imitating President Lincoln; however, Lincoln did not start his beard until 1860, by which time many of his contemporaries were already whiskered.

Whatever its immediate cause, the beard suited the late-nineteenth-century male image. Youthful romantic enthusiasm had been replaced by solid Victorian prosperity, and Victoria herself was no longer a slim young girl but a plump matron. In America too the ideal man had grown older. The young and vigorous revolutionary patriot, explorer or pioneer was no longer of foremost importance to the country's welfare. What was wanted now were men in the prime of life: men of authority, weight and substance—including substance in the physical sense.

These prosperous patriarchs seemed to many authorities to need and deserve beards. According to the *Westminster Review* of 1854, the beard had always been "identified with sternness, dignity, and strength" (now all plus qualities) and

By the mid-nineteenth century, romantic enthusiasm had been replaced by solid Victorian prosperity. Victoria herself was now a plump matron, and Prince Albert a bearded man of substance. Photograph by J. J. Mayall, 1861.

was "the only becoming complement of true manliness." An American guide to etiquette, *The Illustrated Book of Manners,* put it even more strongly:

> . . . the full beard is the most natural, most comfortable, most healthful, most expressive, dignified, and beautiful . . . Nature gave man a beard for use and beauty . . . The Gods and Heroes wore beards . . .

Historically, the universal reign of the beard was brief. In the early 1880s it began to disappear, or rather to shrink. As if by a slow process of deforestation, the forest dwindled into mere patches of shrubbery: sideburns and especially mustaches—some of them admittedly luxuriant. From about 1890 to 1920, the majority of American and British men sprouted hair on their upper lips alone. The reasons for this change are unclear. The mustache, like the beard, tends to add years—though not as many. It also suggests dignity and authority; however, it does not seem to be related to the ideas of patriarchy, wisdom or religious faith. Perhaps, as the Victorian family declined in stability and size with the declining birth rate and the increasing participation of women in the labor force, fewer men wanted to look like The Father of Us All.

VICTORIAN WOMEN: THE ANGEL IN THE HOUSE AND THE QUEEN-SIZE BEAUTY

The ideal woman continued to grow older during the mid-1800s, reaching adulthood about 1850. Now it was no longer enough to be innocent, affectionate and decorative; the really admirable female was a paragon of the housewifely virtues and skilled in domestic management, whether of a country estate and a staff of thirty or of a humble cottage. Though remaining gentle, sweet and modest, she was now also supposed to be resourceful, practical, charitable, devout, and above all strongly maternal, able to train and guide her many surviving children. This was an era of huge families, the result of lowered rates of infant mortal-

The mid-nineteenth century was an era of huge families, the result of lowered infant mortality rates combined with a high birth rate. Dressing all these children "properly," especially if they were girls, was a time-consuming task. The Cocroft family of Staten Island, New York. Photograph by E. Alice Austen, 1886. Copyright © Staten Island Historical Society.

ity; it was also a time of population movement from the country to the city and the suburbs. Fewer men worked at home or nearby, and the Victorian patriarch had to delegate at least some of his authority.

The mid-century ideal woman, at once divine and efficient, the "angel in the house," is well represented by Marmee and her eldest daughter Meg in Louisa May Alcott's *Little Women* (1868). Across the ocean, in a higher stratum of society, she appears frequently in the novels of Trollope.

Again, fashions obligingly altered to suit the altered ideal. Curves grew rounder, materials heavier, colors stronger; the sides of the sheltering poke bonnet drew back from the face, as if allowing the maturing woman to see more of the world metaphorically as well as physically. The beauties in fashion plates and popular illustrations of the time are now older and fuller of figure; above all, they take up more space. This was the age of the crinoline, and later of the bustle, and the increased importance of women in the domestic and social sphere was signaled by their sheer bulk. The oversize fashions also allowed them to display their father's or husband's wealth to the fullest extent.

The outsize American beauty: Charles Dana Gibson's queenly Gibson Girl, who was usually portrayed as larger than her male contemporaries, 1898.

In the final decades of the nineteenth century, the ideal female continued to become larger and older. Her size was a sign of increasing public visibility; in growing numbers now women were going to college, working for a living and campaigning for legal and political equality. But even when she remained at home as a showpiece, the late Victorian and Edwardian woman was an impressive creature physically. Height and weight above the average had ceased to be a liability and become an asset. Authors compared their heroines to goddesses, praising their classic proportions, or described them as regal and queenly—whatever their social origins. George Du Maurier's statuesque Trilby, in the novel of the same name (1894), was only one of many outsize beauties.

For those not properly endowed by nature, like the child heroine of Katherine Anne Porter's "Old Mortality" (1939), there was no hope:

> . . . a beauty must be tall; whatever color the eyes, the hair must be dark, the darker the better; the skin must be pale and smooth . . . she would never be tall; and this meant, of course, that she would never be a beauty . . .

We can see the ideal type in photographs of famous beauties like Maud Gonne, Lily Langtry and Jennie Churchill, as well as in contemporary fashion plates. She was opulently built, with the figure of a woman in prosperous middle age: round, well-fleshed arms and broad shoulders, heavy hips and rear, and a full but low-slung matronly bosom. A small waist, created by rigid and painful corseting, emphasized the bulk above and below. Her carriage was erect, her shoulders square; her chin was prominent, her profile Grecian, her features large and well-defined, her ex-

The ideal woman of the late-Victorian period was tall, generously proportioned and self-confident. Lady Randolph Churchill, the mother of Winston Churchill. Photograph by Barraud, 1888.

pression graciously domineering. The timid, fairylike child of the early nineteenth century had become the confident Junoesque beauty painted by Sargent and drawn by Charles Dana Gibson.

Contemporary fashions showed off this marvelous creature to full advantage, and offered the woman of merely average dimensions hope of emulating her. There were rigid padded corsets to produce the fashionable S-curved figure, corset covers trimmed with waterfalls of starched lace to fill out the bosom, blouses with immense puffed sleeves to extend the shoulders, high collars to elevate and support the chin and heavy trailing skirts. Boots with substantial heels increased the goddess's stature; and her upswept hairdo, puffed out over pads of wire and horsehair and topped with an immense hat, might well add another foot. As contemporary photographs show, in this costume the mature beauty looked glorious. Younger and slimmer women, however, often appeared awkward and cluttered with decoration; thinner women seemed gaunt; and the pocket Venus was reduced to an untidy bundle of expensive washing.

THE TWENTIES: CHILDREN OF THE JAZZ AGE

A second revolution in fashion took place during and just after World War I, when Europe and America politically, economically and culturally entered what was then called "the modern world." Again, youth and novelty were in fashion, and fashion transformed itself to emphasize and proclaim youth. Thousands of women entered the second decade of the century shaped like hourglasses and came out of it shaped like rolls of carpet, though often only with the assistance of painful flattening corsets and starvation diets.

Even before the war the Edwardian figure had begun to diminish, and by 1914 women's clothes followed more or less natural lines. During the war years, fashions remained conservative, though skirts rose slowly from floor level to just above the ankle, easing the life of the many women now working outside the home or serving as nurses or members of the auxiliary corps. After peace broke out hems continued to rise more rapidly and waistlines to expand. Dresses became brief sacks, low-cut and often sleeveless; hats shrunk into tight cloches. Curves were out; instead a "boyish" figure was admired, flat both before and aft, with long thin legs.

Historians of costume have put forward various explanations for the modes of the 1920s. Some have attributed them to the need of the human species to maintain its numbers; to make up for the loss of population in World War I. According to this theory, women's fashions had to be sexually provocative in order to boost the birth rate. But though an unconscious wish for increased procreation may have been responsible for the sexual freedom of the 1920s, it cannot be claimed that the clothes of the period, with their

suppression of secondary sex characteristics, were intrinsi-
cally more provocative than those of the previous generation. It has also been suggested that women were asserting
their new-won rights by dressing like men; or, alternatively,
that they were trying to replace the young males who had
died in World War I.

*Women entered the second decade of the
twentieth century shaped like hourglasses, and
came out of it shaped like rolls of carpet. The
tubular look of the early 1920s, in a British
fashion photograph of "motoring and sports
coats," 1924.*

Possibly some or all of these motives were operating;
but a glance at contemporary photographs and films shows
that women in the 1920s did not look like men, but rather
like children—like the little girls they had been ten to
twenty years earlier, and (to a lesser extent) the little boys
they had played with. Just as before, the clock had been
turned back; but whereas a hundred years earlier the ideal
woman had been a good and innocent little girl, she was now
a daring, even a naughty, tomboy. The "flapper" of the
1920s was high-spirited, flirtatious and often reckless in her
search for fun and thrills. And though she might have the
figure of an adolescent boy, her face was that of a small
child: round and soft, with a turned-up nose, saucer eyes
and a pouting "bee-stung" mouth. Her bobbed hair curled
about her head like a child's, or clung to it like a baby's.
(Only a minority ever adopted the authentic boy's haircut
or "Eton crop," which was unflattering in its severity.)

Fashions by and large imitated the clothes that little girls had worn in the previous two decades, with occasional borrowings from those of little boys. Women wore loose smocklike or sacklike dresses that ended just below the knee and were either waistless or belted at hip level; and the fine thin materials and pale colors of an earlier childhood—cream, beige, white and soft pastels—were favored. After nearly a century of skintight or rather corsettight gowns these loose, short frocks made women look like little girls dressed in their mothers' old blouses. Large-scale trimmings, huge artificial flowers of silk and velvet, and heavy ropes of beads, by making their wearers look small in proportion, added to the childish effect.

One popular style of the 1920s was the dress cut to look like a shirt, with an outsize collar and floppy bow tie of the kind seen on little boys ten or twenty years earlier. Another favorite was the Peter Pan collar, named after James Barrie's hero—who, as you will recall, was chiefly famous for his refusal to grow up. Middy blouses and skirts were now worn by grown women as well as children, and the ankle-strap button shoes or "Mary Janes" once traditional for little girls became, with the addition of a Cuban heel, the classic female style of the 1920s.

It was not only women who grew younger between 1910 and 1920; men too lost their Edwardian bulk and authority. If we follow the ideal man through the advertisements and magazine illustrations of the period we can see him gradually becoming slimmer and younger, with narrower and more sloping shoulders, less chin and less or no facial hair. By the early 1920s he is a good-looking boy rather than a handsome man in middle life, with a character to suit: athletic, daring, romantic, modern: a child of the twentieth century. In literature the same process was at work. Maturity ceased to be in fashion, and the strong, silent, self-reliant father figures who were held up for the admiration of men and the love of women by writers like Shaw, Hardy, Wells and Conrad seemed old-fashioned. They were replaced, more and more, by the son-figures who are the heroes of the novels of Joyce, Lawrence and Fitzgerald: romantic, sensitive, impulsive—and also occasionally weak and often psychologically unsteady.

Fashion, as usual, accommodated itself to the new type. Clothes were no longer designed to make men look as large and powerful as possible. They were made of lighter materials and often in paler colors: white, tan, light gray, cream. The high stiff collar was disappearing; suit jackets were shorter and shoulders were less padded. Trousers became high-waisted, suggesting a youthful, even a preadolescent figure. Sports clothes of all kinds were popular; and on informal occasions, even when they did not intend to play golf or tennis, men often wore the pullover sweaters, knickerbockers and flat peaked caps of their boyhood.

In the 1920s youth was in fashion, and both men and women dressed to look like children or adolescents. The flapper and her boyfriend. Drawing by John Held, Jr., 1926.

THE THIRTIES: TOUGH GUYS AND GALS

The men and women of the Depression years dressed to look like competent adults rather than playful children, in dark, serious clothes. Sinclair Lewis and Dorothy Thompson, New York, 1930.

The childlike fashions of the twenties passed away far more rapidly than those of the previous century. The Crash of 1929 and the economic depression that followed made the flapper and her boyfriend look silly and irrelevant. In ages of anxiety, childish high spirits seem frivolous or even callous: seriousness and maturity are in style; manly men and womanly (not girlish) women are admired. The thirties idea of good looks, as portrayed in advertisements and on the screen, was sophisticated and assured. Heroes had to seem able to withstand the blows of adversity as well as to make love and perform daring deeds; they therefore needed to be larger and stronger. Often they had a rugged, weatherbeaten look which in the age of Barrymore and Valentino would have been considered scruffy if not downright ugly.

The standard of female beauty, too, had changed. The flapper was passé; the ideal woman of the thirties was in her thirties, and classically handsome rather than childishly pretty: Greta Garbo had replaced Clara Bow. At first the thirties' beauty might have been called mannish; but by the middle of the decade the line had softened, and she was not only allowed but encouraged to have breasts. Literature celebrated these new types—perhaps partly invented them—and fashion dressed them. The battered tough-guy heroes and the strong, passionate heroines of Steinbeck, Dos Passos, Farrell, Cain and the later Hemingway appeared to best advantage in the serious, adult-looking clothes of the thirties.

Within a year or two of the Crash men's suits were becoming darker and heavier, as if to shelter them from the wind and rain while waiting on bread lines. Often they were double-breasted, suggesting even greater bulk. Trousers tended to be wider and the jacket had a fuller cut and much higher and squarer shoulders—perhaps to counteract or disguise the owner's slump of discouragement. Overcoats became longer, and many men wore the new-style heavy brogues, which often had thick rubber soles—useful when pounding the pavements looking for work.

Women's clothes too offered more protection from the

elements. As the decade progressed, thicker fabrics and darker colors came in. Skirts descended almost to the ankles at one point, and were covered by longer and heavier coats, often topped with high sheltering collars of fur. Most strikingly, women signified their willingness and ability to help bear the burdens of the world by literally squaring their shoulders. Suits, coats, dresses, blouses, sweaters and even nightgowns were fitted with shoulder pads so as to give an almost horizontal line that might extend up to three inches beyond the natural shoulder, making fashionable women resemble football players in full rig.

MID-TWENTIETH CENTURY: CONVENTION AND SOPHISTICATION

Between 1940 and 1955, though clothes went through many changes, they remained the clothes of grownups. The postwar New Look with its longer skirts added years and dignity to women, and the sober, well-tailored Man in the Gray Flannel Suit was their fit companion. Some men, especially in Britain, went even further, adopting what was called the Neo-Edwardian Look and imitating not their fathers but their grandfathers. The working-class youths known as Teddy Boys (Teddy being short for Edward) wore an exaggerated version of this style, with excessively narrow ties and trousers ("drainpipes"), and shoes or boots with even higher heels and more pointed toes ("winkle-pickers"). They rejected the narrow-cut Neo-Edwardian jacket, however, preferring a wider and more padded shoulder line that gave them a look of muscularity.

In the fifties there was a curious split in fashion. Suddenly it appeared that there were two different sorts of women. One lot was worldly and sophisticated and wore elegant, carefully cut adult clothes; the other was composed of "teens" or "girls" who might be any age from thirteen to thirty, and wore loose sweaters and skirts and jeans and Bermuda shorts. Fashions designed for the first group were photographed on haughty, high-cheekboned, neurasthenic models in their mid-thirties; those designed for the second group on round-faced, conventionally healthy-looking teenagers. In reality, these disparate females were often the same woman on different occasions: cinched into a tight "Merry Widow" girdle and stiffened satin for parties, and in loose casual clothes for everyday.

THE TRIUMPH OF YOUTH

Though some of the clothes of the 1950s were childish, or at least youthful, they were usually the clothes of good, well-behaved, conventional children or teenagers, suitable to a society that was well-behaved and conventional if not particularly good. Then, in the early sixties, a new wave of romantic enthusiasm and innovation—political, spiritual

The sophisticated super-adult look of the 1950s was sometimes also worn by children —even very small ones—on formal occasions. Photograph by Dorothea Lange, 1952.

and cultural, or rather countercultural—broke over the Western world. At first only a few social and aesthetic radicals were involved in what presently came to be called the Youth Culture. The majority of right-thinking and Right-voting persons were offended or bored by the new music, the new art and the new politics, but a shrewd student of fashion, observing what was being worn on the streets of Europe and America, might have predicted that in a few years youth would be adored and emulated everywhere; that, indeed, simply to be under thirty would be accounted a virtue.

Cynical social critics have suggested that this worship of the young was homage paid to economic clout. By the mid-sixties half of the population of the United States was under twenty-five, and a third of the population of France was under twenty. Since times were prosperous these children and young people had a lot of disposable income. And in a commercially sophisticated society the tastes, habits, mores and appearance of the majority tend to be celebrated and encouraged.

The glorification of the young in the late sixties and early seventies is too recent to need much description, and so is the exaggeratedly youthful look of the period. The fashionable appearance for women became that of an eight-to-ten-year-old child, with a child's wide-eyed pouting face and a child's figure: long thin legs, narrow undeveloped body and proportionately big head. This juvenile shape was achieved by strenuous, often medically dangerous dieting (it was in this period that *anorexia* became a household word). The large head was obtained only somewhat more harmlessly, by blow-drying, teasing, back-combing and spraying the hair—often with substances later discovered to be highly toxic. If you were a member of the counterculture, a similar effect could be obtained by allowing your hair to expand in an uncombed tangle or a bushy Afro.

Women's clothes, too, were those of children. Some styles recalled those of the twenties: the loose dresses, the rectangular silhouette, the small hats, and the large—this time often gigantic—collars and fastenings and trimmings. But this time fashion went even further. Skirts, which had

In the late 1960s fashionable young women dressed as if they were little girls, in loose, very short ruffled cotton frocks and flat slippers. Make-up bleached the mouth and enlarged the eyes to create an appealing baby-faced look. London, 1967. Photograph by Ken Heyman.

begun to rise in the late 1950s, cleared the knee about 1963 and a few years later were up to midthigh like a two-year-old's. The baby-doll nightgown and the brief lacy baby-doll dress attempted, with results which now seem ridiculous rather than seductive, to make grown women look like toddlers with a glandular affliction, or like severely retarded nubile teenagers.

Just as before, women's clothes imitated those worn by little girls ten or twenty years earlier. But the period 1930–50 had witnessed important changes in juvenile costume, and these changes were accordingly reflected in the development of sixties' fashion. The sack dress of the early period resembled the shapeless children's frocks of the thirties, while the jeans and trouser suits that became popular later reflected the fact that during and after World War II little girls began to wear pants for play and even to school.

Men, too, grew their hair longer in the sixties and/or had it styled in such a way as to increase the apparent size of their heads. They also readopted—or refused to give up—the clothes of their childhood. The short collarless jackets and long thick bangs in which the Beatles first burst upon the international scene were almost a direct copy of what small middle-class boys had been wearing to parties. But in many cases new styles were not necessary; men simply went on wearing the play clothes of their childhood: jeans, cord pants, sneakers, sweaters, T-shirts, turtlenecks and windbreakers. And, like little boys, they preferred bright colors: red and green and yellow and blue. What has been called "the peacock revolution" was fought by men of many different ages, incomes and political persuasions. Expensive designer shirts and ties patterned with flowers and stars and swirls were just as colorful and sometimes even more childish than the ragbag treasures of hippie chic.

THE GRANNY AND GRANDDADDY LOOK

One interesting exception to the vogue for childish fashions in the sixties and early seventies occurred when some young —often very young—people began to dress as if they were very old. Young men in their teens and early twenties appeared in the square or round gold-rimmed spectacles, collarless stiff-fronted shirts, woolly scarves and unbuttoned vests of stage grandfathers. In even greater numbers, young women of a similar age adopted the "Granny Look." They wore "granny dresses"—floor-length, high-waisted, ruffled frocks made of old-fashioned Gingham-Dog-and-Calico-Cat cotton prints—and "granny glasses," often without any glass in them. Sometimes, to complete the costume, they draped a fringed shawl round their shoulders, pinned their long hair into a bun, and carried their eye make-up, marijuana and small change in a Victorian beaded reticule which their own grandmothers would not have been caught dead with.

For, of course, the "Granny" or "Granddaddy Look" did not in most cases mean looking like the wearers' actual grandparents; it meant looking like the grandparents in a Norman Rockwell Thanksgiving cover of the forties. And the message of the costume was not conservative in the sense in which the kids' parents would have understood the words, but radical. Like other varieties of hippie dress, it expressed scorn and rejection of contemporary adults as uptight, phony, untrustworthy and warmongering. But its message was also in a way hopeful, even romantic, in that it suggested an imagined identification with the good, simple, honest Americans of a much earlier, even a pioneer generation. If she had to grow up, the girl in the granny dress was saying, she would damn well grow up to be like her great-grandmother; not like her disgusting mother who had voted for Johnson and Nixon and saw nothing wrong with dead baby seals and napalmed villages and indoor-outdoor plastic carpeting.

The young—often very young—women who adopted the "Granny Look" were not trying to resemble their own grandmothers, but rather those of a much earlier generation; their models were the pioneer women and feminists of a hundred years ago. An authentic example of the "Granny Look": Susan B. Anthony, women's rights activist. Photograph by Frances B. Johnston, 1909.

TO OZ AND BACK

The sixties and seventies were a time of great exuberance and variety in dress. Clothes were treated as costumes, and an observer on the main street of any large city and many towns in Britain or America might see persons dressed up as babies, grandmothers, cowboys, pirates, gypsies, Indians, soldiers, Christian hermits, Oriental sages, Robin Hood and Little Bo-Peep. The wildest inventions of designers—the see-through blouse, the throwaway paper dress, the plastic silver windbreaker—were enthusiastically purchased. Meanwhile, more conventional fashions languished on the racks while potential customers browsed in secondhand shops and at church sales.

Many social commentators, including some writers on costume, announced that the golden age of youth had arrived. Clothes manufacturers and fashion magazines, eager to reclaim a share of the market and chastened by the expensive failure of the maxiskirt and similar styles, began to assure consumers that they were wonderful, free, creative people whom nobody could possibly push around, or want to push around. We had entered an exciting new period of individualism, they said; the autocratic dominance of Paris and London and New York designers was ended forever. Henceforth, everyone would wear his or her Own Thing.

This pronouncement was wrong twice over. First, as pointed out earlier, it was not true that styles in the past had always been dictated from above. Second, and more sadly, it was an error to believe that the greening of America and the rest of the Western World would go on forever. By the end of the 1970s, a declining economy and a rising population-age bulge had made childhood unfashionable. Doing (and wearing) Your Own Thing had been redefined as narcissism, countercultural life styles as irrelevant, radical politics as disloyal obfuscation of the Real Issues and free sexual experiment as a neurotic incapacity for emotional commitment.

Today, the look of invention and play in costume, the childlike delight in the possibilities of dressing up, are almost gone. The romantic styles of the recent past have been replaced by expensive, conservative clothes—the clothes of responsible adults. The plus-word in fashion is "classic," and within recognized parameters everyone looks alike. Which is, according to your own sentiments, a sign of restored sanity or one of lost innocence and freedom.

IV
FASHION
AND PLACE

A man of sense carefully avoids any
particular character in his dress; he
. . . dresses as well, and in the same
manner, as the people of sense and
fashion of the place where he is.

—Lord Chesterfield, *Letters to His Son,*
LXI

As well as telling us how old someone is—or wishes
to seem—clothes can tell us where he or she comes from,
providing information about national, ethnic or regional origin. Or they can tell us what national, ethnic or regional
group their wearer wishes to be associated with.

FOREIGN LANGUAGES AND FOREIGN ACCENTS

The most obvious case here is that of the foreigner in native
dress—the sartorial equivalent of a foreign tongue. When
we see an Indian woman in a sari, or a Japanese in the
traditional kimono, we identify them just as we might identify a foreign language, without necessarily understanding
what is being said. Only if we ourself "speak" some Indian
or Japanese costume—that is, only if we know the sartorial
code of those cultures—will we have any idea of the particular messages that these garments convey.

Within national borders there may also be the equivalent, both sartorially and verbally, of a foreign tongue; often
the two are found together. The Amish and Mennonite
farmers who live in isolated communities in the United
States and Canada speak a unique language and wear dis-

tinctive clothing, and so do the Hasidic Jews of London and New York. To the outsider they may all sound and look the same, but members of these communities recognize many fine distinctions of meaning. Among the Amish, for instance, beards may be worn only by married men. The dress of Hasidic males in New York City, according to a recent study, indicates six different degrees of religious commitment, from the near-secular *Yid* who wears only the standard dark double-breasted suit buttoning from right to left

Among Hasidic Jews, the degree of religious and cultural commitment is often indicated by the completeness of the traditional costume. The man on the right, for example, wears not only the bekescher *coat and sable hat but also the traditional* schick *and* zocken *(slippers and white knee socks). Photograph by Bernard Hermann.*

to the *Rebbe* who also has a full beard, side-locks, *kapote* (a long black jacket), sable hat, *bekescher* (a Hasidic coat of silky material), and *schick* and *zocken* (slippers and white knee socks).

In other cases we see the sartorial equivalent of a foreign accent rather than a foreign language: garments made abroad that imitate Western dress. As with speech, the accent may be pronounced or it may be so faint as to be difficult to detect or identify. East European visitors to the West often wear suits of native manufacture which, though they resemble our own, are differently cut in ways only a tailor could correctly describe. Though the rest of us could not explain why, we recognize these clothes as foreign.

Sometimes the foreign accent of a costume is obvious and deliberate. The fashionable woman who gets all of her clothes abroad is declaring, to those sophisticated enough to identify them, that she is rich and well-traveled, and also possibly that she does not care for American or British fashions. Hence the national outrage when an American president's wife buys her wardrobe in Paris, as Jackie Kennedy Onassis once did; or the insistence that members of the British royal family patronize native designers. Even when high fashion and large sums of money are not involved, the insistent wearing of foreign-made outfits suggests the rejection of one's native land in favor of another country. The BBC cameraman who buys his gear when on assignment in the States, or the American lady executive whose clothes were made in Italy, are in a sense imaginary citizens of Los Angeles and Rome, and may be expected to manifest some of the traits associated with these cities in the popular mind.

FASHIONABLE AND UNFASHIONABLE COUNTRIES

Fashion, as opposed to mere dress, is traditionally sprinkled with foreign terms, resembling in this the conversation of certain fashionable people. Not just any foreign terms, of course, but those of the countries that are currently in fashion; for at any given period some countries are chic and others dowdy. What makes a country fashionable in most

Costume, like any language, may be "spoken" with a foreign accent that immediately identifies its wearer as a native of some other country. Ellsworth Bunker, President of the American Red Cross, meeting three Soviet Red Cross officials at the United Nations in 1956. Note especially the width and length of the Russians' trousers, and the condition of their hair.

cases is economic and political alliance or political power (though occasionally fashionableness will continue for a while after power begins to wane, as in the case of France). At the deepest level, this phenomenon is the expression of magical thinking. Like the savage who slings a bearskin around his shoulders, or sticks eagle's feathers in his hair, the contemporary European teenager in his Levis is practicing contagious magic: he subconsciously believes that the power and virtu of America is contained in those jeans and will rub off on him.

Whether as the result of magical thinking or of admiration for the outward trappings of success, the process of fashionable imitation has been going on for thousands of years. In Roman Britain prosperous natives wore togas; after the Norman invasion French styles became chic. The alliance between France and Russia in the 1890s and 1900s made fur coats for women fashionable first in Paris and then in London and New York. But the borrowing of the styles of a dominant or rising nation is not just a by-product of alliance; it also involves countries that are politically antagonistic or even at war. In the later sixteenth century, during the Golden Age of Spain, Iberian fashions were popular throughout Europe, and stylish English gentlemen and ladies adopted the stiff, tight-fitting black clothes of the Spanish court. The defeat of the Spanish Armada and the decline of Spanish hegemony were soon reflected in a softening of line and color.

When there is no single powerful nation, the styles of two or more foreign powers may be worn—though usually not by the same people. In the mid-seventeenth century, as Geoffrey Squire has pointed out, English Royalists took their fashions from Catholic France. The hair of both women and men was long and curly, and their clothes were loose, full, soft, richly colored and lavishly trimmed with ribbons and feathers and lace in imitation of the styles of Versailles. The Puritans, in contrast, took their fashions from Protestant Holland: men's hair was cropped short (hence the name "Roundhead," given to Cromwell's soldiers) and that of women was tightly drawn away from the face and covered by a modest cap. Puritan clothes, though they might be made of satin or brocade, were conservative in cut and subdued in hue—black, white and gray being the favored colors. (In Holland itself, as the paintings of Rembrandt and Rubens show, dress might be much more colorful and luxurious, but it did not exhibit the extravagances of ornament found at the French court: the waist-length plumes, the encrustations of gold lace, and the fountains of superfluous ribbon.)

A powerful country need not be near at hand for its styles to become modish. The Crusaders who went to fight in the Holy Land in the eleventh to thirteenth centuries had to endure an arduous voyage of many weeks or months. Yet they were able to bring back to Europe a selection of exotic styles that became the rage of aristocratic Christendom: the Saracen turban, the pointed shoes of the Turks and the

The English Royalists of the seventeenth century announced their political allegiance by wearing fashions based on those of Catholic France: long, curly hair and loose, soft clothes richly trimmed with ribbons and lace. James Stuart, Duke of Richmond and Lennox, *painted by Anthony Van Dyck.*

Jewish steeple headdress. The Crusades also introduced new colors such as azure and lilac, whose names preserve their Persian origin. In the late nineteenth century, the emergence of Japan as an international power was accompanied by a passion for Japanese prints, fans, pottery and—especially among aesthetes—for clothes which, though they look Vic-

In the latter half of the nineteenth century the emergence of Japan as an international power was accompanied by a passion for Japanese prints, fans, pottery, clothing and hair styles. James A. McNeill Whistler, Purple and Rose: The Lange Lijzen of the Six Marks, *1864.*

torian to us, were thought at the time to be Oriental. They can be seen in the paintings of the early Impressionists and also in the work of Whistler and Mary Cassatt. A couple of decades later the entry of Russia into World War I, along with the visit of the Ballets Russes to Paris, established her in the public imagination as a great power and prompted an epidemic of Russian blouses and furs and fringes.

When the styles of some relatively unthreatening country become chic, it is often because that country is currently the site of a popular and at least temporarily successful military or economic campaign. The expansion of the China trade in the late seventeenth and eighteenth centuries resulted in a vogue for real or imitation Oriental silks printed or embroidered with designs of bamboo, chrysanthemums and dragons; and for the loose, kimonolike sack-back dresses and robes seen in pictures by Watteau. Other eighteenth-century paintings show fashionable men in Chinese slippers, and fashionable ladies wearing Chinese coolie hats —possibly in the same spirit that a few years ago prompted some of their modern descendants to affect the padded cotton jackets of modern Chinese coolies. The latter fad, however, was more transitory, mainly because of changes in methods of mercantile distribution. In the eighteenth century it took months to bring even a single coolie hat back from the Orient; today King's Road or Madison Avenue can be flooded with padded jackets in a few weeks—and at a price too low to be fashionable.

Sometimes military or economic campaigns follow one another so rapidly that fashionable gatherings begin to look like United Nations Day at a children's school. In 1804 Napoleon's Egyptian expedition created a demand for turbans, cameos and shawls; the Peninsular War of 1808–14 persuaded Paris and London ladies to wear hats with flattened crowns and cover their shoulders with what were called "Spanish jackets." Mainly, however, Napoleon's military adventures were reflected in styles of ornament and trimming rather than changes in the basic shape of garments; it was almost as if the goddess of fashion herself knew that his empire would be short-lived.

THE PAST AS FASHION: CLASSICAL CHIC

One of the oddest things in the history of the arts is the way in which at certain times some much earlier culture, native or foreign, becomes extraordinarily popular. In the mid-nineteenth century it was the Italian Renaissance; a little later the Middle Ages. But the most striking instance of this phenomenon was the passion for classical Greece and Rome that swept Europe and America at the end of the eighteenth century and persisted into the nineteenth, influencing not only how the Western world looked but how it thought of itself. The founding fathers of the American Republic believed themselves to be the inheritors of the civilization of Greece and Rome. In both the United States and Britain politicians based their speeches on classical models and built their country houses in what they imagined to be the shape of Roman villas. In France the political history of Rome from Republic to tyranny was condensed into a mere three decades as if by some satirical college outline; and Napoleon Bonaparte, who became consecutively First Consul, Consul for Life and Emperor, had himself painted in a toga, reclined on imitation Roman furniture and drank from brand-new Roman goblets.

In the popular imagination of the time the neoclassical style in houses, furnishings and clothes indicated an admiration for the classical virtues and a generally high moral tone. Except when posing for their portraits, men did not wear the toga—which was just as well, since that garment is singularly ill-adapted to the cold, wet climate of Northern Europe —but they gave up their wigs and curls and had their hair cropped to resemble the busts of the Caesars. Women's clothes, on the other hand, became almost violently classical. Disregarding the weather, they shivered in flimsy white muslin gowns, low-necked and short-sleeved, which they believed to be identical with the *chitons* and *stolae* worn by Greek and Roman ladies; they padded through the rain and mud in thin-soled Roman sandals, protected only by a shawl with a Greek-key border. It is perhaps no coincidence that the early nineteenth century was the great period of female

The founding fathers of the American Republic saw themselves as Greek or Roman statesmen. Sculptors, turning the simile into a metaphor, often portrayed them in classical robes that would have been both chilly and embarrassing to their wearers. George Washington *by Horatio Greenough, 1832–41.*

fragility and ill-health, especially of what were called "complaints of the lungs." Ironically, these inconvenient clothes were far from authentic: for one thing, they were cut out and stitched together rather than draped and pinned. Moreover, these dresses were invariably white, whereas the Greek *chiton* and the Roman matron's *tunica* and *stola* had been dyed in many colors. To the neoclassical imagination, familiar only with Greek and Roman statuary, classical costume was always marble-white; and even this was a misapprehension, since as we now know the statues were originally painted in bright hues that wore off over the years. Early nineteenth-century women's clothes did not really reproduce the robes of classical virgins and matrons, but the frocks of contemporary little girls; they expressed not an antique but a juvenile simplicity.

More recent female fashion has not entirely abandoned the classical. The pleated silk gowns of the brilliant and eccentric Spanish designer Mariano Fortuny, popular with rich and artistic women in the early years of this century, were consciously derived from classical models. Even today one still sees an occasional draped and pleated evening gown or nightgown of white or pastel silk or nylon, often worn with a classical or neoclassical hairdo and intended to convey the same qualities of nobility, purity and dignity that it would have indicated in 1800. The woman wearing such a gown is often compared in advertising copy to a nymph or a goddess. Meanwhile, contemporary high style continues to reflect the international power struggle. In the past few years the West has gone through a flurry of Communist-Chinese–inspired styles, an outbreak of Arab caftans and Mideastern turbans and one of Russian embroidered blouses and shawls and skirts—the latter passing under the euphemism "the rich peasant look."

ETHNIC COSTUME AND ETHNIC PRIDE

Twenty or thirty years ago the statement that ethnic groups can sometimes be distinguished by their clothing would

The "classical" or "Grecian" draped gown has continued to reappear in fashion, though it has never again been as popular as it was in the 1800s. Today it is usually made of nylon or polyester, but it is still traditionally white, and still thought to indicate nobility, purity and dignity; the woman who wears it is often compared to a nymph or a goddess. Photograph by Horst P. Horst, 1938.

have been apt to arouse uneasiness if not downright hostil-ity. The fact that most people in the "developed nations" had access to inexpensive Western dress was a matter for self-congratulation, not only by the manufacturers but by advocates of a united world. It was taken for granted that the homogenization of Western civilization was both inevi-table and basically a Good Thing, in spite of the loss of picturesque cultural variety. Almost the first act of many immigrants to America had long been to discard the gar-ments that identified them as "greenhorns"; and most edu-cated Blacks and American Indians deliberately avoided anything suggesting folk costume. The first generation to cross the ocean or leave the fields and reservations might continue to wear head scarves or beaded leather; but for their descendants the wearing of ethnic outfits—except on holidays or for the amusement of tourists—was almost un-known.

Today the expression of national origin and ethnic identity through dress is often a matter of personal pride, and sometimes also a graphic form of political statement. The London-bred Scot in Highland garb, or the American Black in a dashiki, are determined that no one shall forget who they are for a moment. Such costumes are not only a reminder or a challenge to the outsider; they can also be a rebuke to other minority group members who are still wam-bling around town in the garb of the majority. The more total the ethnic outfit, the more seriously it is intended to be taken. The Scot whose only sign of his ancestry is a plaid clan tie, or the Black who wears a modest Afro with his or her business suit, do not threaten the rest of us but merely inform us politely if firmly of their sympathies.

When persons of foreign origin or ancestry deliberately adopt native dress, they tend to wear outmoded styles, those that they or their forefathers wore when they left the home-land. The ceremonial costume of Japanese-Americans, for instance, is more conservative than that of most contempo-rary Japanese. Similarly, those British Colonials who remain in former colonies often preserve the fashions—and the po-litical attitudes—current in Britain thirty or more years ago.

ETHNIC CHIC

The adoption of ethnic costume by nonmembers of the group in which it originated has social implications of another kind. If the clothes are what the fashion magazines call "ethnic," that is, third world, they suggest social welfare and/or countercultural interests, or a combination of both. This is true of native peasant garments of every sort: Eastern Indian print shirts, skirts, scarves and drawstring pants; embroidered caftans and djellabas from Morocco; Indonesian batiks; Western Indian fringed vests and turquoise bracelets; Mexican serapes, sandals made out of water-buffalo hide and so on. To be authentic these garments must be of "natural" materials: cotton, silk, wool and leather. If they are secondhand, so much the better, since they then possess the mana of their original owners who are in imagination, though not usually in reality, authentic natives.

The wearer of "ethnic" costume of this sort is almost always into one or several of the following: acupuncture, astrology, cannabis, Eastern religion, ESP, folk song and folk dance, homeopathic medicine, Indian or Near-Eastern music, massage, meditation, natural childbirth and lactation, organic gardening, Oxfam, solar energy, vegetarianism, weaving, yoga and Zen. The number of interests and degree of commitment can be gauged by noting how much of the outfit is exotic. A complete ethnic getup, especially one in which items from several different third-world countries are combined, usually indicates a full-time member of the counterculture, someone who is professionally involved in one of the interests listed above. At the other end of the spectrum, conventional clothes spiced up with exotic accessories (an Indian-print scarf and a heavy silver bracelet, for instance) suggest a merely avocational concern with one or two of the more respectable items on the list.

During the late sixties and early seventies ethnic costume temporarily became high fashion, and for a time it simply signified membership in the "with-it" generation. The results were picturesque; Tom Wolfe, always an acute observer of contemporary modes, described the scene in a fashionable London club, the Arethusa:

In the grand salon, only the waiters wear white shirts and black ties. The clientele sit there roaring and gurgling and flashing fireproof grins in a rout of leather jerkins, Hindu tunics, buckskin skirts, deerslayer boots, dueling shirts, bandanas knotted at the Adam's apple, love beads dangling to the belly, turtlenecks reaching up to meet the muttonchops at midjowl, Indian blouses worn thin and raggy to reveal the jutting nipples and crimson aureolae underneath . . . The place looks like some grand luxe dining-room on the Mediterranean unaccountably overrun by mob-scene scruffs from out of *Northwest Passage, The Informer, Gunga Din,* and *Bitter Rice.*

The wearing of what fashion writers call "ethnic" costume suggests social welfare, artistic and/or countercultural interests. When the clothes are "authentic"—that is, of natural materials and made by natives—the commitment of their wearers is greater than when they are merely copies. Advertisement in The New York Times, *1981.*

Today, though these carnival scenes are no longer visible, third-world styles are sometimes still featured in the pages of *Vogue* and worn by fashionable women. The garments they choose, however, tend to be the festival or ceremonial dress of the cultures from which they come, and are usually remarkable either for their rarity or for their expensiveness or both: Mexican wedding dresses with handmade lace and hundreds of tiny pleats, hand-tooled leather boots,

elaborately embroidered blouses and shawls, saris heavy
with gold thread and brocade, intricately carved African
ivory beads and the like. Although these garments are
mainly a form of conspicuous consumption, they also suggest a wish to appear original or exotic and at least a flirtatious interest in Zen, yoga, vegetarianism, etc. After all, the
society woman in the silk caftan could have bought a designer dress instead.

SECOND-WORLD CHIC: LATINS AND GYPSIES

What might be called second-world costume is less often
seen today. The folk dress of European peasant communities, for example, appears mostly at festivals and family
reunions, where the degree of identification with the Old
Country correlates fairly well with the completeness of the
native dress. A particularly becoming embroidered skirt or
lace mantilla may also sometimes be worn to ordinary parties by a woman who wishes to look piquantly foreign or
simply to provoke conversation.

A few folk garments, such as the head scarf, have become part of mainstream fashion and no longer have any
special ethnic significance. Others, only half assimilated,
remain ambiguous in meaning. The Latin-American
guayabera shirt, with its narrow bands of vertical pleats and
button trim, is beginning to be worn on holiday by men of
non-Latin descent, especially in Florida and Southern California. On a Cuban or Mexican-American, the guayabera
shirt is merely a sign that he is dressed up for dinner, a party
or an evening out. On a non-Latin, however, such a shirt
suggests familiarity with Latin America and/or makes a
claim to such stereotypical Latin qualities as relaxation,
spontaneity and a sense of rhythm. Attempts are now being
made to sell this shirt by mail order through *The New Yorker*
as "synonymous with graceful and casual living." Whether
this campaign will succeed and what the semiotic effect will
be if it does remain to be seen. Ethnic fashions, like national
fashions, go in and out of style, and as they do, their meanings change. The Tyrolean hat, once a common sight on

The popularity of ethnic dress in the sixties was soon extended to Native American costume. In 1968 both sexes began wearing clothes of fringed leather decorated with feathers and beads that made them look like children playing cowboys and Indians. These frontier costumes were especially popular with feminists, who found the trailing skirts and ballooning harem pants of many other ethnic female styles a physical and psychological handicap. Photograph by Jill Krementz.

commuter trains, now marks its wearer as either (a) of Swiss/Austrian/German descent; (b) a member of a bird-watching expedition; or (c) a bit of a ninny.

Certain ethnic groups, though not associated with any single nation, have managed to maintain distinctive styles for hundreds of years: the best-known of these is the Gypsies. Every little girl who has been to a costume party thinks she knows what Gypsy dress looks like, since it is one of the easiest to improvise out of available materials: a long, brightly colored skirt or dress, a bandanna knotted around the head and all the beads in mother's top drawer. (A Gypsy *dress,* in reality, is a contradiction in terms: in Romany belief women are *marimay*—taboo, unclean—from the waist down, and must always wear two-piece garments.) From time to time "Gypsy" clothes reappear as a fashion, and models are photographed in full flowered skirts, loose gathered blouses, fringed silk shawls, colorful head scarves, dangling hoop earrings and an abundance of gold necklaces and bracelets. When these styles reach the shops certain brunettes who feel themselves to be (or wish to appear) passionate, impulsive, tempestuous and possessed of strange powers (in a respectable way, of course), buy and wear them. So, misguidedly, do some blondes and redheads, who end up looking not like Carmen but like performing canaries. For men the Gypsy style is both easier to assume and more difficult, since what it mainly demands is looks of a certain sort. Men who are naturally muscular, dark-skinned and black-haired, with flashing white teeth, can manage it with just a dark shirt and a bright scarf knotted round the neck. For a stronger effect, a single gold earring may be worn.

When Gypsies are not in fashion the man or woman who choses to wear Gypsy costume is usually giving off danger signals: making a strong statement about his or her violent passions, restless habits, quick temper, jealous nature and possibly even financial unreliability. Of course this message may be undercut by a conventional demeanor or the simultaneous wearing of garments with contradictory meanings—a modest white blouse with a gypsy skirt, or jogging shoes with the male equivalent. People in such getups should probably be avoided, since they are likely to become fretful and restless with the routines of everyday life, and to chicken out in the middle of any adventure.

BLACK AND JEWISH FASHION: THE DANDY AND THE JAP

Black costume, especially that of Black men, is almost a language of its own like Black English, and one equally

Today urban Blacks often show a sense of style in dress that is lacking in many other groups. Black men, especially, are noticeable for the originality and superb fit of their clothes. An elegant New York couple. Photograph by Coreen Simpson, 1980.

difficult for the outsider to understand. Though highly distinctive, it is hard to describe except in general terms, both because it changes rapidly and because it has had so much influence on mainstream fashion. As many writers have pointed out, what the Black dude is wearing today is apt to be in *Esquire* in a year or so. This is not a recent phenomenon: according to one expert the so-called Ivy League or Preppie Look for men originated in Harlem, and the red-flannel shirts, plaid caps and checked cotton shirts now sold to prosperous suburban woodsmen by L. L. Bean were once worn almost exclusively by Blacks.

Urban Blacks are the dandies of today, the true heirs of Beau Brummell; their "boss vines" show a concern for fit and detail rare elsewhere, and a talent for daring combinations of color and fabric that a professional designer might envy. The special elegance of Black shoes and hats has often been noted, and some writers have suggested that they represent an attempt to minimize anthropomorphic differences: that the slim pointed shoes and wide-brimmed hats favored by Blacks serve to disguise their larger feet and longer and narrower heads. This seems doubtful; it might equally well be claimed that such shoes and hats proudly call attention to racial characteristics.

High-style, innovative clothes are worn not only by Black hustlers, but by Blacks in many legitimate occupations: sports, advertising, journalism, the theater and films, popular music and business. Lawyers, politicians and clergymen, too, are sometimes seen in a modified version of the look. The Black talent for dress is often celebrated in interviews with sports and media stars, and is an important feature of the folk "toasts" that relate the adventures of legendary underworld characters such as Honky-Tonk Bud:

> He was choked up tight in a white-on-white
> > And a cocoa front [suit] that was down [sophisticated].
> A candy-striped tie hung down to his fly,
> > And he sported a gold-dust crown [hat].

It takes money as well as taste to be a successful dandy, and in the past Blacks above the poverty line have spent much of their disposable income on clothes; according to one study, in 1950 their average expenditure was twenty percent greater than that of whites. Many writers have noted the Black enthusiasm for expensive and elegant clothes, and also for expensive and elegant automobiles. It has been suggested that these tastes, and the associated spending patterns, are related to the problems Blacks have traditionally had in acquiring other kinds of status symbols, such as membership in country clubs and houses in middle-class suburbs. If this is so, as equality of opportunity increases the relative elegance of Blacks may decline.

The one aspect of the Black language of costume that even outsiders understand is the hairdo. Straightened or "processed" hair is now recognized as a sign of accommodation to white values, while the "natural" or Afro hairdo— or, more recently, cornrows—indicates racial pride and intransigence. A striking phenomenon of the sixties and seventies was the imitation of the Black natural hairstyle by radical whites. What came to be known as a "Jewish Afro" (even when it appeared on WASPS) was not only adopted by those who could do so easily because of the texture of their hair. It was also achieved with the help of a drastic permanent wave by some "white Negroes" whose natural locks were as straight as a plumb line. The effect, especially on blondes, was extremely odd. More recently, in 1979, the cornrow braids of native African and ethnically conscious Black women were imitated: first by the white star of the film *10*, Bo Derek; and then by fashionable women attracted to the style by its obvious difficulty and expense: the beauty-shop version cost up to a hundred and fifty dollars and took three hours to complete.

The existence of typically Jewish styles, apart from those prescribed to members of Orthodox congregations by religious law, is more doubtful. The getup of the Jewish American Princess, or JAP, has been the subject of a comic poster widely sold in American bookstores, but the clothes pictured do not seem to differ from those of any rich, spoilt, contemporary college girl. Informants tell me that a passion for high leather boots and cashmere sweaters is characteristic.

The Black natural hair style, or Afro, is now recognized as a sign of ethnic pride—especially when, as here, it is allowed to become strikingly large. Coney Island. Photograph by Jerry L. Thompson, 1973.

It has also been claimed that the extravagantly bouffant and stiff hairdos worn by some Jewish matrons repeat, perhaps unconsciously, the wigs traditionally adopted by married women in Orthodox Jewish communities.

A current joke also suggests that certain fabrics may be associated in the popular mind with Jewish origins. It relates the story of two women who meet on a golf course. One introduces herself as Mrs. Cohen, the other, a Nordic-looking blonde, as Mrs. Smith. During the game Mrs. Smith hits her ball into the rough and exclaims, "Oy vey!"

"Say, are you Jewish?" asks Mrs. Cohen.

"That's right."

"I can't believe it. Say something else Jewish."

"Okay," replies Mrs. Smith. "Ultrasuede."

BRITISH REGIONAL COSTUME: URBAN CAMOUFLAGE

Before the present century regional dress, like regional speech, was extremely distinct; in some cases almost a separate language. Today the sartorial equivalent of the dialect is less striking, but most persistent. Persons of the same age, occupation and tastes dress differently according to what part of America or the British Empire they hail from; because of the static caused by individual variations, however, such regional differences are most easily observed en masse, for example at a national political assembly or at a professional convention.

Within the British Isles sartorial dialects, like spoken ones, are beginning to die out. Educated Welshmen, Scotsmen and Irishmen (and their womenfolk) are now difficult to distinguish on sight from the educated English. The only important remaining difference is between city clothes and country clothes; or to put it another way, between London and provincial styles—with the understanding that "London styles" can sometimes be seen in cities such as Manchester, Edinburgh and Dublin. Usually, however, provincial British fashion even in large cities is from two to ten years behind that of London and environs.

The most striking thing about British dress, both urban and rural, is its tendency to follow the principle of camouflage. City clothes are most often made in colors that echo the hues of stone, cement, soot, cloudy skies and wet pavements: black, white, navy and the darker shades of gray. (In places with a somewhat better climate, such as Brighton, lighter grays are more common.) These subdued and gloomy hues, like those of many British towns, are brightened here and there with color: the red of a pillar-box or a tie, the orange and yellow of a bed of marigolds or a flowered blouse. British city clothes are also cut and ornamented so as to make the naturally rounded human figure seem more rectangular, helping it to merge into the urban landscape. The disguise is most complete in the case of the male, whose city suit turns him into an assemblage of oblongs accentuated by a rolled umbrella and a rectangular attaché case.

Urban camouflage costume: these clothes repeat the dark or drab hues, rectangular outlines, parallel lines and grid patterns of the city. The shape of the men's hats is echoed by the roofs of the buses and (upside down) by the hanging street lamps. Commuters crossing London Bridge. Photograph by Henri Cartier-Bresson, 1951.

Hard-surfaced plain materials are favored; if there is any pattern it tends to be rectangular, narrow stripes being especially popular. This style of male dress was established in the mid-nineteenth century, a period of very rapid urbanization, and has persisted ever since. The only significant change has been in headgear: the tall "chimney pot" or top hat gradually died out as coal furnaces were replaced by gas and electricity, reducing the number of actual chimney pots and thus the usefulness of such hats as deceptive form.

Nineteenth-century women's dress did not follow the principle of camouflage, but rather the reverse. Brilliant or pale colors, broad trimmings and a profusion of rounded draperies and ornament made the female as visible and as vulnerable as a pink angora rabbit in Piccadilly Circus. Over the last fifty years, however, women's business and street wear has become almost as rectangular and subdued as that of men, and now they too can merge with the urban landscape if they choose. Today urban camouflage costume can be seen in all the cities of the world, though it is naturally most common in those that most resemble London in architecture and climate. Whether it mainly serves to conceal city-dwellers from possible predators, or makes it easier for them to sneak up on their prey, or both, probably depends on the individual. It can be observed, however, that the better camouflaged people are, the more subdued and rectilinear their dress, the more successful they generally prove to be—in the urban sense of the word "successful."

RURAL CAMOUFLAGE
AND THE SHEEPLESS SHEPHERDESS

Rural British dress is also based on the principle of harmony with the surroundings. The favored colors are those of the country landscape: browns, tans, blues and greens, particularly the muted shades associated with damp weather. Lavender and heather tones are also seen, especially in the regions where these plants grow wild. And whereas urban clothes tend to be hard-surfaced, like the polished stone and worn asphalt of an urban landscape, rural fabrics are usually soft and fuzzy. Tweed and wool and homespun repeat the textures of grass and bark and leaf, while corduroy, the traditional rural fabric, mimics not only the feel of moss but the look of a plowed field. These materials are made into baggy, rumpled, rounded garments that echo the uneven rounded shapes of the landscape—of bush, tree and hill. For centuries, these have been the clothes of the countryman, and often of the countrywoman.

There are also, however, what might be called theatrical country clothes: garments meant to suggest rural associations but unsuited to rural life. At the moment the most conspicuous example is the English shepherdess costume, known also as the "Laura Ashley Look." This style imitates the clothes worn, not by real shepherdesses at any time or place in history, but by Little Bo-Peep in children's books. It features figured cottons in pastels and white, trimmed with ruffles and bows and lace edgings of the sort that would make actual farm work impossible; white cotton Victorian nightgowns; lacy hand-crocheted shawls; and flat thin-soled shoes or delicate sandals that would be ruined in five minutes in any farmyard. This fragility, of course, is no error of design but half the point of the shepherdess outfit, which is intended to suggest rural values and pleasures without any hint of rural toil—indeed to proclaim that its wearer is no more a real sheep farmer than Marie Antoinette was a real dairymaid. Clothes like these demand constant washing and ironing, whether worn in the country or in the city (one of the saddest sights in London on a rainy spring day is the wet draggled hems of the urban shepherdesses). They are really only suited to a leisured life in the better-manicured outer suburbs.

As well as pretending to be country wear, these clothes are associated with innocence, youth and dainty femininity; they imply an interest in old-fashioned creative domestic pursuits: gardening, hand-weaving, jam-making, sewing and embroidery. When they are worn in town the message is "I don't really belong here, behind this desk or in this flat; my rightful place is in the garden of a rather large country house." Over the years the shepherdess outfit has gradually become more conservative in meaning; or possibly history

Modern shepherdess or dairymaid fashions, like those worn by Marie Antoinette two hundred years ago, are a very idealized version of rural costume, and are meant to suggest dainty feminine simplicity rather than a familiarity with the barnyard. Clothes by Laura Ashley. Photograph by Sally Fear, 1978.

has passed it by. Originally associated with Hampstead political parties and progressive schools, it now suggests a liberal or even Tory bias and what are called "old-fashioned values." It seems to appeal to the conservative, protective instinct in men. "I'd wear that sort of getup," said a London secretary who wouldn't be caught dead in it, "if I wanted some older man in the office to notice me—some guy who wants a nice little wifey."

Genuine folk costume still survives here and there in the British Isles, though because of the efforts of tourist boards and the manufacturers of post cards, it now has a rather theatrical look. The Welsh countrywoman's black buckled hat, shawl and long full skirt is probably seen more often on English, Scottish and Irish actors, folk dancers and waitresses than on ordinary Welshwomen. In Scotland, though fuzzy tweed suits are the preferred male garment, the kilt is sometimes worn by genuine Scots. Unless they are in the armed forces, however, these men are almost always sportsmen, intellectuals or members of the gentry and aristocracy. Visitors should be warned that the adoption of the kilt (never *a* kilt) by tourists is considered ridiculous and even shameful.

AUSSIES AND CANUCKS

Though the costume of regional Britain is beginning to blur, British colonial dress has remained highly distinctive. Australians, for instance, can often be recognized by their fondness for garments suggesting the pursuit of kangaroos across the outback: khaki shirts and jackets, clumsy sheepskin vests, high leather boots and the famous bush hat. These clothes may be worn by women as well as men. Another peculiarity of visitors from Down Under is their fondness for shorts, which is not only visible abroad but, according to travelers, gives the urban landscape of Australia a unique appearance. Both businessmen and working men may go to their jobs bare-kneed during the summer months, and informants have reported seeing doctors in white coats and shorts, professors in academic gowns and shorts, and law-

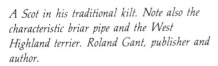

A Scot in his traditional kilt. Note also the characteristic briar pipe and the West Highland terrier. Roland Gant, publisher and author.

yers formally dressed in dark jacket, stiff collar and regimental tie, bowler hat and shorts. Below the area of brown, hairy, muscled Australian leg these men wore conventional black oxfords, socks and sometimes even garters. It is presumably not just a desire for comfort that prompts these outfits, but also the need to remind observers that even the most respectable Aussie is essentially a manly bushwhacker.

Canadian styles, appropriately, are more subtle, and like the Canadian accent often hard to distinguish from those of the northern American states. There is a tendency toward long woolly scarves, bulky sweaters (often with woven-in designs of cubistic reindeer and snowflakes) and padded down vests. In warm weather the individual English-speaking Canadian resembles a Midwestern American; though when they are seen in a group they can sometimes be identified by their fondness for plaids and checks. French-speaking Canadians, on the other hand, affect a somewhat more European style, and the women especially tend to dress more elegantly or more showily; even on sub-zero winter days they can be seen negotiating the icy snow-heaped streets of Montreal in nyloned legs and spike-heeled boots.

BRITONS AND AMERICANS ABROAD

According to the popular stereotype North American and British fashion are two separate and mutually incomprehensible languages. In reality, however, (like American and British speech) they are merely different dialects, not hard to understand once the basic linguistic principles have been grasped. The misconception has arisen mainly because natives of other countries are most visible to us as tourists, and British tourists dress very differently from American ones—largely because their notion of what it means to travel abroad is profoundly different.

America has a history of political isolation and economic self-sufficiency; its citizens have tended to regard the rest of the world as a disaster area from which lucky or pushy people emigrate to the Promised Land. Alternatively,

they think of other nations as mere showplaces for picturesque scenery, odd flora and fauna and quaint artifacts. The
American tourist abroad therefore wears clothes suitable for
a trip to a disaster area, or for a visit to a museum or zoo:
comfortable, casual, brightly colored, relatively cheap: not
calculated to arouse envy or pick up dirt.

Britain, on the other hand, remains in imagination a
world empire. Its citizens go abroad as representatives of the
Top Nation, concerned to uphold its reputation and present
a good example to lesser races. Britons therefore dress up
rather than down for travel, whatever the local conditions.
Even today one can see British tourists (especially those

Many Americans think of the rest of the world as a kind of Disneyland, a showplace for quaint fauna, flora and artifacts. They dress for travel in cheap, comfortable, childish clothes, as if they were going to the zoo and would not be seen by anyone except the animals. Tourists, 1970, *by Duane Hanson.*

born before World War II) silently and courageously perspiring in three-piece suits and ties—or in long-sleeved dresses, panty hose and tight pumps—in the extreme summer climates of Athens, Rome, Los Angeles and Washington, D.C. The legendary British custom of changing for dinner under the most unauspicious colonial conditions also survives as a tendency to dress up even more uncomfortably after dark.

Of course there are many British and American tourists who do not dress up or down and are therefore indistinguishable from citizens of the sister nation. But since they are indistinguishable, they are not distinguished, and the stereotype continues to thrive. As a result many Americans assume that the British are stiff and formal; while some Britons, equally misled, expect all Americans to be relaxed and simple, even crude. The degree of misunderstanding, however, depends on what region of the United States is involved, just as it does with speech. It is much harder for the average Bostonian to understand the speech of someone from Atlanta, for example, than it is for him or her to understand a middle-class Englishman. The traditional Bostonian language of clothes, too, is closer to that of London than to that of the Deep South.

AMERICAN REGIONAL COSTUME

Even today, when the American landscape is becoming more and more homogeneous, there is really no such thing as an all-American style of dress. A shopping center in Maine may superficially resemble one in Georgia or California, but the shoppers in it will look different, because the diverse histories of these states have left their mark on costume.

Regional dress in the United States, as in Britain, can best be observed at large national meetings where factors such as occupation and income are held relatively constant. At these meetings regional differences stand out clearly, and can be checked by looking at the name tags Americans conventionally wear to conventions. Five distinct styles can be distinguished: (1) Old New England, (2) Deep South, (3)

New Englanders like classic, conservatively cut clothes and, especially when in the city, prefer tan, gray, beige and black. If they are nearsighted they are less likely to get contact lenses, and may even prefer the serious, intellectual look their eyeglasses give them. The man is wearing a vest and the woman a sweater under her blouse, not only because layering is stylish, but because it is often cold and damp in this part of the country.

Middle American, (4) Wild West and (5) Far West or California. In border areas, outfits usually combine regional styles.

Americans who do not travel much within their own country often misinterpret the styles of other regions. Natives of the Eastern states, for instance, may misread Far Western clothing as indicating greater casualness—or greater sexual availability—than is actually present. The laid-back-looking Los Angeles executive in his open-chested sport shirt and sandals may have his eye on the main chance to an extent that will shock his Eastern colleague. The reverse error can also occur: a Southern Californian may discover with surprise that the sober-hued, buttoned-up New Englander he or she has just met is bored with business and longing to get drunk or hop into bed.

NORTHEAST AND SOUTHEAST: PURITANS AND PLANTERS

The drab, severe costumes of the Puritan settlers of New England, and their suspicion of color and ornament as snares of the devil, have left their mark on the present-day clothes of New Englanders. At any large meeting people from this part of the country will be dressed in darker hues—notably black, gray and navy—often with touches of white that recall the starched collars and cuffs of Puritan costume. Fabrics will be plainer (though heavier and sometimes more expensive) and styles simpler, with less waste of material: skirts and lapels and trimmings will be narrower. More of the men will also wear suits and shoes made in England (or designed to look as if they had been made in England). The law of camouflage also operates in New England, where gray skies and dark rectangular urban landscapes are not unknown.

The distinctive dress of the Deep South is based on a climate that did not demand heavy clothing and an economy that for many years exempted middle- and upper-class whites from all manual labor and made washing and ironing cheap. Today the planter's white suits and fondness for fine

Natives of the Deep South often enjoy dressing up; the men's clothes may suggest not only the Southern gentleman but also the dandy, and their hair is apt to be a little longer than a Northerner's. The women tend to look ruffly and ladylike, and by Northern standards are sometimes overdressed. This is also one of the few parts of the United States where hats are still worn.

linen and his wife's and daughters' elaborate and fragile gowns survive in modern form. At our imaginary national meeting the male Southerners will wear lighter-colored suits —pale grays and beiges—and a certain dandyism will be apparent, expressing itself in French cuffs, more expensive ties, silkier materials and wider pin stripes. The women's clothes will be more flowery, with a tendency toward bows, ruffles, lace and embroidery. If they are white, they will probably be as white as possible; a pale complexion is still the sign of a Southern lady, and female sun tans are unfashionable except on tourists.

MIDWEST AND WILD WEST:
PIONEERS AND COWBOYS

The American Midwest and Great Plains states were settled by men and women who had to do their own work and prided themselves on it. They chose sturdy, practical clothes that did not show the dirt, washed and wore well and

Midwesterners like practical, sporty clothes cut more generously than those worn back East. Lapels are wider, patterns larger, and there is often a fondness for monogrammed accessories. The hair, especially that of men, tends to be shorter than in any other part of the country.

needed little ironing, made of gingham and linsey-woolsey and canvas. From these clothes descends the contemporary costume of Middle Americans. This style is visible to everyone on national television, where it is worn by most news announcers, politicians, talk-show hosts and actors in commercials for kitchen products. A slightly dowdier version appears in the Sears and Montgomery Ward catalogues. But even when expensive, Middle American fashion is apt to lag behind fashion as it is currently understood back East; it is also usually more sporty and casual. The pioneer regard for physical activity and exercise is still strong in this part of the country, and as a result the Midwesterners at our convention will look healthier and more athletic—and also somewhat beefier—than their colleagues from the cold, damp Northeast and the hot humid South. Their suits will tend toward the tans and browns of plowed cornfields rather than the grays of Eastern skies. More of them will wear white or white-on-white shirts, and their striped or foulard ties will be brighter and patterned on a larger scale than those purchased in sober New York and Boston.

The traditional Western costume, of course, was that of the cowboy on the range. Perhaps because of the isolation of those wide open spaces, this is the style which has been least influenced by those of other regions. At any national convention the Wild Westerners will be the easiest to identify. For one thing, they are apt to be taller—either genetically or with the help of boots. Some may appear in full Western costume, the sartorial equivalent of a "he-went-thataway" drawl; but even the more conservative will betray, or rather proclaim, their regional loyalty through their dress, just as in conversation they will from time to time use a ranching metaphor, or call you "pal" or "pardner." A man in otherwise conventional business uniform will wear what look like cowboy boots, or a hat with an enlarged brim and crown. Women, too, are apt to wear boots, and their jackets and skirts may have a Western cut, especially when viewed from the rear. Some may wear red or navy-blue bandanna-print shirts or dresses, or an actual cotton-print bandanna knotted round their necks.

THE FAR WEST: ADVENTURERS AND BEACH BOYS

The men and women who settled the Far West were a mixed and rather raffish lot. Restlessness, the wish for excitement, the hope of a fortune in gold and sometimes a need to escape the law led them to undertake the long and dangerous journey over mountains and deserts, or by sea round Cape Horn. In more than one sense they were adventurers, and often desperadoes—desperate people. California was a territory where no one would ask about your past, where unconventionality of character and behavior was easily accepted. Even today when, as the country song puts it, "all the gold in California is in a bank in the middle of Beverly Hills in somebody else's name," the place has the reputation of an El Dorado. Men and women willing to risk everything on long odds in the hope of a big hit, or eager to put legal, financial and personal foul-ups behind them, often go west.

Present-day California styles are still in many ways those of adventurers and eccentrics. Whatever the current fashion, the California version will be more extreme, more various and—possibly because of the influence of the large Spanish-American population—much more colorful. Clothes tend to fit more tightly than is considered proper elsewhere, and to expose more flesh: an inability to button the shirt above the diaphragm is common in both sexes. Virtuous working-class housewives may wear outfits that in any other part of the country would identify them as medium-priced whores; reputable business and professional men may dress in a manner which would lose them most of their clients back east and attract the attention of the Bureau of Internal Revenue if not of the police.

Southern Californians, and many other natives of what is now called the Sun Belt (an imaginary strip of land stretching across the bottom of the United States from Florida to Santa Barbara, but excluding most of the Old South), can also be identified by their year-round sun tans, which by middle age have often given the skin the look of old if expensive and well-oiled leather. The men may also wear the getup known as Sun Belt Cool: a pale beige suit, open-collared shirt (often in a darker shade than the suit), cream-colored loafers and aviator sunglasses. The female version of the look is similar, except that the shoes will be high-heeled sandals.

REGIONAL DISGUISE: SUNBELT PURITANS AND URBAN COWBOYS

Some long-time inhabitants of California and the other sartorially distinct regions of the United States refuse to wear the styles characteristic of that area. In this case the message is clear: they are unhappy in that locale and/or do not want anyone to attribute to them the traits associated with it. Such persons, if depressed, may adopt a vague and anonymous mode of dress; if in good spirits they may wear the costume of some other region in order to proclaim their sympathy with it. In terms of speech, what we have then is not a regional accent, but the conscious adoption of a dialect by an outsider.

In the urban centers of the West and Far West bankers and financial experts of both sexes sometimes adopt an Eastern manner of speech and a Wall Street appearance in order to suggest reliability and tradition. And today in Southern California there are professors who speak with Bostonian accents, spend their days in the library stacks, avoid the beach and dress in clothes that would occasion no comment in Harvard Yard. New arrivals to the area sometimes take these men and women for visiting Eastern lecturers, and are surprised to learn that they have lived in Southern California for thirty or forty years, or have even been born there.

The popularity of the various regional styles of American costume, like that of the various national styles, is also related to economic and political factors. Some years ago modes often originated in the Far West and the word "California" on a garment was thought to be an allurement. Today, with power and population growth shifting to the Southwestern oil-producing states, Wild West styles—particularly those of Texas—are in vogue. This fashion, of course, is not new. For many years men who have never been nearer to a cow than the local steakhouse have worn Western costume to signify that they are independent, tough and reliable. In a story by Flannery O'Connor, for instance, the sinister traveling salesman is described as wearing "a broad-brimmed stiff gray hat of the kind used by businessmen who would like to look like cowboys"—but, it is implied, seldom succeed in doing so.

The current popularity of Western costume has been increased by the turn away from foreign modes that has accompanied the recent right-wing shift in United States politics. In all countries periods of isolationism and a belligerantly ostrichlike stance toward the rest of the world have usually been reflected in a rejection of international modes in favor of national styles, often those of the past. Today in America the cowboy look is high fashion, and even in New York City the streets are full of a variety of Wild West types. Some are dressed in old-fashioned, well-worn Western gear; others in the newer, brighter and sleeker outfits of modern ranchers; while a few wear spangled, neon-hued Electric Cowboy and Cowgirl costumes of the type most often seen on Texas country-rock musicians.

When the cultural climate is right, styles worn in childhood are often revived later as adult fashions. The overdecorated, obviously ersatz Western outfits seen today on the streets of British and American cities derive directly from the cowboy costumes popular with little boys—and some little girls—in the thirties, forties and fifties. Tucson, 1938.

V

FASHION
AND STATUS

Man from the earliest times has worn
clothes to overcome his feelings of
inferiority and to achieve a conviction
of his superiority to the rest of creation,
including members of his own family
and tribe, and to win admiration and to
assure himself that he "belongs."

—Lawrence Langner

Clothing designed to show the social position of its
wearer has a long history. Just as the oldest languages are
full of elaborate titles and forms of address, so for thousands of years certain modes have indicated high or royal
rank. Many societies passed decrees known as *sumptuary
laws* to prescribe or forbid the wearing of specific styles by
specific classes of persons. In ancient Egypt only those in
high position could wear sandals; the Greeks and Romans
controlled the type, color and number of garments worn
and the sorts of embroidery with which they could be
trimmed. During the Middle Ages almost every aspect of
dress was regulated at some place or time—though not always with much success. The common features of all
sumptuary laws—like that of edicts against the use of certain words—seem to be that they are difficult to enforce
for very long.

Laws about what could be worn by whom continued to
be passed in Europe until about 1700. But as class barriers
weakened and wealth could be more easily and rapidly con-
verted into gentility, the system by which color and shape
indicated social status began to break down. What came to
designate high rank instead was the evident cost of a costume: rich materials, superfluous trimmings and difficult-
to-care-for styles; or, as Thorstein Veblen later put it,

Conspicuous Consumption, Conspicuous Waste and Conspicuous Leisure. As a result, it was assumed that the people you met would be dressed as lavishly as their income permitted. In Fielding's *Tom Jones,* for instance, everyone judges strangers by their clothing and treats them accordingly; this is presented as natural. It is a world in which rank is very exactly indicated by costume, from the rags of Molly the gamekeeper's daughter to Sophia Western's riding habit "which was so very richly laced" that "Partridge and the post-boy instantly started from their chairs, and my landlady fell to her curtsies, and her ladyships, with great eagerness." The elaborate wigs characteristic of this period conferred status partly because they were both expensive to buy and expensive to maintain.

By the early eighteenth century the social advantages of conspicuous dress were such that even those who could not afford it often spent their money on finery. This development was naturally deplored by supporters of the status quo. In Colonial America the Massachusetts General Court declared its "utter detestation and dislike, that men or women of mean condition, should take upon them the garb of Gentlemen, by wearing Gold or Silver lace, or Buttons, or Points at their knees, or to walk in great Boots; or Women of the same rank to wear Silk or Tiffiny hoods, or Scarfes . . ." What "men or women of mean condition"—farmers or artisans—were supposed to wear were coarse linen or wool, leather aprons, deerskin jackets, flannel petticoats and the like.

To dress above one's station was considered not only foolishly extravagant, but deliberately deceptive. In 1878 an American etiquette book complained,

> It is . . . unfortunately the fact that, in the United States, but too much attention is paid to dress by those who have neither the excuse of ample means nor of social claims. . . . We Americans are lavish, generous, and ostentatious. The wives of our wealthy men are glorious in garb as are princesses and queens. They have a right so to be. But when those who can ill afford to wear alpaca persist in arraying themselves in silk . . . the matter is a sad one.

In Colonial America farmers and artisans wore simple, practical clothes of coarse linen, wool and leather. Paul Revere, *by John Singleton Copley, 1768–70.*

CONTEMPORARY STATUS: FINE FEATHERS AND TATTERED SOULS

Today simple ostentation in dress, like gold or silver lace, is less common than it used to be; but clothes are as much a sign of status as ever. The wives of our wealthy men are no longer praised for being glorious in garb; indeed, they constantly declare in interviews that they choose their clothes for ease, comfort, convenience and practicality. But, as Tom Wolfe has remarked, these comfortable, practical clothes always turn out to have been bought very recently from the most expensive shops; moreover, they always follow the current rules of Conspicuous Consumption, Waste and Leisure.

At the same time, as high-status clothes have become superficially less gorgeous they have increasingly tended to take on an aura of moral virtue. A 1924 guide to good manners clearly suggests this:

> An honest heart may beat beneath the ragged coat, a brilliant intellect may rise above the bright checked suit and the yellow tie, the man in the shabby suit may be a famous writer, the girl in the untidy blouse may be an artist of great promise, but as a general rule, the chances are against it and such people are dull, flat, stale, and unprofitable both to themselves and to other people.

The implication is that an ill-dressed person is also probably dishonest, stupid and without talent. Today this idea is so well established that one of our foremost historians of costume, Anne Hollander, has refused to admit that true virtue can shine through ugly or ragged clothes, as in the tale of Cinderella:

> In real life . . . rags obviously cannot be "seen through" to something lovely underneath because they themselves express and also create a tattered condition of soul. The habit of fine clothes, however, can actually produce a true personal grace.

In a society that believes this, it is no wonder that many of those who can ill afford to wear alpaca—or its modern equivalent, polyester—are doing their best to array themselves in silk. Popular writers no longer complain that those of modest means wear clothes above their rank; instead they explain how best to do so: how to, as the title of one such book puts it, *Dress for Success.* At the moment there are so many such guidebooks it may seem surprising that their advice is not followed by more people. However, as my friend the lady executive remarks, "wardrobe engineering won't do much for you if your work is lousy . . . or if you're one of an army of aspirants in impeccable skirted suits all competing for the same spot. As with investment advice, once everyone agrees that it's the thing to do, it's time to look for value somewhere else."

There are other problems with dressing to advance your status professionally. First and most obviously, it is very expensive. The young executive who buys a high-priced suit instead of a stereo system or a week's vacation in Portugal or the Caribbean is giving up certain present pleasure for possible future success in a society that regards hedonistic self-fulfillment as a right. Second, there are one's colleagues to consider. For many people, agreeable working conditions and well-disposed birds are worth more than a possible promotion in the bush. The clerk who dresses like his boss is apt to be regarded by other clerks as a cold fish or an ass-kisser; the secretary in her severe skirted suit is seen as snotty and pretentious: Who does she think she is, in that getup? Moreover, somebody who is distrusted and disliked by his or her equals is very unlikely ever to become their superior. It is also a rare boss who wants to have employees who dress exactly as he or she does—especially since they are usually younger and may already have the edge in appearance. Fortunately for the manufacturers, however, there are more ways than one of advertising high status. Today, "simple," "easy-care" and "active" may be the bywords of fashion copy; but fashionable luxury, waste and inconvenience continue to flourish in new forms.

CONSPICUOUS ADDITION: EATING AND LAYERING

The most primitive form of Conspicuous Consumption is simply to consume so much food that one becomes conspicuous by one's bulk, a walking proof of having dined often and well. Fatness, frequently a sign of high status in primitive tribes, has also been admired in more civilized societies. In late nineteenth-century Europe and America it was common among well-to-do men, who often, as Robert Brain has remarked, "were as proud of their girth as a Bangwa chief, the big belly being a sign of imposing male power. It was a culture trait among German men, for whom fatness reflected wealth and status." The late-Victorian woman, too, was often as handsomely solid and well-upholstered as her furniture.

In the nineteenth century fatness—especially in men—was often a sign of wealth and status: visible evidence that one had consumed conspicuously, and thus a matter for pride rather than shame. De Witt Clinton, 1844, by William H. Brown.

In general, the fashionable size seems to vary according to real or imagined scarcity of food. When a large proportion of the population is known to be actually going hungry, it is chic to be well-padded and to dine lavishly. When (as in England and America in the 1960s) there seems to be at least enough starchy food to go around, it becomes chic to be thin, thus demonstrating that one is existing on an expensive protein diet rather than on proletarian bread, potatoes, franks and beans. Today, when food prices are rising astronomically and the facts of world hunger have come to the attention even of café society, it is again no longer necessary to be very thin in order to be 'chic.

Another simple and time-honored way of consuming conspicuously is to wear more clothes than other people do. "More" of course is relative: when most people went naked, the mere wearing of garments conferred prestige. In ancient Egypt, for instance, slaves and servants often wore nothing, or at most a brief loincloth; aristocrats put on clothes not out of modesty or for warmth, but to indicate rank. Even in colder climates and more Puritanical societies it has generally been true that the more clothes someone has on, the higher his or her status. This principle can be observed in medieval and Renaissance art, where peasants wear relatively few garments, while kings and queens (including the King and Queen of Heaven) are burdened with layers of gowns and robes and mantles, even in indoor scenes. The recent fashion for "layered" clothes may be related, as is sometimes claimed, to the energy shortage; it is also a fine way of displaying a large wardrobe.

In any contemporary gathering, no matter what its occasion, the well-to-do can be observed to have on more clothes. The men are more likely to wear vests; the women are more apt to wear panty hose, superfluous scarves and useless little wraps. Even in hot weather the difference is plain. At an outdoor restaurant on a summer day the customers who have more money and have had it longer will be the ones in jackets and/or long-sleeved shirts and dresses. If it gets frightfully hot they may roll up their sleeves, but in such a way that there is no doubt about their actual length. On the beach, though the rich may splash into the waves in suits as skimpy as anyone else's, the moment they

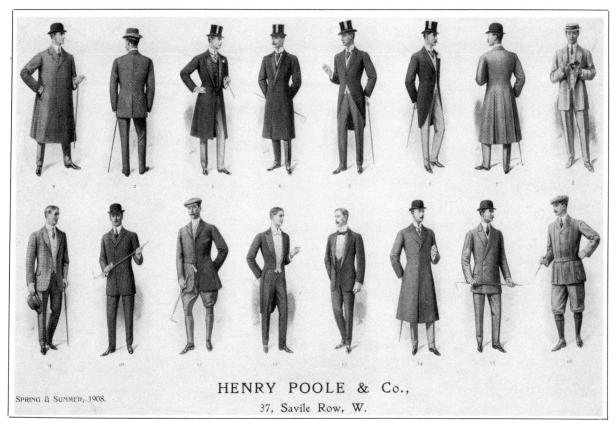

HENRY POOLE & Co.,
37, Savile Row, W.

SPRING & SUMMER, 1908.

In order to be correctly dressed for every possible high-status activity, the Edwardian gentleman needed sixteen different costumes. Advertisement for the Savile Row tailor Henry Poole, 1908.

emerge they will make a dash for the conspicuous raw-silk beach kimono, terry swim dress or linen shirt that matches their bathing suit and restores the status quo.

CONSPICUOUS DIVISION

It is also possible to advertise one's rank by wearing more clothes consecutively rather than simultaneously. Traditionally, the more different outfits one can display, the higher one's status; high society in the past has made this sort of display possible by the division of daily life into many different types of activity, each of which demands a special costume. As a 1924 book on etiquette puts it:

> In the world of good society, dress plays an important part in the expression of culture. There is proper dress for afternoon wear, and another for evening functions. There are certain costumes for the wedding, and others for the garden fête. The

gentlemen wears one suit to business, and another to dinner. Where civilization has reached its highest point, there has dress and fashion reached its finest and most exquisite development.

The contemporary man does not need to have a morning coat, a frock coat, a dress coat and a dinner jacket (and the appropriate trousers, shirts and shoes) as he did in the 1900s. Nor must the contemporary woman possess morning

By 1945 the number of outfits necessary for a gentleman's wardrobe had been somewhat reduced, but the returning soldier still needed at least eight complete costumes, seven hats and a tweed jacket to replace his army uniform. Cover by Alájalov for **The New Yorker**, 1945. Drawing by Alájalov copyright © 1945, 1973, The New Yorker Magazine, Inc.

On ritual occasions, social status—and the importance of the proceedings—is proclaimed by the wearing of expensive and specialized costumes that would be considered inappropriate in daily life. London church wedding, 1961.

costumes, walking costumes, afternoon costumes, tea gowns, motoring outfits and evening dresses—all of which it would have been considered extremely improper and embarrassing to wear at the wrong time or place. Today, the conspicuous multiplication of clothing continues to thrive, but now the emphasis is on sports rather than on social life. The truly fashionable person will have separate getups for tennis, jogging, hiking (winter and summer), bicycling, swimming, skiing, golf and that anonymous and disagreeable sport known simply as "exercise." If he or she also goes in for team sports or dancing (ballet, modern, tap, folk or disco) yet more costumes must be acquired, each one unique. From a utilitarian point of view there is no reason not to play golf in jogging clothes, or ride your bike in a bathing suit on a hot day—except of course that it would cause a drastic loss of prestige.

In order to maintain (or better yet to advance) status, it is not merely necessary to have separate costumes for each sporting activity; one must also have costumes—and where relevant, equipment—of properly high prestige. Just any jogging shoes, tennis racket or leotards will not do; they must bear the currently correct brand and model names, which tend to change so fast that if I were to list them here they would be out of date by the time this book appears.

CONSPICUOUS MULTIPLICATION

Wearing a great many clothes at once is a burdensome and often unpleasantly hot form of Conspicuous Consumption; changing into different outfits for different activities is a nuisance. An alternative or supplementary way of demonstrating high status is to own many similar garments, so that you almost never wear exactly the same costume. The extreme case of this is the person who—like Marie Antoinette—never wears the same thing twice. Today such extravagance is rare and felt to be excessive, but the possession of a very large wardrobe is still considered charming by those who follow what Veblen called "pecuniary canons of taste."

F. Scott Fitzgerald, in a famous scene, describes the effect of Jay Gatsby's extensive collection of shirts on Daisy Buchanan:

> He took out a pile of shirts and began throwing them, one by one, before us, shirts of sheer linen and thick silk and fine flannel, which lost their folds as they fell and covered the table in many-colored disarray. While we admired, he brought more and the soft rich heap mounted higher—shirts with stripes and scrolls and plaids in coral and apple-green and lavender and faint orange, with monograms of Indian blue. Suddenly, with a strained sound, Daisy bent her head into the shirts and began to cry stormily. "They're such beautiful shirts," she sobbed, her voice muffled in the thick folds. "It makes me sad because I've never seen such—such beautiful shirts before."

The particular type of Conspicuous Consumption that consists in the multiplication of similar garments is most common among women. In men it is more rare, and usually associated either with dandyism or with great and rapidly acquired wealth, as in the case of the bootlegger Gatsby. A man who gets a raise or a windfall usually buys better clothes rather than more of them, and he has no need to wear a different outfit each day. Indeed, if he were seen to vary his costume as often as his female colleagues do he would be thought vain and capricious—perhaps even unstable. Monotony of dress is only a minor fault, though a man who wore the same tie to the office every day for a week would probably be considered a dull fellow.

For a woman, on the other hand, variety in dress is essential, and the demand for it starts very early. In America many girls in secondary school or even younger feel acute embarassment about wearing the same outfit twice in the same week—let alone on consecutive days. Even if they own relatively few garments they will go to great lengths to combine them differently and to alter the total effect with accessories. So strong is this compulsion that quantity is usually preferred to quality, and shoddy new garments to well-made old ones. In terms of the struggle for status, this may be the right decision: young girls may not be able to recognize good clothes, but they can certainly count.

This female sense of the shamefulness of repetition

persists into adult life. One of the most double-edged compliments one woman can give another is "Oh, you're wearing that pretty dress *again!*" (Men, who know no better, are forgiven such remarks.) Often the compulsion continues into old age: my mother, when nearly ninety, still liked to appear in a different outfit each day "so as not to be boring." But it seems to be strongest among women in offices, for whom the fact that a colleague arrives at work on Tuesday in the same costume she was wearing on Monday is positive proof that she spent the intervening night unexpectedly at somebody else's apartment.

The constant wearing of new and different garments is most effective when those you wish to impress see you constantly—ideally, every day. It is also more effective if these people are relative strangers. If you live and work in an isolated country village, most of the people you meet will already have a pretty good idea of your rank and income, and they will not be much impressed if you keep changing

In the thirties both men and women occasionally exhibited their wealth by wearing fur coats—sometimes identical fur coats. Harlem, New York, 1932; the automobile, also a sign of Conspicuous Consumption, is a Dusenberg, which cost $7,000; the raccoon coats were $300 each. Photograph by James Van Der Zee.

your clothes. If you live in or near a city and work in a large organization, however, you will be seen often by the same people, but most of them will know little about you. Having a large and up-to-date sartorial vocabulary then becomes a matter of the first importance, especially if you have not yet established yourself socially or professionally. For this reason, it is not surprising that the most active supporters of the fashion industry today are young women in places like London and New York.

What is surprising, though, is the lengths to which this support can go. Many young working women now seem to take it for granted that they will spend most of their income on dress. "It's awfully important to look right," a secretary in a London advertising agency explained to me. "If a girl lives at home it'll be her main expense. If she's living in town, even sharing a flat, it's much harder. I'm always in debt for clothes; when I want something I just put it on my credit card. I know things cost more that way. But, well, take these boots. They were eighty-nine pounds, but they were so beautiful, I just had to have them, and they make me feel fantastic, like a deb or a film star. All my friends are the same."

CONSPICUOUS MATERIALS: FUR AND LEATHER

Through the centuries, the most popular form of Conspicuous Consumption has been the use of expensive materials. For a long time this meant heavy damasked satins, patterned brocades and velvets that were handwoven at tremendous expense of time and labor. Today, when the machine-weaving of such fabrics is relatively simple, but hand labor and natural resources scarce, the desirable materials are wool, silk, leather and hand-knits. When "artificial silk" (rayon) and nylon first appeared they were expensive and highly fashionable. But since the prestige of any fabric tends to vary in direct relation to its price per yard, the synthetic materials lost distinction as they became cheaper to produce; today "polyester" is a dirty word in many circles. "Natural" fabrics are chic now not only because of the current prestige

Today a fur coat on a man is apt to express personal originality or eccentricity rather than Conspicuous Consumption. Edward Gorey, American artist, writer and illustrator. Note the peaked cap, sunglasses and white gym shoes. New York, 1981. Photograph by Bill Cunningham.

of nature, but because they cost more than the man-made alternatives.

The wearing of the skins and pelts of animals to indicate wealth has a varied history. In the past, when the world population of beasts was larger in proportion to that of people, only the furs of the least common animals conferred prestige. Those who had been enriched by their rapacity in war or trade might cover their floors or their beds with rugs made from the skins of the larger and more rapacious beasts, such as the tiger and the bear; or they might on formal occasions wear garments decorated or lined with the pelts of rare animals. Merchants wore robes trimmed with beaver, noblemen preferred sable; kings and queens (as they still do on ceremonial occasions) decked themselves in ermine. But common hides and furs were the dress of the common people. A leather jerkin meant a peasant, a sheepskin jacket a shepherd; the furs of common wild animals like the fox and the rabbit were associated with hunters and outlaws.

In the nineteenth century, however, as wildlife grew rarer, fur collars and cuffs began to appear on outdoor clothing, and fur muffs and tippets became popular. In the 1880s it suddenly became fashionable to decorate women's costumes and accessories with real or imitation dead animals, birds and even insects, and little capes of opossum, raccoon and marten fur were worn. By the 1890s an entire coat made of or lined with fur had begun to suggest a large bank account rather than too great a familiarity with life in the backwoods.

The first fur coats were usually worn by men; it was not until the turn of the century that they were generally seen on women. For a while the fashion was unisexual; a stylish couple, for instance, might appear in public in identical raccoon coats. After the Depression, however—in spite of the efforts of manufacturers and fashion columnists—a fur coat on a man was a sign either of personal eccentricity or of sports or entertainment stardom—often of both. On a woman it was a conventional way of displaying wealth, with the rarer and more expensive furs such as mink and sable naturally ranking above the pelts of more common beasts.

Leather, particularly that of domestic animals like the cow and the sheep, took somewhat longer to become fashionable. Even today garments made of hide only have real status if they come from rare and disagreeable animals like the llama and the alligator, or if they can be seen at a glance to have necessitated much tedious hand labor (dyeing, piecing, tooling, etc.).

In the sixties and seventies, when it became clear that many species of animals were threatened with extinction, fur coats became less popular. Many women refused to buy them, and hid any furs they already owned in the closet. Today, though coats made of the skins of rare wild beasts continue to be sold and worn, they have become associated with disregard for environmental values and a slightly murderous disposition. Wearing the fleece of sheep or the skins of cattle, on the other hand, is thought to be consistent with humanitarian views, and is still acceptable except to vegetarians.

CONSPICUOUS WEALTH: WEARING MONEY

Another primitive and simple way of displaying wealth is the wearing of actual money. In the past sharks' teeth, wampum and coins, as well as many other forms of legal tender, have been made into jewelry or used to trim garments. Today, even in parts of the world where they cannot be used to buy lunch, such pieces retain some of their original prestige, and are often worn as accessories to high-fashion dress, to which they are believed to lend a barbaric glamour. Contemporary currency, which has no intrinsic value, is seldom or never made into jewelry, though the silver dimes and sixpences that have now been replaced by cheaper alloys are occasionally attached to bracelets and necklaces.

More common today, as well as in the past, is the decoration of the person with lumps of high-priced rock and metal. This method of announcing one's wealth also has the advantage of simplicity, since more people are aware of the approximate cost of such substances, especially when the local currency is based on them. The recent rise in the price of gold has made gold jewelry far more chic than it used to be, and diamonds, though their rise has not been so spectacular, retain their appeal. Materials such as rubies and emeralds, whose market price is less well-known, or which can more easily be imitated, are naturally less popular. Instant identification is desirable: platinum, though more costly than gold, never really caught on because most people couldn't tell it from silver or aluminum.

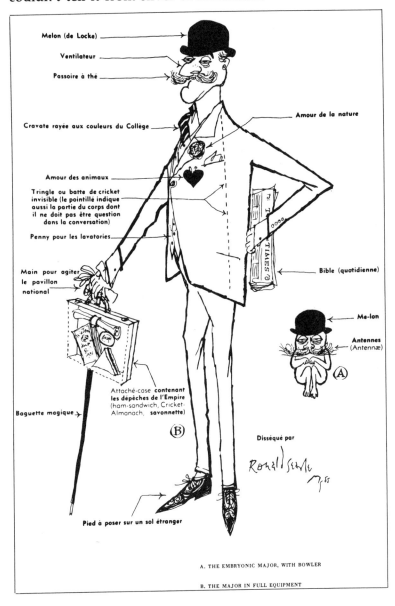

Melon (de Locke)

Ventilateur

Passoire à thé

Amour de la nature

Cravate rayée aux couleurs du Collège

Amour des animaux

Tringle ou batte de cricket invisible (le pointillé indique aussi la partie du corps dont il ne doit pas être question dans la conversation)

Penny pour les lavatories

Bible (quotidienne)

Main pour agiter le pavillon national

Me-lon

Antennes (Antennæ)

Ⓐ

Attaché-case contenant les dépêches de l'Empire (ham-sandwich, Cricket-Almanach, savonnette)

Baguette magique

Ⓑ

Disséqué par

Ronald Searle '55

Pied à poser sur un sol étranger

A. THE EMBRYONIC MAJOR, WITH BOWLER

B. THE MAJOR IN FULL EQUIPMENT

The costume of the upper-class British male is designed to be "read" in detail by his peers. In this cartoon by Ronald Searle, 1955, note especially the bowler from the best London hatter, the exceptionally narrow trousers, the extra button on the sleeve, the carelessly protruding handkerchief, the college tie and the mustache.

IN-GROUP SIGNALS

Sheer bulk and the wearing of many or obviously expensive garments and decorations are signs of status that can be read by almost anyone. More subtle sorts of Conspicuous Consumption are directed toward one's peers rather than toward the world in general; they are intended not to impress the multitude but to identify one as a member of some "in" group.

The costume of the upper-class British male, for example, is a mass of semiotic indicators. According to my informants, he customarily wears striped shirts, sometimes with white collars, leaving plenty of cuff showing and always fastening at the wrist with cuff links. The shirt collars must be neither too long and pointed nor too round, and never button-down: "In fact, the obsession of the gentleman is to avoid all extremes at all times." His suits, made by a "good" —i.e., superb—Savile Row tailor, are embellished in a number of small ways that will be noted by observant people: for instance, they may have extra buttons on the jacket cuff that can actually be buttoned, and a ticket pocket. The trousers will be cut fairly high in the waist and usually provided with buttons to which to attach braces or suspenders: "Wearing a belt is not done except with country suits, sometimes in the City called 'Friday suits,' since they are worn preparatory to going out of town. Older public-school men prefer to wear a tie around the waist rather than a belt." Ideally, the suit will be a dark pin stripe with a vest. The latter must never have lapels, which are "flashy" and "suggest the dandy or even the pouf." Recently, when one British politician became involved in a homosexual scandal, my informants remarked to one another that they were not really all that surprised: though his suit, hat and watch chain were very reputable, "the lapels on his waistcoats were a nasty giveaway."

It is not only the clothes themselves that must be correct, but the haircut and the accessories. "A gentleman practically never wears sideburns or a hairstyle that covers his ears"; if he has a mustache it must be of moderate size. His eyeglasses must be of real tortoise shell or gold-rimmed, and he must carry the right umbrella. "Umbrellas are as talismanically magic as fairies' wands. They must be tightly rolled, and preferably never unrolled even in heavy rain." Old Etonians, however, always carry an unrolled umbrella.

Though the ordinary casual observer might miss or misinterpret these details, those in the know will recognize proper London tailoring—just as they will recognize the accent that means someone has gone to the right (i.e., sufficiently expensive) sort of school. Since they too have shopped abroad, they will also notice expensive foreign-made clothes, just as they would notice foreign words that happened to be dropped in conversation. To be acceptable, these must be the right sort of clothes, and from a currently fashionable country. Ideally, they should not be available at home; foreign fashions, like foreign words, are most prestigious when not too famillar. Once they have become naturalized they are no longer very chic—like the word chic itself. French T-shirts and Italian sandals, once high fashion, now cause no more thrill than the words boutique and espresso.

A similar law of diminishing returns affects foreign *types* of garment. The triangular head scarf tied under the chin, originally featured in *Vogue* as an exotic accessory, was so useful and soon became so familiar that it was a negative status indicator. The Oriental kimono, a glamorous import at the turn of the century, was by the 1930s associated with slatternly females of easy virtue, and today is one standard pattern for terry-cloth bathrobes. If such styles are to retain any of their initial prestige they must be made up in very costly materials: the head scarf must be of handwoven wool and sprout handprinted roses; the kimono must be of silk embroidered with golden dragons.

CONSPICUOUS LABELING

Not long ago, expensive materials could be identified on sight, and fashionable men and women recognized Savile Row tailoring or a Paris designer dress at a glance. In the twentieth century, however, synthetics began to counterfeit wool, silk, linen, leather, fur, gold and precious stones more and more successfully. At the same time, manufacturing processes became more efficient, so that a new and fashionable style could be copied in a few months and sold at a fraction of its original price. Meanwhile, the economic ability to consume conspicuously had been extended to millions of people who were ignorant of the subtleties of dress, who could not tell wool from Orlon or Schiaparelli from Sears Roebuck. As a result there was a world crisis in Conspicuous Consumption. For a while it seemed as if it might actually become impossible for most of us to distinguish the very rich from the moderately rich or the merely well-off by looking at what they were wearing.

This awful possibility was averted by a bold and ingenious move. It was realized that a high-status garment need not be recognizably of better quality or more difficult to

In art, the display of expensive material on the human body was also extended to the background, and painters increased the prestige of their sitters by surrounding them with yards of nonfunctional velvet and satin. James, Seventh Earl of Derby, His Lady and Child, *by Anthony Van Dyck, 1632–41.*

produce than other garments; it need only be recognizably more expensive. What was necessary was somehow to incorporate the price of each garment into the design. This was accomplished very simply: by moving the maker's name from its former modest inward retirement to a place of outward prominence. Ordinary shoes, shirts, dresses, pants and scarves were clearly and indelibly marked with the names, monograms or insignia of their manufacturers. The names or trademarks were then exhaustively publicized—a sort of saturation bombing technique was used—so that they might become household words and serve as an instant guide to the price of the clothes they adorned. These prices were very high, not because the clothes were made of superior materials or constructed more carefully, but because advertising budgets were so immense.

When this system was first tried, certain critics scoffed, averring that nobody in their right mind would pay sixty dollars for a pair of jeans labeled Gloria Vanderbilt when a more or less identical pair labeled Montgomery Ward could be purchased for twelve. Others claimed that consumers who wanted a monogram on their shirts and bags would want it to be their own monogram and not that of some industrialist they had never met. As everyone now knows, they were wrong. Indeed, it soon became apparent that even obviously inferior merchandise, if clearly labeled and known to be extravagantly priced, would be enthusiastically purchased. There was, for instance, a great boom in the sale of very ugly brown plastic handbags, which, because they were boldly stamped with the letters "LV," were known to cost far more than similar but less ugly brown leather handbags. Cotton T-shirts that faded or shrank out of shape after a few washings but had the word Dior printed on them were preferred to better-behaved but anonymous T-shirts. Those who wore them said (or were claimed in advertisements to say) that they felt "secure." After all, even if the shirt was blotchy and tight, everyone knew it had cost a lot of money, and if it got too bad you could always buy another of the same kind. Thus Conspicuous Consumption, as it so often does, merged into Veblen's second type of sartorial status.

CONSPICUOUS WASTE: SUPERFLUOUS DRAPERY

Historically speaking, Conspicuous Waste has most often involved the use of obviously unnecessary material and trimmings in the construction of clothing. The classical toga portrayed in Greek and Roman sculpture, for instance, used much more fabric than was really needed to cover the body, the excess being artistically if inconveniently draped over one arm.

Anne Hollander has written most perceptively about the use of superfluous draped cloth in medieval, Renaissance and Baroque art. In preindustrial Europe, as she points out, cloth was the most important manufactured commodity, "the primary worldly good." Beautiful material was as admirable as gold or blown glass, and occupied far more space. The ownership of elaborate and expensive clothing was an important proof of social dominance. A single aristocrat sitting for his portrait, however, could only wear one luxurious outfit at a time. The display of many yards of velvet or satin behind him would suggest that he owned more such stuff and was able, in modern terms, to fling it around. Even after immensely full and trailing garments ceased to be worn, at least by men, excess drapery survived in art: it is notable for example in the paintings of Hals and Van Dyck and the sculptures of Bernini. The Frick Collection portrait of the Earl of Derby and his family "shows the family out of doors, standing on bare earth with shrubbery in the foreground and trees behind. But on the right side of the painting, behind the earl, next to a column that might conceivably be part of a house, fifty yards of dark red stuff cascade to the ground from nowhere. So skillfully does Van Dyck fling down these folds that their ludicrous inconsequence is unnoticeable . . ."

Traditionally, as Ms. Hollander remarks, superfluous drapery has been a sign not only of wealth and high rank but of moral worth: angels, saints, martyrs and Biblical characters in medieval and Renaissance art often wear yards and yards of extra silk and velvet. Drapery derived additional prestige from its association with classical art, and thus with nobility, dignity and the ideal. Marble columns and togalike folds (occasionally, actual togas) were felt to transform the political hack into a national statesman and the grabby businessman into a Captain of Industry. As Ms. Hollander notes, Westminster Abbey and the Capitol in Washington, D.C., are full of such attempted metamorphoses, frozen into soapy marble.

Excess drapery survives today in middlebrow portrait painting, causing over-the-hill industrialists, mayors and society women to appear against stage backgrounds of draped velvet or brocade, the moral and economic prestige of which is somehow felt to transfer itself to them. Successful academics, I have noticed, are often painted in this manner: posed before velvet curtains, with their gowns and hoods and mortarboards treated in a way that recalls the idealized drapery and stiffened halos of Renaissance saints. (Appropriately, the halos of professors and college presidents are square rather than round.)

The use of superfluous fabric in costume never died out completely. During most of the period between 1600 and 1900, for instance, respectable middle-class and upper-class women wore a minimum of three petticoats; fewer than this was thought pathetic, and indicated negligence or poverty. Skirts were inflated with hoops or bustles to provide a framework on which to display great quantities of cloth, while overskirts, panniers, flounces and trains demanded additional superfluous fabric. A fashionable dress might easily require twenty or thirty yards of material. Elaborate trimmings of bows, ribbons, lace, braid and artificial flowers permitted yet more prestigious waste of goods. Men's clothing during the same period used relatively little excess fabric except in outerwear, where long, full coats and heavy capes employed yards of unnecessary cloth, adding greatly to their cost and to the apparent bulk of their wearers.

A glance through any current fashion magazine will show that the use of superfluous fabric today, though on a much more modest scale, is by no means outmoded. Expensive clothes are often cut more generously, and fashion photography tends to make the most of whatever extra material the designer provides, spreading it over prop sofas or blowing it about in the air. Even the most miserly excess of cloth

may now be touted as a sign of prestige: a recent advertisement in *The New York Times* boasts of an extra inch in the back
yoke of Hathaway shirts which, the manufacturer sobs,
costs them $52,000 a year.

Wastage of material in the form of trimming, though
less striking than it was in the past, still persists. Today,
however, it is often thinly distinguished as practical. A prestigious shirt, for instance, has a breast pocket into which
nothing must ever be put; the habit of filling it with pens
and pencils is a lower-middle-class indicator, and also suggests a fussy personality. A related ploy, especially popular
between the two World Wars, was the custom of embroider-
ing everything with the owner's initials. This may in some
cases have had a practical function, as in the separation of
laundry, but—and more importantly—it also added conspicuously to the cost of the garment.

SUPERFLUOUS PERSONALITIES

Changing styles, of course, are another and very effective
form of Conspicuous Waste. Although I do not believe that
fashions alter at the whim of designers and manufacturers
—otherwise they would do so far more often—it is certainly
true that when social and cultural changes prompt a shift in
the way we look the fashion industry is quick to take advantage of it, and to hint in advertising copy that last year's
dress will do our reputation no good. When new styles do
not catch on other ploys are tried. A recent one is to announce with disingenuous enthusiasm that fashion is dead;
that instead of the tyranny of "this year's look" we now
have a range of "individual" looks—which are given such
names as Classic, Feminine, Sporty, Sophisticate and Ingénue. The task of the well-dressed liberated woman, the ads
suggest, is to chose the look—or, much better and more
liberated, *looks*—that suit her "life style." She is encouraged,
for instance, to be sleek and refined on the job, glowingly
energetic on holiday, sweetly domestic at home with her
children and irresistibly sexy in the presence of what one
department at my university has taken to calling her

The sack suit repeats the rectangular lines and drab colors of the urban landscape. If well tailored, it is becoming to men who do little or no work, since it can disguise both a skinny figure and a somewhat portly one. Photograph by Sir Benjamin Stone.

"spouse-equivalent." Thus, most ingeniously, life itself has been turned into a series of fashionable games, each of which, like jogging or scuba-diving or tennis, demands a different costume—or, in this case, a different set of costumes (winter/summer, day/night, formal/informal). The more different looks a woman can assume, the more fascinating she is supposed to be: personality itself has become an adjunct of Conspicuous Waste.

Men traditionally are not supposed to have more than one personality, one real self. Lately, however, they have been encouraged by self-styled "wardrobe engineers" to diversify their outward appearance for practical reasons. According to these experts, the successful businessman needs different sets of clothes in order to "inspire confidence in" (or deceive) other businessmen who inhabit different regions of the United States. This idea is not new, nor has it been limited to the mercantile professions. A former journalist has reported that as a young man he consciously varied his costume to suit his assignment. When sent to interview rich and powerful Easterners, he wore clothes to suggest that he was one of them: a dark-grey flannel Savile Row suit, a shirt from André Oliver or Turnbull & Asser, a

Cartier watch of a sort never available at Bloomingdale's and John Lobb shoes. "What you have to convey to rich people anywhere," he explained, "is that you don't have to try; so what you're wearing shouldn't ever be brand-new." New clothes, on the other hand, were appropriate when interviewing the *nouveau riche;* and since they might not recognize understated wealth, he (somewhat reluctantly, but a job is a job) would also put on a monogrammed shirt and Italian shoes with tassels.

When assigned to official Washington, this particular journalist took care to be three or four years behind current New York modes. "Washington hates fashion, especially New York fashion. The message should be, I am not attempting style; I am a man of the people, a regular fellow." He would therefore wear a somewhat rumpled pin-striped suit, a white shirt and a nondescript tie. Before leaving Manhattan he would get his hair cut shorter than usual. On the other hand, if he were sent to California, or were interviewing a writer, artist or musician anywhere in the country, he would try to let his hair grow or rumple it up a bit. He would wear slacks and a good tweed jacket over a turtleneck shirt; if the interviewee were financially successful he would add an expensive watch or pair of shoes to this costume. Still other getups were appropriate—and available—for the Midwest, Texas, the South, Continental Europe and Britain.

When this system works it is no longer Waste; nor, since the clothes are deliberately chosen to blend into their surroundings, can they be called Conspicuous. But as the journalist himself remarked, clothes alone cannot disguise anyone, and the traveling salesman or saleswoman who engineers his or her wardrobe but not his or her voice, vocabulary or manners may simply be practicing Conspicuous Waste without its usual reward of enhanced status—let alone a rise in sales figures.

CONSPICUOUS LEISURE: DISCOMFORT AND HELPLESSNESS

Once upon a time leisure was far more conspicuous than it usually is today. The history of European costume is rich in styles in which it was literally impossible to perform any useful activity: sleeves that trailed on the floor, curled and powdered wigs the size, color and texture of a large white poodle, skirts six feet in diameter or with six-foot dragging trains, clanking ceremonial swords, starched wimples and ruffs and cravats that prevented their wearers from turning their heads or looking at anything below waist level, high-heeled pointed shoes that made walking agony and corsets so tight that it was impossible to bend at the waist or take a normal breath. Such clothes proclaimed, indeed demanded, an unproductive life and the constant assistance of servants.

These conspicuously uncomfortable and leisurely styles reached an extreme in the late eighteenth century at the court of Versailles. The political and sartorial revolution that followed freed both sexes temporarily, and men permanently, from the need to advertise their aristocratic helplessness. Men's clothes became, and have remained ever since, at least moderately comfortable. Women's fashions on the other hand, after barely ten years of ease and simplicity, rapidly became burdensome again and continued so for the next hundred years.

Urban middle-class clothing today, though it does not usually cause pain, makes anything more than limited activity awkward. It is hard to run or climb in a business suit and slick-soled shoes; and the easily soiled white or pale-colored shirt that signifies freedom from manual labor is in constant danger of embarrassing its wearer with grimy cuffs or ring-around-the-collar. Urban women's dress is equally inconvenient. It should be pointed out, however, that inconvenience may be an advantage in some situations. A friend who often does historical research in libraries tells me that she always gets dressed up for it. If she is obviously handicapped by high heels, a pale, elegant suit and a ruffled white blouse, the librarians will search the stacks for the heavy volumes of documents and old newspapers she needs and carry them to her, dusting them on the way. If she wears a sweater, casual slacks and sensible shoes, they will let her do it herself. The same ploy would probably work for a man if he were middle-aged or older.

THE RISE AND FALL OF THE SACK SUIT

It is now almost two hundred years since the more extreme manifestations of Conspicuous Leisure in male clothing, but this principle, in a modified form, continues to separate white-collar from blue-collar men. Though the shirt may now be light blue, tan or striped, "white-collar" status is still signaled by the sack suit, which became standard in the mid-nineteenth century when the middle class had become largely urban and its occupations largely sedentary. As noted earlier, the sack suit is a kind of camouflage costume; it echoes the colors and shapes of the urban landscape.

Working men tend to be broader in the chest and shoulders than middle-class men, and to have larger muscles. When they buy a sack suit off the rack, it is apt to be either too long or too tight, making them look misshapen, and thus putting them at a disadvantage in any confrontation with their "betters." Photograph by Sir Benjamin Stone.

When well-tailored, the loose, square-cut jacket and tubular trousers also have a personal camouflage function: they conceal the soft belly and spindly legs characteristic of inactive persons who are no longer young.

The sack suit, as John Berger has recently pointed out, not only flatters the inactive, it deforms the laborious. It was designed for men who did little or no physical work and were therefore tall in relation to their breadth; it accommodated and emphasized the gestures of walking, sitting, speaking and pointing, but not those of running, lifting, carrying, hauling and digging. In addition, since it rumpled and soiled easily, it demanded to be worn indoors or on city streets. When physically active men with broad shoulders, deep chests and well-developed muscles put on cheap versions of the sack suit they looked misshapen, even deformed: as Berger puts it, they seemed "uncoordinated, bandy-legged, barrel-chested, low-arsed . . . coarse, clumsy, brutelike." Today backbreaking physical labor and the physique that goes with it are less common; but the same brutish effect is produced whenever a professional football player or wrestler appears in a suit off the peg.

The triumph of the sack suit meant that the blue-collar man in his best clothes was at his worst in any formal confrontation with his "betters." This strategic disadvantage can still be seen in operation at local union-management confrontations, in the offices of banks and loan companies, and whenever a working-class man visits a government bureau. Also, since the suit deforms the athlete and disguises the weakling, it may give the latter an undeserved edge in sexual competition. Not all social situations favor the sack suit, however: imagine, for instance, a bureaucrat climbing up out of his flooded cellar in a muddy, bedraggled helpless condition, followed by a plumber in rubber boots and sturdy, good-looking work clothes that show no sign of damage.

Recently the sack suit seems to be losing ground, especially outside large cities and in professions such as teaching, journalism and architecture. This change may be related to the recent shift in fashion from ambulatory sports such as golf and shooting to more vigorous pastimes like jogging and tennis. New styles have appeared to suit the man who has jogged himself into muscularity and no longer needs to conceal a pot. The unathletic white-collar male who affects such styles, however, is taking a risk: presently he may find himself looking remarkably feeble and podgy in his tight designer jeans and sport shirt while he (and if he is really unlucky, his girl friend) wait for some trim, well-built auto mechanic to diagnose his engine trouble.

THEATRICAL CONSUMPTION:
THE TRIUMPH OF EXTRAVAGANCE

In modern times the most conspicuous showcase for consumption has been films and television. Waste on a grand scale is one of the characteristics of movie-making: waste of talent, waste of energy, waste of materials, waste of money and waste of time—as anyone who has spent even a couple of hours on a movie set knows. From a Veblenite point of view, what could be more attractive and generate more prestige?

Film costumes, which are worn only once, are an extreme example of Conspicuous Consumption. This is the most expensive of them all: worn by Ginger Rogers in Lady in the Dark *(1944)*, it was covered with sequins and trimmed with mink, and cost $35,000.

Theatrical extravagance, of course, has a long history; yet it has been exceeded by the extravagance of the film industry. Stage costume, however elaborate, is made to be worn many times: if a play is successful each garment may get more hours of vigorous use than it would in real life. In the movies, however, months of work and thousands of dollars can be spent on something that will be worn for only a few minutes. Perhaps the most famous example is the dance outfit for Ginger Rogers in *Lady in the Dark* (1944), directed and in part designed by Mitchell Leisen. This costume, billed in publicity releases as the most expensive costume in the world, was paved with red and gold sequins and trimmed in mink, and cost $35,000.

Granted, the principles of theatrical costuming could not be transferred directly to films or television. Clothes for the stage must be designed for large-scale effect: subtle tailoring and delicate patterns are invisible beyond the second row, and everything must be exaggerated so that it can be seen at the back of the auditorium. In a movie, on the other hand, an inch of ribbon can appear ten feet long on the screen, showing every stitch. Yet the importance given to costume in Hollywood, almost from the start, was well beyond the requirements of the medium. It may be no coincidence that most of the early movie magnates started out in the fashion business. Harry Warner was a shoemaker, Samuel Goldwyn a glovemaker and Adolph Zukor a furrier before they went to Hollywood, and all three men brought friends and colleagues from the garment trade with them into the film industry.

Because of dramatic convention and the visual distance from performer to viewer, stage costume has been able to emphasize appearance rather than reality. Great theater, as Roland Barthes remarks in "The Diseases of Costume," relies on the imaginative power of the spectator, who is capable of "transforming rayon into silk and lies into illusion," rather than attempting to overwhelm his disbelief with authentic historical detail, formal beauty or obvious expenditure. Even at Stratford-on-Avon the king's ermine and sable robes are either dyed rabbit or—more often—synthetic fur, which not only costs less but is lighter to carry onstage; and the jewelry is paste.

The Hollywood producers, however, were not content with appearance; they demanded the use of the most expensive materials even when a cheaper substitute would deceive the camera. Adolph Zukor, for instance, insisted on real fur trimmings for all the costumes in his films, declaring that it was "good for the business." In some of the film extravaganzas of the thirties and forties even the extras were dressed like kings and queens. For *Marie Antoinette* (1938) Adrian designed four thousand lavishly authentic costumes, using real eighteenth-century silks, velvets, lace and embroidery. Norma Shearer, the star of the film, had thirty-four costume changes and eighteen wigs, one frosted with real diamonds. In these getups her mobility, like Marie Antoinette's, was severely limited; this was no novelty for Hollywood period films, where skirts were often so wide that it was impossible to get in or out of a dressing room. Or, at the other extreme, so tightly fitted to the body and armored with beading and embroidery that the actor or actress could not sit down or even walk naturally.

Clothes like these, in their elaborate decoration, fantastic cost, physical inconvenience and infrequency of use, recall not so much stage costume as the extravagantly trimmed and bejeweled vestments of religion, assumed only for a few moments of supernatural importance. This is as it should be, for (as has often been said) the stars of Hollywood and TV are our demigods and goddesses—the deities of what is in more ways than one a pagan society. Pure monotheism has always been a difficult and abstract faith. The popular mind is uncomfortable with the idea of a single god who embodies all known qualities. What it prefers is something closer to the Greek or Roman pantheon, with appropriate gods and goddesses for each admired virtue—or admired vice: a Venus, a Diana, a Mercury, a Mars. And, like some pagans, we tend to destroy our gods, or rather their human avatars, at frequent intervals, replacing them with new ones—thus even in our spiritual life following Veblen's principle of Conspicuous Waste.

VICARIOUS CONSUMPTION

In the nineteenth century, as Veblen pointed out in *The Theory of the Leisure Class,* men were relieved of the need to display their wealth through expensive, wasteful and uncomfortable dress; instead they delegated the task to their wives and daughters. Women became the vehicles of what Veblen called Vicarious Ostentation, and the richer a man was the more luxurious and inconvenient would be the costumes of his female relatives, and possibly his mistress. The well-to-do Victorian and Edwardian woman was an elaborate and expensive object. Heavily corseted, and wearing up to ten petticoats under her long skirt, she needed both height and muscular strength to carry an outfit that often weighed over ten pounds—not counting a hat loaded with flora and fauna, a muff, a reticule and a ruffled parasol. From about 1880 on a high, tight collar kept her chin elevated at an angle that suggested pride if not disdain, and made it difficult for her to look down at lesser mortals; it also helped to conceal the double chin that often accompanied the full late-Victorian figure.

Today many women—especially those who are not gainfully employed—still serve as vehicles of Vicarious Ostentation, as they are exhorted to do by commercial interests in advertisements that encourage their readers to "make him proud of you" or "proud to be seen with you." Certain concessions have been made to female emancipation, and extremes of discomfort are usually avoided. But any woman who is honest will admit that the full-length mink coat that advertises her husband's wealth is heavier and harder to manage than the down jacket she wears in the country, and that her diamond and gold jewelry is a constant invitation to mugging and murder. Vicarious Consumption on the part of males is much rarer, since it is usually thought to reduce the status of those who practice it. Nevertheless, the handsome young man whose elegant costume displays the wealth of some less handsome woman—or more often, man—can occasionally be seen in certain resorts.

One of the principal functions of the upper-class Victorian and Edwardian woman was the display of her father's or husband's wealth on her person. The more lavish her clothes, and the more they obviously unfitted her for any useful activity, the greater her value as a showcase. Mrs. Jay Gould, wife of the financier, wearing her $500,000 pearl necklace.

As Veblen points out, Vicarious Consumption has never been limited to the official and unofficial loved ones of a high-status individual. From the earliest times, the rich and the royal have delegated the task of exhibiting wealth to their servants as well as to their relatives. In the eighteenth and nineteenth centuries the grandeur of one's butler, footmen and coachmen—their height, and the elegance of their formal wear or the amount of gold braid on their liveries—was an important sign of rank. As several authorities on costume have noted, the dress of these functionaries tended to be many years behind current styles—possibly in order to suggest inherited money and position. Today, when only the very few have servants, this custom survives in the outfits of public rather than private functionaries: the employees of grand hotels and restaurants: doormen, elevator operators, bellboys, maîtres d'hôtel and waiters. Thus the very rich, at least symbolically, continue to display their wealth on the backs of their servants.

CONSPICUOUS OUTRAGE

Quentin Bell, whose fascinating study *On Human Finery* follows Veblen in designating economic competition as the principal force behind the vicissitudes of fashion, has suggested that to the categories of Conspicuous Consumption, Waste and Leisure should be added Conspicuous Outrage, or the deliberate wearing of clothes that do not conform to the standards of "good taste." It is effective because of the rule that the more important any occasion is to the participants, the more careful and formal will be their dress. At job interviews, for example, the prospective employer may if he or she wishes appear in slacks and sweater; the candidates, even if of higher status, must wear suits or dresses. Sometimes the relative importance of an occasion to its different participants is ritual rather than economic, as for example at a wedding, where costumes range from the elaborate outfits of the wedding party to the less formal ones of distant relatives and acquaintances. The friend who, disapproving of the match or of marriage in general, comes to the ceremony in faded jeans and an old flannel shirt is practicing Conspicuous Outrage. The same rule causes us to attend parties given by those to whom we feel superior in relatively casual clothes; when this casualness is carried to a point where our contempt for the event is obvious we become Conspicuously Outrageous. A similar ploy is also frequently, and perhaps more forgivably, adopted by artists when visiting patrons whose wardrobes are far better equipped for the display of consumption, waste and leisure. Here it is not a direct insult that is intended, but merely an evasion of "pecuniary canons of taste."

People who decide to practice Conspicuous Outrage, of course, must be sure they will be instantly recognizable at the event in question. If they are not, they run the risk of being roughly escorted out by those who assume they have crashed the party to get free drinks. I once saw this almost happen to a rock star in a two-day beard and stained T-shirt who, through motives of boyhood friendship—mixed, it must be admitted, with scorn of the whole affair—came to an elaborate publisher's party. His error was to assume that his face would be as well known in the literary world as it was in the music industry.

The wearing of outrageous clothes primarily in order to attract negative attention—to annoy and offend—may also in a sense be a claim for status. The teenage punk in the torn, filthy T-shirt, and his or her formal equivalent, the Punk Rocker in the artificially torn T-shirt silk-screened with a symbolic representation of filth in the form of four-letter words, may be admired by their peers if not by us. Moreover, the wearers of such garments are often persons of low status and power, for whom to be noticed at all is a step up.

STATUS THROUGH ASSOCIATION: SUPERSTARS AND SUPERJOCKS

Though luxury, waste, inconvenience and outrage are the main determinants of status in dress, other factors may operate. Magical thinking of a primitive kind sometimes causes styles associated with so-called fashion leaders—in the past, usually members of the aristocracy—to take on an aura of prestige. The pompadour hairdo, first worn by Madame de Pompadour, the mistress of Louis XV, was presently adopted by fine ladies all over Europe, who, however strict their own morals, enjoyed a fantasy identification with the famous courtesan. Today fashions are often inaugurated by individuals of the sort known as People, with a capital letter (to distinguish them from the rest of us nonpersons, mere percentage points on a Nielsen scale). Initially these styles are taken up by fans of the Person, both as a form of homage and as sympathetic magic. The teenager in the Kiss outfit of slashed leather and vinyl, with his face painted chalk-white, hopes that his peers will be thrilled and squares frightened and annoyed by him, just as they are by his idols; the young woman in the Farrah Fawcett hairdo hopes to become, and be perceived as, equally athletic and tirelessly sexy. Such styles may later be taken up by the media, and through a process that the British writers Ted Polhemus and Lynn Proctor have called "fashionalization" lose much of their original meaning. In a few cases—as with the Farrah-do, though not the Kiss costume—fashionalization is so complete that most of the original associations vanish, and a style merely indicates stylishness.

Clothes may also acquire prestige through association with a high-status activity such as war (the trench coat, the Eisenhower jacket) or space exploration (silver-hued vinyl, calendar watches). The costumes worn for high-status sports have always had a marked influence on fashion. A high-status sport, by definition, is one that requires a great deal of expensive equipment or an expensive setting or both; ideally, it will use up goods and services rapidly. Golf, for instance, demands the withdrawal from cultivation, housing or commercial use of many acres of valuable land; the resulting golf course must be constantly weeded, watered, mown and rolled with high-cost machines. It is played with a collection of pricey and specialized clubs so numerous and so heavy that it must be carried about by a caddie or a gas-powered vehicle; the game gains additional prestige from the constant loss of expensive small balls. Soccer, on the other hand, can be played on any flat half-acre of ground with only a single large ball that is seldom misplaced. As a result, the clothes traditionally worn for golf have become high fashion; those worn for soccer have not.

The most prestigious sports, traditionally, have been those involving that expensive animal, the horse. Among them are polo, show riding and above all fox-hunting, which Quentin Bell describes as "the most English of sports and that which has had the most decided effect upon clothes. [It consists] in the pursuit of an 'inedible animal,' with an expensive pack of hounds, a great assembly of expensive horses and expensive ladies and gentlemen, many of them wearing a kind of uniform and with a stiff bill for damages at the end."

Today an aura of status clings to horsey clothes of all sorts: wideskirted, side-vented coats that vaguely resemble hacking jackets; glossy high-heeled boots; polo shirts and caps; scarves and ties printed with equine portraits; gold pins and cuff links in the shape of horses' tack. People who wear such clothes are informing us (often truthfully) that they know how to ride, and also (less reliably) that they themselves own a horse or move in circles where horses are customarily owned.

In the early twentieth century, when the high-status recreations were golf and yachting, informal men's and women's wear was a clutter of plus fours, golf caps, V-necked sweaters and checked socks; of white flannel trousers, middy blouses, navy-blue blazers and yachting caps. When tennis and skiing became fashionable there was an epidemic of thick white socks and canvas shoes, short-sleeved knit shirts, heavy sweaters, knitted caps and insulated gloves. These garments were not only worn when pursuing the sport in question, but at every conceivable opportunity; there were, for example, both sailor-boy and ski pajamas. Many of these sporting styles have now become such popular status signals that they cannot be taken as a sign that their wearer knows how to play golf, sail, ski or hit a tennis ball—or even wishes to do so. The wearing of symbolic sports insignia, on the other hand (shirts printed

Sports such as golf, which require a lot of expensive equipment and the withdrawal from productive use of many acres of valuable land, have always had a strong influence on fashion. Golfing costume at the height of its vogue in the twenties: a magazine cover by Edward Hopper.

with marine signal flags, for instance, or jeweled pins shaped like tennis rackets), may be assumed to indicate some degree of enthusiasm and perhaps even expertise.

There are also symbolic garments that confer status because they bear the insignia of prestigious clubs, schools, regiments and the like. Here the rule is that you must actually have been associated with the organization whose badge you wear. The man in the horseshoe-patterned shirt who cannot ride is merely pathetic; the one in the Oxford blazer who was never up at Oxford is a cad or a crook. Ignorance is no excuse, as many American tourists have discovered when they appeared in ties they had bought because of their attractive stripes, but which turned out to be those of some famous British regiment. Americans in turn become indignant when they meet on the streets of Munich or Rome some scruffy-looking youth who doesn't even speak English but is wearing a sweat shirt emblazoned with the name of their own alma mater. Back home nobody wears such sweat shirts unless he or she has an official connection with that university, or is currently sleeping with somebody who does. (An exception is made for small children, who may be given miniature college sweat shirts by alumni who hope that one day they will legitimately wear the larger size.) To judge by the shopping districts of many European cities, most American university sweat shirts are now being sent overseas. This may be in part because at many more sophisticated American universities it is considered callow to wear such garments on campus after one's freshman year— though those of close friends at other universities are admissible. Sweat shirts and jackets bearing the insignia of some college team of which one is a member, on the other hand, are not only admissible but highly prestigious.

REVERSE CHIC

Once upon a time, a low-status garment was simply one that did not manifest Conspicuous Consumption, Waste or Leisure: which was instead economical, practical and comfortable to wear. It was not subject to the vicissitudes of style; it did not get in the way of hard work, nor did it wrinkle, tear or soil readily. It was uncomplicated in cut, untrimmed and of some durable material such as homespun, corduroy, calico or leather.

Today such clothes, where they still exist, are relatively expensive to manufacture and have therefore risen in prestige. In terms of language, they are the equivalent of colloquial, down-homey words and phrases, and inspire the same kind of warmth and confidence. Nowadays the extensive dress vocabulary of expensive persons is apt to include some of these colloquial items: a plaid flannel work shirt, for instance, or a mechanic's khaki jump suit. The high-fashion wearer, however, must deploy these garments so as to ensure that the total effect will be sexy, piquant or ironic rather than in any sense vulgar. The rule, as with the spoken language, seems to be that only one such garment may appear in a total costume, and that its practical or lowbrow associations must be canceled out by another item or items that are conspicuously expensive. Therefore the work shirt is slung over tan suede pants and a silk shirt; the coveralls are worn with hundred-dollar boots and hung with half-a-dozen heavy gold chains. Low-status foreign clothing is sometimes used in the same manner; though because it is exotic as well as plebeian more such items can be worn at one time. The standard garb of Chinese peasants, Indian laborers or Greek fishermen needs only one or two expensive accessories to transform it into high-status chic.

Simple, old-fashioned work clothes have now been replaced at the low end of the status ladder by garments that imitate recent high-fashion styles as cheaply as possible. Orlon and polyester replace wool and cotton and silk, vinyl replaces leather, glued-on trim replaces tucks and pleats and embroidery; seams are narrow and badly sewn, hems skimpy, linings sleazy or missing. When they are brand-new these clothes may fool some of the people some of the time, especially at a distance; but once they have been through the washer or the do-it-yourself dry-cleaning machine their true nature is revealed. Curiously enough, this built-in obsolescence creates its own variety of Conspicuous Waste. Certain sections of the public, for whom low prices and instant chic are more important than quality or durability, prefer such clothes. They are especially popular with kids in their early teens, whose first priorities are to look like the rest of the gang and to keep up with changes in their own size and shape. For this reason, it is often difficult to tell the class origin of a thirteen-to-fifteen-year old unless he or she belongs to the top or bottom strata of society and is either rich enough to buy a well-made version of the latest fad, or too poor to buy any version of it.

JUVENILE STATUS

The clothes of young children indicate status very clearly, but in ways different from those of adults. At first glance, working-class children look better dressed than middle-class ones, especially when they are with their parents. On a Sunday at the zoo, for instance, the little girls will have on fancy and relatively fragile dresses; the boys will wear miniature suits, or brightly colored jackets bearing the insignia of some sports team. The middle-class kids will be the ones in overalls, jeans and T-shirts.

This apparent inversion of the rules of Conspicuous Consumption is the result of different attitudes toward childhood. For a respectable working-class or lower-middle-class family, their children express status aspiration; they are therefore dressed to indicate (perhaps magically to predestine) their hoped-for futures. Well-to-do girls and boys, on the other hand, are not expected to do more than equal their parents' status, and at the moment they are on probation. It is not surprising therefore that, as several writers on costume have noted, such children have since the late eighteenth century often been dressed in the clothes of servants and laborers. Little boys in mid-Victorian England wore linen or cotton smocks like those of farm workers; the starched and ruffled white pinafore apron of the Victorian schoolgirl imitated that of the parlormaid. Today upper-middle-class kids wear farmers' bib overalls and factory workers' zip-up boiler suits. Occasionally, however, especially on small children, these outfits are only plebian in shape, not in substance.

Though the designs are the same, they are made up in more expensive and/or more delicate fabrics, and in paler colors. Thus we see toddlers in pinafore aprons of dotted swiss and coveralls of pale pink or blue velour that will never get within a mile of a farmyard—materials that proclaim consumption and leisure. These clothes perfectly express the status of the well-to-do child, who is a small person of no importance compared to his parents, and is usually engaged in simple low-status activities; but, we are asked to note, is essentially of finer substance than his contemporaries.

VI
FASHION
AND OPINION

Man's earthly interests are all hooked
and buttoned together, and held up, by
Clothes.

—Thomas Carlyle, *Sartor Resartus,*
Book I, Chapter VIII

Strangers to any language or dialect have difficulty in communicating any but the simplest ideas. When those who share not only a language but an accent and a vocabulary come together, on the other hand, conversation readily becomes fluent and complex. In the same way, those who share a language of clothes can read one anothers' costumes for information on more individual and subtle matters than age, national or regional origin, and status. Through signs that might be invisible to an outsider, they can identify one another as radical, liberal, conservative or reactionary, and often make a good guess as to occupation and cultural tastes.

Though it might be convenient, it is not as easy to distinguish supporters of one political party from those of another as it was for a time in eighteenth-century England, when Whigs wore beauty patches on their right cheek only, and Tories on the left. Nevertheless, even today political and social views are often eloquently conveyed by costume. The smaller and more unified the group, of course, the more subtle and expressive its language. A room full of high school or university students, sartorially homogeneous to an outsider, can instantly be sorted out by one another into jocks (heavy-knit sweaters, team shirts and jackets, athletic socks), grinds (dress shoes, clip-on pens and pencils, unfashionable spectacles), artsies (longer hair than the norm, excess or worn denim, Indian shawls, etc.) and awkward, naïve nurds (ill-fitting, unbecoming garments evidently purchased by their mothers).

CONSERVATIVE FASHIONS

"He won't sunbathe—he says he doesn't like to attract attention."

Conventional dress, like conventional opinion, demands a static social setting. When it is stubbornly maintained in the wrong circumstances it ceases to be conventional and becomes instead highly eccentric. Cartoon by Jackson in Punch, *1950.*

Even in gatherings that are not homogeneous in terms of age and occupation, certain general rules apply. The conservative members of the group will tend to wear what by group standards are "conservative" clothes, made of heavier fabrics, relatively subdued in color and restrained in cut; compared to the rest, they will be dressed more like adults. This is true regardless of the overall political inclination of the group, and applies equally to a meeting of the Daughters of the American Revolution and to a bunch of unemployed teenagers on a street corner.

When the group consists of persons in early middle age or beyond, its more conservative members will usually avoid current fads. Often their dress will be some years behind contemporary high fashion—the symbolic manifestation of their attachment to the past. This is particularly common in educational circles, and to judge by the evidence of fiction has always been so. In Charles Dickens's *Dombey and Son,* for instance, the old-fashioned pedantry of the schoolmaster Dr. Blimber is signaled by his old-fashioned black suit "with strings at his knees, and stockings below them"—that is, at a time when most men had adopted the long trousers that came in after the French Revolution, Dr. Blimber clung to the knee breeches of the late eighteenth century. Today the same time-lag can be observed at academic meetings. The more pedantic and conservative professors still wear 1950s styles: dark three-piece suits, white or pale-blue Oxford cloth shirts and narrow dark ties. The few female professors who have survived from this patriarchal era without becoming radicals or feminists are dressed in an equally antique manner.

When fashion itself becomes suddenly youthful, the

reluctance of older people to abandon outmoded styles is more widespread. This happened after World War I, and as a result family photographs of the early 1920s often show a strange assortment of costumes. Some of the older subjects are dressed much as they would have been ten or fifteen years earlier, and they often retain their portly Edwardian figures. Others in the same picture are much slimmer and wear the skimpy, childish fashions of the Jazz Age. The same phenomenon can be seen in photographs from the late sixties, where those who are out of sympathy with the Youth Culture wear elegant, formal adult clothes that contrast oddly with the flowing hair and picturesque garments of their relatives. In some photos from this period, members of different generations do not even seem to belong to the same nationality, let alone the same family.

When fashion shifts from a look of youth to one of maturity, as it did during the 1970s, the transition is smoother. Since the new styles are becoming to those over thirty they are readily adopted by the mature, while the fashionable young can grow up along with fashion. Some adolescents may continue to dress childishly and casually, but when they leave school and begin looking for jobs, which are usually scarce in such periods, they succumb to the prevailing mode. As a result, in family photographs almost everyone over twenty seems to belong to the same culture—a clear sign that generational conflict has diminished.

THE LAST TO LAY THE OLD ASIDE

A special sort of sartorial conservatism occurs in those who continue to wear the clothes and hair styles that were most becoming to them in youth. This phenomenon is not limited to political conservatives; indeed, it may be more widespread among radicals, who lack the same impulse to conform to the times. It has been suggested that a woman's age can be accurately dated by her hairdo, even if she is dressed in the latest fashions and has had her face lifted. According

In popular music clothing is an essential semiotic indicator. The costume and hair style of the performer tell his audience what to expect: the fringed leather outfit and beard suggest folk music, the Afro and sharply tailored polka-dot suit mean soul, the cowboy getup indicates country-and-western and the greased pompadour and psychedelic shirt, rock. A musician who wore the wrong clothes for his kind of sound would probably be booed off the stage.

to this theory, the flat waves of the 1930s indicate someone born between 1905 and 1915; longer, straight locks breaking into curls at the end (as in the 1940s) suggest a birth date between 1915 and 1925. The elaborate, smoothly lacquered constructions of the sophisticated 1950s and the alternative but equally tidy "feather cut" of that time are still favored by many women born between 1925 and 1935, while hair puffed, teased, back-combed or otherwise induced to occupy extra air space, as in the 1960s, indicates a birth date between 1935 and 1945. And, though it is perhaps too soon to judge, there are already signs that many women born between 1945 and 1955 will keep the straight, geometrically shaped "Sassoon" haircuts of their first youth.

This same retention of one's youthful hair style also occurs in men, who may continue to ask their barbers for the same as before or a light trim for fifty years—or at least until a receding hairline makes adjustment necessary. Some early admirers of Fred Astaire now in their sixties are still walking around with a low side part and smooth top hair; while certain dedicated fans of Elvis Presley now in their forties retain a modified shiny pompadour and duck-tail. President Reagan's characteristic puffy toplock dates from his days as a film star in the 1940s.

Since what is available in the stores changes over time, it is more difficult and thus less common to adhere to the styles of one's youth, though a favorite (perhaps magically endowed) garment may be preserved and worn for a very long time. In certain cases, this clinging to outmoded costumes can become highly neurotic or even pathological. In literature the classic example is that of Miss Havisham in Dickens's *Great Expectations,* who was jilted on her wedding day and wore her bridal gown for the next thirty years:

> She was dressed in rich materials—satins, and lace, and silks —all of white. Her shoes were white. And she had a long white veil dependent from her hair, and she had bridal flowers in her hair, but her hair was white . . . [Then] I saw that everything . . . which ought to be white, had been white long ago, and had lost its lustre, and was faded and yellow. I saw that the bride within the bridal dress had withered like the dress, and like the flowers.

FUN-CLOTHES VS. GOOD INVESTMENTS

Among reasonably sane persons, whether a specific costume should be read as radical or as conservative depends on many factors, among which are the age and status of the wearer, the social context and the current political and economic situation. In periods of expansion, such as the 1960s, clothes as a whole tend to be more childlike, informal, inventive and brightly colored. (Occasionally they become positively silly.) Expensive garments are recommended in advertisements as "exciting" and "fun." Muted tints seem drab and dowdy, and any restraint in dress—a few inches more hem and less flare to a skirt, or a plain white shirt and dark tie—becomes a sign of political and social conservatism.

Plain, unimaginative clothes in neutral colors, euphemistically referred to at the time as "classics," are the sign of periods of economic and social anxiety or depression. In such periods the fashionable buzz words of the previous era take on negative connotations. "Exciting" and "daring" are out; the "fun-clothes" of last year look faddish and freaky, and too much originality in dress suggests unreliability or a failure to grasp the serious realities of life. Brilliant hues and patterns appear gaudy or even vulgar, and rummage-sale racks are suddenly full of splashy ruby and purple and sunset orange and emerald-green paisley and Art Nouveau print dresses and ties and shirts that nobody wants.

Flashy, splashy clothes may be fashionable in conservative periods—but only in certain isolated places, of which the best current example is the disco. One of the characteristics of a conservative era is that day and night, or formal and informal, clothes and manners are much more sharply differentiated than at other times. In the eighteenth century, for instance, the public manners of fashionable persons were highly formalized, and their discourse on polite occasions was ceremonial and elaborate. In private, or on less proper occasions, both formal dress and formal manners were laid aside. When the powdered and curled wigs were removed they revealed cropped and often untidy hair; in the same way, when eighteenth-century men and women did not

Parents and children in family pictures taken in the 1960s sometimes seem to be members of different cultures or even different nationalities. California, 1972. Photograph by Bill Owens.

converse in eighteenth-century prose their speech was coarse, blunt and often bawdy.

During the cultural revolution of the sixties and seventies, when everyday wear was a kind of costume, getting dressed for a party often merely meant putting on a clean or favorite shirt. Today, a complete transformation may take place, as anxious young men and women shed the drab gray and navy cocoons in which they have Dressed for Success and change into butterfly-hued dance outfits—which, though sometimes as colorful, tend to be both more expensive and more restrained in cut than the clothes of a decade earlier.

In anxious and conservative times there is a preference for solid value in all areas. Expensive garments (a camel's-hair jacket, diamond jewelry, a fur coat) are advertised not as thrilling luxuries but as "good investments," talismans that will give their wearer "a sense of security." Large, solid-looking houses are favored; furniture tends to be heavy—and often antique—in style. If the swing to conservative values is pronounced, any marked originality or informality in dress may indicate political and/or social radicalism. The person whose clothes become more conservative then may simply be responding to the spirit of the times, or he may be expressing a change in his own outlook—or both. When Jimmy Carter first became president he was often photographed in blue jeans and a pullover sweater. After a year or so, he was seen only in conventional dark suits.

When an age of anxiety is accompanied, as often happens, by increased national chauvinism and distrust or envy of foreign nations, there is apt to be a wholesale rejection of foreign styles and foreign garments. It is no longer chic to look as if one's clothes had been made in France or Italy, or inspired by the native costumes of Africa and Asia. Instead, fashion turns to the national past for its inspiration. The result in Britain is a rash of tartans and tweeds and knits; in America there is a corresponding outbreak of quilting, patchwork, crochet and cowhide.

Another guide to the political temper and international outlook of a group or an individual is the extent to which their clothes echo the color of their country's flag. Currently, at political meetings in both Britain and America—especially those of the more conservative parties—there is a striking prevalence of red, white and navy blue. When appearing on television, American political candidates almost always wear these colors in combination, though the red element (no doubt because of its Marxist associations) is usually kept to a minimum.

RADICAL AND LIBERAL FASHIONS

The sort of political radicalism that involves an identification with the working class often expresses itself in the wearing of "workers'" clothing: boiler suits, denim shirts, heavy boots with reinforced toes and in extreme cases the rumpled blue or gray cotton uniforms of Chinese peasants. Among the young, bib overalls are the current sign of the uncompromising political or social radical—someone who still goes on protest marches, pickets the visits of foreign heads-of-state, and/or lives in a radical commune.

To be significant, workers' clothes must be worn as a complete costume; a single item combined with more fashionable gear will simply suggest fashionable chic. Radical costume is also most effective in situations where it constitutes Conspicuous Outrage: a formal party, a conservative family reunion, a business meeting. When it is worn only informally in the country or around the house, the radical-

Ronald Reagan, even as President, often wears Western gear of the Good-Guy type, reminding us—and possibly himself—of his mythological role as a noble cowboy. Of course he never was a cowboy, but he now has a ranch to go with the costume. Photograph by Michael Evans from The New York Times, *1981.*

ism of its owner is usually a matter of private rather than public commitment. A special case is the working-man's garb favored by some painters, writers and musicians—and more recently, film and stage directors—on the job: what Antonia Fraser has called the "artists-are-workers-too" costume. For the painter or sculptor, of course, this outfit has practical advantages; its adoption by those whose tools are pencil and paper, or by actors and actresses, is purely symbolic. Sometimes the costume of these "workers" is only superficially or symbolically authentic, as in William Trevor's *Other People's Worlds* (1980), in which the director of a television play is described as

> attired in what appeared to be the garb of a plumber but which closer examination revealed to be a fashionable variation of such workman's clothing: his dungarees were of fawn corduroy, his shirt of red and blue lumberjack checks. He wore boots that were unusual, being silver-coloured; and beneath each arm-pit, in a shade of fawn that matched his dungarees, were sewn-on patches, appearing to symbolise a labourer's excretion of sweat.

It is not only conservatives and radicals who can be identified by their clothes. Middle-of-the-road views are appropriately indicated by soft, comfortable, woolly-liberal garments in pleasantly blurred hues (heather mixtures are a favorite). In Britain socialists of the older generation also wear such clothes. The current leader of the Labor Party, Michael Foot, according to report, "is famous for his baggy, hairy tweed suit and other furry woolly shapeless garments." Extremism, on the other hand, whether of left or right, tends to express itself in sharp outlines, hard-surfaced (often shiny) fabrics and definite colors. Anthony Wedgwood Benn, the ambitious Labor politician, is reported to wear well-cut suits in definite colors and is "practically never seen without a red tie to proclaim where he stands in politics."

SOCIAL PROTEST: THE PUNK LOOK

Social protest and social disaffection both tend to adopt some characteristic costume. The Beatniks, Teddy Boys and

In the past many writers deliberately dressed as aesthetes; today they are more likely to wear clothes designed for physical labor, the "artists-are-workers-too" costume. Anne Jones, author and feminist. Photograph copyright © 1981 by Thomas Victor.

Zoot Suiters of the postwar period, the Mods, the Rockers of the 1950s, the Skinheads and the Hippies of the 1960s, all expressed themselves eloquently in the language of clothes. Today alienation from mainstream values is just as fluently set forth by what were known first as Punk and later as New Wave styles.

The Punk Look that swept Britain in the late 1970s was intended to—and did—arouse disturbing and conflicting emotions: rage, fear and pity. Though it originated among working-class teenagers, it was soon taken up by many middle- and upper-class youths, some of whom are pictured here in a remarkably complete disguise.

The original Punk Look appeared in London in the late 1970s among marginally employed or unemployed working-class teenagers. It featured hair cropped to a fuzz and dyed startling, unnatural colors: often very pale yellow, sometimes red, green, orange or lavender. Faces were powdered pasty white, with sooty eyes and heavy lipstick. In clothing, red, black and white were the favorite colors. Punks wore black leather jackets and jeans decorated with metal studs and superfluous zippers; T-shirts printed with vulgar words and violent and/or pornographic pictures—often images of rape and murder. Artificially torn and soiled clothing, held together with outsize safety pins, exposed areas of pale, unhealthy flesh, which were often bruised and scratched. One favorite accessory was the dog or bicycle chain, which might be pulled tight round the neck or used to fasten one leg to the other. Punk chicks might also wear this costume, or they might vary it with hot pants, side-slit skirts, tight angora sweaters and spike-heeled sandals; their boyfriends favored heavy "shit-kicker" boots.

In the language of clothes, the Punk style was a demand for attention, together with a cry of rage against those who should have paid attention to these kids in the past but had not done so: parents who were too immature or too exhausted; callous or helpless teachers and social workers; a welfare state that seemed uninterested in their welfare and had no jobs for most of them. The motorcycle-gang outfits, the chains and razor blades, the real and artificial bloodstains and scars, the exposure of flesh, were intended to offend and to frighten. It was necessary to go to these extremes to get any reaction because the street costumes of the late sixties and early seventies were already fairly outrageous, and because the ordinary man and woman had become so familiarized with violence and sex through the media.

At the same time, other aspects of the Punk Look appealed not only for attention, but for the love and care that we give to very small children, especially to injured ones. After all, where else had we seen that fluffy Easter-chick hair, those pale scratched faces and scraped knees, those torn shirts and jeans, those ill-fitting, often half-undone jackets and leggings? As for that Punk trademark, the outsize safety pin stuck through a cheek or earlobe, it could not help but remind every mother of the awful moment when she ran one just like it into her darling instead of into his nappie. The chain that linked one leg to the other not only suggested violence, bondage and sexual perversion—it also gave its wearer the short, halting, appealing gait of a toddler.

It was this double message, as of a viciously angry, miserable baby, that made the Punk Look so deeply disturbing. Most new styles cause only surprise, scornful amusement or admiration; the Punk Look made people in Britain feel rage, guilt, compassion and fear simultaneously; it was fashion moving toward political protest, possibly toward political action. The recent American equivalent, known as

New Wave, is a watered-down version of its original, more theatrical than serious in intent. It is not associated with the working class, and it de-emphasizes the damaged-baby indicators—quite logically, since American children are more apt to be spoiled than neglected. New Wave fashions, too, are usually worn at night, to parties and bars and discos and concerts; they seldom appear in public in the daytime. As might be expected, therefore, the New Wave Look has aroused relatively little public outrage; its principal message seems to be that some American teenagers are bored and restless (so what else is new?) and looking for cheap, relatively safe thrills.

SOCIAL CONFORMITY: THE PREPPIE LOOK

The other emergent style of the late seventies, the so-called Preppie Look, originated in North America rather than in Britain and expressed not social protest but social conformity. In fact, it was not a new style, but a revival of the most conventional American suburban styles of the 1950s and early 1960s, what at the time were called "country-club fashions." It was very popular in Ivy League colleges: the Radcliffe glamour girl and sports buff Brenda Patimkin in Philip Roth's *Goodbye, Columbus* (1959) usually appears in tan Bermuda shorts, a tartan belt and a white polo shirt with a small turnover collar.

The Preppie Look featured the sort of clothes worn by adolescents at expensive American and Canadian boarding schools: tweeds, tartan kilts, blazers, Shetland and Fair-Isle sweaters, chino pants, polo shirts, Oxford-cloth and madras and plaid flannel shirts. All these garments followed the usual rules for conservative dress: they were of relatively heavy (usually natural) fabrics, backward-looking in design and allowed very little scope for personal taste or imagination. The choice of styles was extremely limited, and to be correct everything had to have the "right" manufacturers' labels and come from the "right" stores. Simple primary colors were preferred, with an emphasis on the patriotic triad of red, white and blue, plus a neutral tan. The aim was to look as if not only you but your family had been rich and

The Preppie Look of the 1980s has its origin in the casual, rather uninteresting sports clothes worn by upper-middle-class suburbanites in the conservative fifties and early sixties. Cleveland, 1967: cotton shirts in checks and small-flower prints, Bermuda shorts, penny loafers. Photograph by Burk Uzzle.

The Preppie Look in 1980. Note the layered shirts.

Are You A Preppie?

...hopefully not. However, in recent years college officials have become increasingly alarmed by the dramatic population boom of the **Homo Gatorus**; i.e. the **PREPPIE**. According to experts, the "Preppie disease", which strikes thousands of youths each year, invariably leaves its victim suffering from **clotheserphobia** - an intense desire to dress like Mr. Rummage Sale of 1960. Most Preppies also experience an insatiable thirst for alcoholic beverages which often results in the unique honor of graduating from college **Magna Cum Loaded.** Experts have further distinguished Preppie victims by their dancing style, mannerisms, social rank, monetary worth, and self-love. Currently, there are only two known cures for this disease: Reincarnation or Bankruptcy. To determine if you have contacted and been infected by the Preppie germ, study the picture below and rank yourself according to the following scale: 18 -21 Ultra Prep; 14 - 17 Moderate or Intermediate Prep; 10 -13 Pseudo Prep; 9 or less Normal.

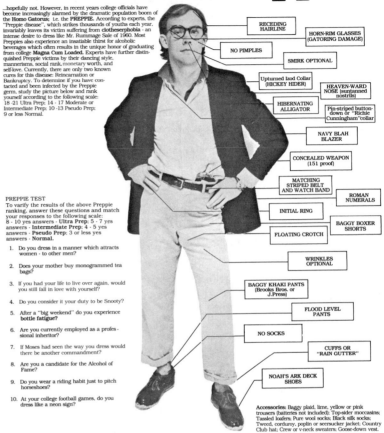

RECEDING HAIRLINE

HORN-RIM GLASSES (GATORING DAMAGE)

NO PIMPLES

SMIRK OPTIONAL

Upturned Izod Collar (HICKEY HIDER)

HEAVEN-WARD NOSE (suntanned nostrils)

HIBERNATING ALLIGATOR

Pin-striped button-down or "Richie Cunningham"collar

NAVY BLAH BLAZER

CONCEALED WEAPON (151 proof)

MATCHING STRIPED BELT AND WATCH BAND

ROMAN NUMERALS

INITIAL RING

BAGGY BOXER SHORTS

FLOATING CROTCH

WRINKLES OPTIONAL

BAGGY KHAKI PANTS (Brooks Bros. or J.Press)

FLOOD LEVEL PANTS

NO SOCKS

CUFFS OR "RAIN GUTTER"

NOAH'S ARK DECK SHOES

Accessories: Baggy plaid, lime, yellow or pink trousers (batteries not included); Top-sider moccasins; Tassled loafers; Pure wool socks; Black silk socks; Tweed, corduroy, poplin or seersucker jacket; Country Club hat; Crew or v-neck sweaters; Goose-down vest.

PREPPIE TEST
To varify the results of the above Preppie ranking, answer these questions and match your responses to the following scale:
8 - 10 yes answers - **Ultra Prep;** 5 - 7 yes answers - **Intermediate Prep;** 4 - 5 yes answers - **Pseudo Prep;** 3 or less yes answers - **Normal.**

1. Do you dress in a manner which attracts women - to other men?

2. Does your mother buy monogrammed tea bags?

3. If you had your life to live over again, would you still fall in love with yourself?

4. Do you consider it your duty to be Snooty?

5. After a "big weekend" do you experience **bottle fatigue?**

6. Are you currently employed as a professional inheritor?

7. If Moses had seen the way you dress would there be another commandment?

8. Are you a candidate for the Alcohol of Fame?

9. Do you wear a riding habit just to pitch horseshoes?

10. At your college football games, do you dress like a neon sign?

Nathaniel Elliot Worthington III

Punch Posters. P.O. Box 2001 Falls Church, VA 22042

dull for several generations—denying, and at the same time of course suggesting, a deep-seated social anxiety.

What distinguished the Preppie Look from the country-club styles of the 1950s was the range of its wearers. These casual garments were now being worn not only by adolescents in boarding schools and Ivy League colleges, but by people in their thirties and forties, many of whom would have considered such styles dreary rather than chic a few years earlier. Moreover, the Preppie Look was now visible in places and on occasions that in the 1950s would have demanded more formal clothing. Preppies of both sexes in madras check shirts and chino pants and Shetland sweaters could be seen eating lunch in elegant restaurants, in the offices of large corporations and at evening parties—as well as in class and on the tennis courts.

Though the elements that composed the Preppie Look were old-fashioned, it had certain original features. One was the custom of what was called *layering:* wearing three, four or even more visible thicknesses of cloth over the upper body. A Preppie might wear (moving outward) a turtleneck jersey, one or two cotton shirts, a crew-neck sweater, a down vest or wool blazer and a loose coat, often with a large wool scarf draped over the whole. Such extreme layering must have been intended partly as Conspicuous Consumption, but it also suggests concern with the world energy crisis and an anxiety about warmth and survival so severe that even overheated American schoolrooms and offices seem cold. A secondary effect of layering on this scale was the blurring of the body image and even of sexual differences, so that except for the length of their hair the Preppie young were often indistinguishable from one another. When they projected a sexual aura at all it was one of healthy athleticism or of prepubescent cuddliness: a sort of teddy-bear warmth.

The other outstanding characteristic of Preppie fashion was its use of unnecessary fastenings. Shoes were trimmed with nonfunctional ties and hooks and latches; the pleats of kilts were safety-pinned or buckled together; leather and cloth straps unnecessarily secured the wrists of gloves, the waistbands of skirts and jeans and the shoulders of raincoats; even the corners of shirt collars were buttoned down so they could not get away. Clothes like these are a sign that someone or something is being confined or restrained. Significantly, an even greater excess of fastenings appeared in Punk clothing, but here the effect was of a barely controlled, sexually charged violence and energy. The ubiquitous Punk zippers were usually left sagging open, and the safety pins fastened torn and skimpy garments that seemed about to fall away from the naked body; stuck through the cheek or earlobe, they suggested that the flesh itself was splitting. Though Preppie and Punk Looks were in almost every particular as disparate as the people who wore them, both styles graphically conveyed the sense of a world, or a personality, in grave danger of coming apart.

Middle-of-the-road political and social opinions are indicated by soft, comfortable, woolly-liberal clothes, while extremism tends to express itself in sharp outlines, shiny fabrics and strong colors. Cartoon strip by Posy Simmonds from "Mrs. Weber's Diary," 1979.

HAIR: ROUNDHEADS AND CAVALIERS

As anyone who has lived through the 1960s knows, hair styles (especially those of men) can be an important political indicator. Ever since the Romans cut the locks of captured barbarian tribesmen for the slave market, shorter hair than the norm has been a sign of servitude, and by extension a sign of conformity and self-restraint. The Marine Corps and prison crew cut, and the shaved heads of monks, imply regimentation and discipline, whether enforced from without or self-imposed. Longer hair than the norm, on the other hand, has always indicated freedom and license. Which length signifies the conservative and which the radical, however, depends on the style of contemporary politics.

At the time of the English Civil War radicalism was austere and short-haired. The Puritan followers of Oliver

Cromwell were known as "Roundheads" because of their cropped hair; their Royalist opponents or "Cavaliers," who dressed luxuriously and enjoyed the pleasures of life, had long, curly locks. In Puritan New England, a law against long hair for men was passed as early as 1634, and later in the century the Overseers of Harvard College forbade their students to wear curls or powder. The association between radicalism and short hair continued into the eighteenth century. Many leaders of the American Revolution as well as French Jacobins had hairdos that would seem only slightly untidy today, while Tories and aristocrats favored long, elaborate wigs and powder.

The Romantic movement introduced a new sort of radical, wild-haired rather than crop-headed. Daring young men brushed their hair the wrong way on purpose as a sign of their independence from conventional restriction. The loose, disheveled curls familiar to us from portraits of English Romantic poets were associated in the popular mind with radical sympathies as well as with poetic license. By the late nineteenth century, a man whose locks were unusually long was assumed to be a writer, an artist, a musician or—especially if he also wore a beard—a revolutionary anarchist (later, a Bolshevik or a Communist). These associations still operate today, although many artists now have quite short hair and the male population of countries such as Russia and China is noticeably crop-headed.

Although long hair on a man not believed to be artistic has for many years suggested radical views, no absolute length can be designated as correlating with a certain degree of radicalism; what counts is the relative length. In a world of crew cuts and short-back-and-sides, the tidy hair styles of the early Beatles seemed (depending on the observer) thrillingly or threateningly long. During the 1960s and early 1970s, male political opinion could be estimated on sight by the length of the hair and sideburns (female hair, to the relief of many women, was less communicative). However, as time passed a sliding scale had to be applied. At one point, in about 1970, all but the most hidebound conservatives had haircuts that in the 1950s would have marked them as crazy Beatniks, and many committed social and political radicals

When the Beatles first became internationally famous their thick Christopher Robin bangs and collarless suits duplicated almost exactly what well-bred little British and American boys were wearing to parties. These outfits were perceived as dangerously radical, however, because they announced that John, Paul, George and Ringo did not intend to behave like responsible grownups, but had granted themselves—and their audiences—the childish privileges of noisy play and free impulse release.

went around with three-foot Afros or lank, near waist-length curls. Hair had become so important symbolically that a smash musical comedy was devoted entirely to celebrating it.

In the 1970s, as the economic boom tapered off and the climate of opinion became more conservative, men's hair began to shrink, and by the end of the decade it was hardly longer, though somewhat more full, than it had been in the 1920s. The standard range of variation was now much smaller, but it was still possible to classify hairdos as conservative or radical. William Thourlby, one of the new American "wardrobe engineers," warned his students that to most people, "long hair connotes the artistic, aesthetic, romantic, and casual mode of life. Discipline, seriousness, and business ethics are not suggested by long hair . . . Every study I've been able to find indicates that people over forty in American society don't trust a man whose hair covers his ears or drops below the upper edge of his collar."

For women, the main message of hair has always been sexual rather than political and social, though occasionally it has taken on a political meaning by association. The girl who bobbed her hair in the second decade of this century was suspected of wanting the vote along with more personal sorts of freedom; and in the 1960s a bushy female Afro might indicate political radicalism as well as countercultural tastes. More generally, women's hair that is tightly curled or closely restrained (whether by nets, caps or pins) suggests habits of self-restraint that are often accompanied by conservative views. Among British and American women politicians, members of the Conservative and Republican parties can often be observed to have more highly stylized hairdos than their Socialist and Democratic opponents. The same thing is true of politician's wives—at least of those who are in sympathy with their husbands.

THE BEARD AND THE MUSTACHE: FROM VIRTUE TO VILLAINY

Over the centuries male facial hair has provided great opportunities for the expression of opinion. The full beard, for example, has at various times signified paternal authority, spiritual inspiration, radical violence and artistic genius, its particular meaning being determined by other details of the costume and appearance and whether or not beards were respectable at the moment. Facial hair has also often been a guide to occupation. A little treatise could be written on the meaning of the various types of late-nineteenth-century beards and whiskers. It would include the Biblical mane of the religious leader; the rectangular beards of engineers and scientists such as Charles Darwin; the bushy but well-trimmed ones of Army and Navy officers; the pointed Vandyke popular among artists like Whistler; the long side-whiskers or dundrearies associated with English peers and statesmen like Gladstone (and, in a wispier and more attenuated form, with clergymen); and the untidy, flowing locks of poets such as Whitman, Longfellow and Tennyson. The imaginary representatives of nations also wore typical styles: John Bull could be recognized by his curly flyaway whiskers, and Uncle Sam by his straggly white goatee.

In the 1880s beards and side whiskers began to shrink, often leaving a growth of hair on the upper lip. Here too many styles, and many messages, were possible. A mustache

Between 1860 and 1880 men grew an amazing variety of informative facial foliage. Among many others, there was the full, square-cut beard popular among military men such as U. S. Grant; the sparser and more untidy intellectual beard (worn here by Charles Dickens) and the long hair and bushy beard of poets such as Walt Whitman. Clergymen and scholars often favored drooping "muttonchop" whiskers like those of Matthew Arnold, while a more active and belligerent character was expressed by the luxuriant sideburns associated with, and named after, General Ambrose Burnside; Benjamin Disraeli (like Uncle Sam) announced his shrewdness and determination by displaying a goatlike tuft of hair at the end of his chin.

General Ambrose Burnside, one of the leaders of the Union forces in the American Civil War, gave his name to the whiskers known as sideburns; his personal version of the style was particularly luxuriant and impressive.

might be wide or narrow, short or long, full or sparse, straight or trained and curled into elaborate shapes. The large soup-strainer or walrus mustache was favored by Army officers and Wild-West frontiersmen, and in a slightly abbreviated version by the ex-Army officer and would-be frontiersman Theodore Roosevelt. The handlebar mustache with its baroque swoop and waxed ends was associated with barbers and therefore (as it still is today) with barbershop quartets. A slim curled mustache was often preferred by artists and musicians, some of whom also retained the long, narrow pointed beard or Imperial.

According to the Chicago *Chronicle* of 1903, character as well as occupation could be read from the mustache. Vanity and dandyism were indicated by upcurled ends; stoicism by a straight bristly mustache, which appeared to reinforce or stiffen the traditional British stiff upper lip. Sensitivity and artistic tastes were shown by a soft, silky mustache with drooping sides. The opinionated egotist had long, narrow side whiskers, while those of the refined or scholarly gentleman were close-clipped.

To this list could certainly be added the long black mustaches worn by fictional and later by stage and film villains—the sort the wicked landlord twists when foreclosing the mortgage or tying the poor but honest heroine to the railroad tracks. In Hardy's *Tess of the D'Urbervilles*, the "well-groomed black moustache with curled points" of Tess's seducer, Alec D'Urberville, is noted on his first appearance, along with his too-fashionable dress: "a dandy cap, drab jacket, breeches of the same hue, white neckcloth, stick-up collar, and brown driving-gloves," described as the typical getup of a "handsome, horsey young buck." It is in this aspect that he pursues and betrays Tess. Later, during a brief period of repentance, he appears in "half-clerical" dress with a black coat, white neckcloth, and "neatly trimmed, old-fashioned whiskers." But his guilty passion is too strong for Alec, and he reverts to his former ways, cuts off his whiskers, and in "a tweed suit of fashionable pattern" and a "sable moustache," twirling "a gay walking cane," sets about the total ruination of Hardy's heroine.

Unfortunately for novelists, stage designers and stu-

In the Victorian period, long, narrow "muttonchop" whiskers, which narrowed the face and gave it a serious expression, were often worn by clergymen and scholars. Matthew Arnold, English poet and critic.

dents of the male character, by the 1920s most mustaches had shrunk to a vestigial tuft or vanished altogether, and the few beards that survived belonged to elderly men, artists or eccentrics. During the subsequent thirty years almost all American men were clean-shaven. In Britain small mustaches continued to be worn. Some of these styles became associated with certain ranks or branches of the military service, so that it became possible to speak of a Brigade of Guards mustache and later of a Royal Air Force mustache. In both America and Britain larger and more elaborate mustaches were considered foreign and undesirable. Depending on their shape, they suggested Latin suavity and illicit passion, French dandyism, Mexican or Sicilian banditry, Scandinavian stoicism and gloom, Chinese inscrutability, Russian melancholy and Bolshevism and (after the rise of Hitler) Teutonic paranoia. The average man regarded such growths on Anglo-Saxons as he would that of a strange and dangerous weed in his garden. The beard, unless attached to a reputed sage like Shaw or Freud, was considered a rather nasty affectation, probably adopted to conceal a weak chin.

A full but well-trimmed beard and neatly cropped hair were frequently worn by military men. Ulysses S. Grant, general of the Union Army and later president.

THE BEARD TODAY

In the past twenty years, however, the landscape has changed. On both sides of the Atlantic there has been what might be called a reforestation project. New types of beards and mustaches, with new meanings, have sprung up, and some of the old styles have been revived. Full, flowing beards are rarely seen today except in pictures of Santa Claus, God and the Biblical patriarchs and prophets. Men who wear them, whatever their original motives, are apt to be regarded as eccentric father figures. The pointed Vandyke beard, on the other hand, is now associated with less benevolent authority. The Devil is popularly portrayed with just such a beard, and today it no longer designates an artist; rather it suggests someone who has or wants to appear to have the characteristics associated with Satan in the popular mind: he is proud, elegant, well-mannered, formally charm-

In the nineteenth century, just as today, relatively long hair and a somewhat untidy beard often expressed artistic or literary interests. Charles Dickens, English novelist.

ing, rich, meticulous, sinister, and foreign in his tastes and habits.

The short chin beard, which in the nineteenth century was typically worn by sailors, is today most often seen on commercial artists and interior decorators, who like its archaic look; in a modified version, in which the whiskers are allowed to grow above the line of the jaw, it is connected with Abraham Lincoln, and therefore, at least in the United States, with pioneer wisdom and integrity; it is still occasionally seen on men whose self-image it fits or flatters.

At present, however, these idiosyncratic styles of beard are comparatively rare. Medium-length, well-trimmed beards of no particular shape, on the other hand, are fairly common today, though less so than they were ten years ago. They were associated, as they have been for over a century, with creative activity, and are therefore worn by some painters, writers, musicians and inventors; they are also, though less often, seen on editors, critics, architects and theater people.

The message of the standard modern beard depends a good deal on the length of hair that goes with it. With long hair, it implies bohemian tastes and interests, and/or a career in the arts. With medium-length hair it becomes more respectable and suggests maturity and an interesting, but not antisocial or disruptive, originality. Many professors have beards and hair of this type (in the English Department at Cornell, seven out of a possible thirty-eight). It is impossible to look boyish or utterly stupid in a beard—hence perhaps their popularity in the academic world, especially among young faculty members concerned not to be mistaken for their own students.

When the standard beard is combined with shorter-than-average hair it suggests seriousness, specialized knowledge and often a slight inflexibility of views. This combination is often seen on research scientists, doctors and engineers, and is almost standard for "experts" presenting their discoveries in public, whether they are real scientists or actors on TV dressed up to look like scientists. For some reason, the less familiar and reassuring these discoveries are,

the more likely they are to issue from behind facial shrubbery. What we are dealing with here, no doubt, is the old
stereotype of the bearded alchemist or magician—wise but
very possibly dangerous.

In certain circles, even today, any kind of beard is suspect. Businessmen, politicians, and members of the more
conventional professions tend to dislike them, perhaps in
part because of their association with the radical movements
of the sixties. As William Thourlby puts it:

> Beards are like sunglasses. As long as they are on your face,
> no one will really get to know you or trust you. Creative
> people, artists, art directors, and writers are the exceptions
> who may wear beards. Their background, education, trust-
> worthiness and future is of no importance to you when you
> evaluate their work.

The longer and more unconfined the hair and beard of a writer, the greater the claim of its wearer to free self-expression and creative inspiration. Walt Whitman, American poet.

In other words, creative people come from bad backgrounds,
go to the wrong schools, can't really be trusted and will
usually come to a bad end.

The mustache today seems to be in a period of transition, possibly one of decline. A few years ago it was very
popular. The most favored style was full and extended
slightly beyond the mouth: it was thought to imply male
energy, dominance and power. The larger the mustache, the
stronger the message; some approached Mexican-bandit
proportions. This macho mustache was popular among
Madison Avenue and Mayfair desperadoes; it was also worn
by many working-class men, especially those of non-Anglo
background. But the very success of the macho mustache as
a sign may have been its undoing. In the late 1970s it started
to become popular with homosexuals, and by the end of the
decade it had become a gay indicator in places such as New
York and San Francisco. Men in these cities who disliked
being followed and propositioned by members of their own
sex then began shaving off their mustaches. Whether this
trend will spread to regions without a significant gay culture,
or whether homosexual fashion, always volatile, will shift
again, allowing the macho mustache to survive, remains to
be seen.

TEMPORARY FOLIAGE

Some men are bearded all their lives; for others the beard is a shrub that springs up overnight and is soon cut down. When a man has been clean-shaven for many years the deliberate growth of a beard is always meaningful—the more so, of course, if it proves to be permanent. Various causes may bring this about. The discovery of artistic talents or inclinations often expresses itself in the growth of facial foliage, and so does identification with some religious or intellectual belief system, particularly those whose founders were notably bearded (Marx, Freud, Jung). The longer and more luxuriant the new growth, and the more it resembles that of God the Father, the more likely its owner is to have designated himself a prophet or sage of the system in question.

A beard also may appear temporarily on men who have recently severed some important professional or personal tie. College students away from home for the first time often grow facial hair as soon as they are physiologically able to do so, as a test or proof of adulthood. Such growths are usually short-lived, and if they survive into senior year nearly always vanish before the first important job or graduate-school interview. Later, during the male midlife crisis of the forties and fifties, there is a new growing season. The man who has just left his wife or his profession or both often stops shaving temporarily. The resulting beard, as it develops, will most obligingly give him the different successive aspects appropriate to the stages of psychological and social development he is about to pass through. That is, first it makes him look like someone caught in a natural disaster—flood, earthquake, fire; then it makes him look like a bum; then like a shipwrecked mariner; and finally like a desperado. Eventually the man either returns to his wife and/or job (or to a very similar wife and job) and shaves off his beard; or else he changes his life permanently, in which case the beard (if allowed to survive) takes its final form and becomes part of his new persona.

The removal of a long-established beard or mustache is

A hundred years ago, the wearing of a goatlike tuft of hair at the end of the chin was thought to indicate shrewdness and determination. The mythical Uncle Sam wore such a beard, and often still does; and so, in real life, did Benjamin Disraeli, Prime Minister of Great Britain.

also significant. Often it suggests a move towards conventionality; on the other hand, it may be related to the maintenance of an existing image. Facial hair tends to lose its natural color sooner than the hair on the head; and men who grew beards to announce themselves as young radicals, artists, intellectuals or authority figures, may, as the gray hairs appear, shave them off.

THE SYMBOLIC HAT AND THE UTILITARIAN HAT

Traditionally whatever is worn on the head, whether or not it grows there naturally, is a sign of the mind beneath it. The hat therefore, like the hair, expresses ideas and opinions. Since the head is one of the most vulnerable parts of the body, many hats also have a protective function, shielding their wearers from extremes of climate and from human aggression. The man's hat of the nineteenth and early twentieth century, which was derived ultimately from the medieval helmet, protected its wearer both physically and psychologically. The heavy crown deflected blows; the brim shaded the face from strong sunlight and close scrutiny; the conventional shape expressed the conventionality of the mind it covered. The stiffer the hat, in general, the higher the social class of its wearer and/or the more conventional his views: the aristocrat in his topper, the City man in his bowler, were literally hard-headed. The symbolically appropriate disadvantage of such hats was that they were easy to knock off if anyone dared to do so. Working men and boys, on the other hand, wore soft cloth caps, less formidable-looking but harder to remove; their prestige, such as it was, was less easily damaged by direct assault.

Women's hats, too, once had important symbolic meanings, though here social role rather than social status was uppermost. Throughout most of the nineteenth century all respectable wives, widows and spinsters wore not one but two symbolic head coverings. Except for young unmarried girls, an indoor cap of muslin or silk, trimmed with lace and/or ribbon, was an essential part of the everyday costume. It was donned on arising, and could be dispensed with

For European immigrants to the New World, clothes were an important sign of status and of the successful achievement of an American identity. Men who could afford it wore suits and hats to distinguish themselves from more recently arrived "greenhorns," and dressed their wives and children as well as they could manage. Duluth, Minnesota, 1890.

only for formal evening entertainments. Usually this cap was white, expressing the conventional purity and delicacy of the mind within; if the woman was in mourning it might be black (more suitable as a container of sad thoughts) or trimmed with a black ribbon.

When the middle-class woman left her house, even to walk in the garden, she put on a hat or bonnet—over her cap if she wore one. She thus shielded her pure and private thoughts, covering them with an elaborate and conventional representation of contemporary public femininity. A well-dressed female who appeared out of doors without her hat, or indoors without a cap (if she was old enough to wear one), was assumed to be emotionally distracted, mentally disturbed or of loose morals.

By the 1890s caps had been given up by all but the elderly or exceptionally prim; but men's and women's hats continued to flourish for the next half-century, offering a remarkable variety of expressive form. In America the hat was a status symbol of a special kind. These were the great years of European immigration, and as boatload after boatload of hatless peasants landed, those who wanted to make it plain that they were not themselves ignorant "greenhorns," or that they were of a higher class origin than most immigrants, took care to wear hats.

THE DECLINE AND FALL OF THE SYMBOLIC HAT

After World War II, the symbolic hat began to disappear. Women who a few years earlier would never have left home without a hat, even to go down to the corner store, were now tying a scarf over their hair or going bareheaded. In the 1950s the symbolic female hat was obligatory only for formal occasions: lunches in town, business meetings, church; by 1960 it was optional everywhere. Women's hats continued to be manufactured and sold, but now mainly as decorative accessories.

The symbolic man's hat also disappeared after World War II, though more gradually. By 1970, though the British businessman may have owned a bowler, the lawyer or doctor a soft felt, the commercial traveler a porkpie and the working man a cap, more often than not he did not wear it. In America the same thing happened; eventually, even in a large city, a man who was wearing a symbolic hat in good weather was assumed to be either (1) a conscious dandy or eccentric, (2) on his way to some ceremonial function or (3) over sixty.

Strictly utilitarian hats were still occasionally worn: knitted wool caps for cold weather, plastic or waterproofed sou'westers for rain, floppy straws and cotton baseball caps (some with green celluloid visors) for glaring sun. The prestige of all such hats, however, was very low, and many people preferred to be cold, wet or blinded rather than wear them, especially on formal occasions. Sometimes, for protection from the elements, they wore an old symbolic hat, inefficient as this usually turned out to be. The standard man's fedora needed reblocking after every rainstorm, and the soft felt became a sodden pudding. Women's symbolic hats were even more vulnerable. The New Look cartwheel blew off in the slightest breeze, the ladylike straw of the fifties wilted and the Jackie Kennedy pillbox with its wisp of symbolic veil was of no use whatsoever.

The disappearance of the symbolic hat over the last thirty years is one of the oddest chapters in the entire history of costume. After covering their heads ceremonially for centuries most people simply gave up doing so, and this in spite of frantic sobs and threats from the fashion industry. A tremendous advertising campaign was mounted: consumers were reminded that no real lady or gentleman was ever seen in public hatless; they were warned that their desertion of the hat would throw thousands of deserving persons out of work, and afflict millions with head colds and pneumonia. It was all to no avail; every year, more and more men and women went bareheaded.

During the late sixties and early seventies the only real enthusiasm for headgear was among members of the counterculture, who adopted eccentric varieties of symbolic hats in a spirit of play or satire. For a while every political demonstration or outdoor concert was a seething mass of coonskin caps, Mexican sombreros, calico sunbonnets, gypsy

Dramatic, passionate red, shading toward crimson and trimmed in glittering black; an elegant transvestite at Studio 54, New York, 1979. As usual, the disguise is not quite complete: the hairy, muscular forearms deliberately inform us that this is a man in woman's clothes. Photograph by Sonia Moskowitz.

Bright red stands for life, strength and vitality—all ideal qualities for the patron of a roller disco. Christie Brinkley, model and member of the U.S. Women's Olympic Hockey team, at Roxy, New York, 1979. Photograph by Sonia Moskowitz.

Orange clothing signals a demand for attention, and sometimes warns us of danger. Perhaps partly for this reason, members of the Hare Krishna sect in Britain and America are seen as obtrusive or threatening. Photograph by Burt Glinn.

Brilliant yellow, the color of the sun, is associated with youth, life and hope. Mary Cassatt's Mother and Child *(c. 1905) is full of solar imagery: the sitters are bathed in warm light, the mother wears a giant sunflower and the child's face, reflected in the round gold mirror, becomes a personified sun.*

British country camouflage, June 1977. The soft, thick tweeds and woollens in muted shades of green, tan and blue worn by this father and his sons repeat both the textures and the colors of the rural English landscape. Photograph by Ken Heyman.

Amish women's dress is made according to traditional patterns, though variation in color is allowed as long as the material is plain and the apron and scarf match the dress. Blue, the color of work and service, is a common choice. Before marriage girls wear a black head scarf or cap. Married women, like this young mother, always wear a white cap, the style and size of which indicate membership in a particular Amish community. Mifflin County, Pennsylvania, 1976. Photograph by by Rowan P. Smolcha.

Warm browns and tans suggest stability, security and domestic comfort, as in this cosy late-Victorian scene. The brown of the young man's jacket is echoed in the young woman's skirt, a common phenomenon in the clothes of well-suited lovers. The direct sexual implication of the scene seems obvious today; if earlier viewers noticed it they may have been reassured not only by the brown costumes but by the placing of the couple between ivy (the symbol of fidelity) and that most heavenly of instruments, the harp. The Music Lesson, by John George Brown, 1870.

Today a drab brownish or faded green is the standard color of army dress, and therefore of obedience and conformity. These quasi-military getups, however, are intended to parody; they thus recall the ancient connection between green clothes and freedom or even license. Punks at the Mudd Club in New York, 1979. Photograph by Marcia Resnick.

Dramatic Black at its most intense: Sargent's Madame X *(Mme. Virginie Gautreau). If such clothes are elegant and of rich materials they suggest worldly power and sophistication, often with an undertone of evil or danger. Above her superb low-cut gown, however, Madame X is seductively naked, creating a high tension between attraction and fear. Perhaps it was for this reason that when Sargent's portrait was shown at the Paris Salon of 1884 it caused such a scandal that he had to remove it.*

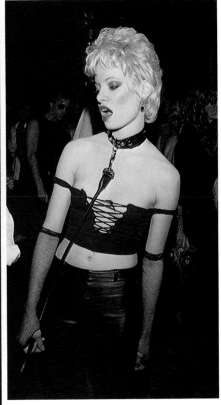

Dramatic Black today: Sargent's Madame X *reduced to the lowest common denominator, with the psychological conflict between desire and danger, sex and death made crudely—but still effectively—manifest. Studio 54, New York, January 1980. Photograph by Sonia Moskowitz.*

A rosy pink shading toward lavender rather than coral is the traditional color of romance and sentiment—and also of sentimentality. *Advertisement in* The New York Times, *1981.*

The innocent blonde in the fragile white dress (often trimmed with blue to suggest loyalty and sincerity), and the more mature and sophisticated brunette in black (worn here with a red rose for romantic passion) are both traditional and powerful female stereotypes. The Vickers Sisters, *by John Singer Sargent, 1884.*

In a conservative era daytime and nighttime clothes are sharply distinguished. Disco fashions like these may be brilliantly colored and daringly cut, but they are, as it were, subject to quarantine, and are limited to certain times and places. To wear them anywhere else is to invite serious moral disapproval. New York, 1979. Photograph by Sonia Moskowitz.

An old-fashioned item of dress, like an archaic word in poetry, may make the ephemeral timeless or universal. Here the effect of the top hat is enhanced by the purple shirt, which, like all clothes of this hue, claims special status for its wearer. Hatless, and in a plain white shirt, this man would be only a hippie sitting in a field; instead he becomes an almost supernatural figure. Photograph by Don Snyder.

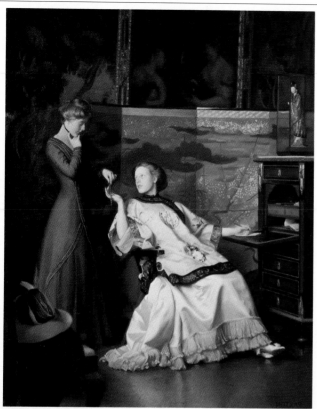

The deliberate mixing of foreign and native garments, like the use of foreign words in conversation, is by no means a recent phenomenon. The young woman in the pink silk kimono and the pale-orange satin skirt tells us that she is rich, well-educated, romantic and worth noticing. Her companion, in modest gray, literally fades into the background. **The New Necklace,** *by William McGregor Paxton, 1910.*

When there is a conflict between the outer and inner selves the top layer of clothing may represent the public person and the one beneath his or her private desires or fears. Here the central figure conceals her emotion under a dark-gray coat, but her flame-red dress reveals them, at least to us. **The Subway,** *1950, by George Tooker.*

scarves, shiny black toppers, antique military helmets and garden-party straws trimmed with fading real or paper flowers. Those who did not wear hats often tied a leather thong or a beaded or embroidered band around their heads Indian fashion (occasionally with an upstanding feather), possibly to keep their rather scattered thoughts together, possibly to symbolize the fact that their mind was in the grip of some obsessive idea.

Interestingly enough, the disappearance of the conventional hat was accompanied and paralleled by a severe simplification of formal etiquette. On all but the most formal occasions, rules of precedence and seating were forgotten. Strangers were introduced by their first names alone, often without regard for rank, age and sex; bank tellers, waitresses and airline stewards presented themselves to the public as "Hi, I'm Billie." Instead of talking about the weather or the news of the day, people one had known for five minutes would begin to describe their current emotional state and reveal intimate details of their lives; this process, known as "letting it all hang out," was often literally echoed in the costume. What seemed to be taking place both in terms of dress and in terms of manners was the abandonment of the formal public self symbolized by the hat. Men or women who had once been willing or even eager to assume a standardized role in public now wanted to operate at all times as spontaneous individuals. A "gentleman" no longer tipped his symbolic hat to a "lady" to show the conventional respect due her sex; he no longer had a hat to tip.

THE RETURN OF THE HAT: COWBOY CHIC AND THE SCARF

In the sixties and seventies the symbolic hat seemed almost as sure of extinction as the passenger pigeon. Currently, however, it seems to be making a limited comeback. This movement began some years ago in the American Wild West with the increasing popularity of cowboy hats among noncowboys. Today a majority of men in this part of the country, especially in Texas, wear some type of "Western" hat—and so do a number of the women.

The cowboy hat, originally part of the practical working garb of men who had to ride long distances in an extreme climate, has over the past century become heavy with symbolic meaning. Basically it suggests toughness and independence, but many subtle variations of this message are possible, depending among other things on the color and shape of the hat and on its trimmings. The Hollywood convention White Hat=Good Guy, Black Hat=Bad Guy still operates: men who wish to appear as rebels or desperate characters prefer the darker shades, and straight arrows the lighter ones. Ambiguous, subtle or secretive types may favor grayed hues, while the more common tans and browns that repeat the colors of the Western landscape are worn (or thought to be worn) by natural, down-to-earth men. Plain leather hatbands, no doubt on the principle of contagious magic, suggest the simple approach to life and physical energy of the beef cattle to which the leather once belonged; expensive hand-tooled bands and decorations of silver and feathers imply a high-flying life style and an extensive bank account. The shape of the Western hat is also a form of communication. In general, the higher the crown, the higher the self-esteem of the wearer; the wider the brim, the closer his connection to the realities of outdoor life on the Western plains, where shelter from sun, rain, dust and wind are of primary importance.

The Western or cowboy hat today is a complex symbolic object. An actor wearing a black hat that is high in the crown and expensively decorated with feathers, for instance, tells us that the character he plays is evil, egotistical and extremely rich. This publicity photograph of Larry Hagman was supplied by Lippin & Grant, Los Angeles.

In the past few years Western hats have begun to multiply outside the Wild West. Today they are on sale in both New York and London—although those who can afford the prices (among them, Bob Dylan and the King of Sweden) still order theirs from Texas Hatters in Houston. Sometimes the message of these hats is merely one of fashionable chic, but often, especially when they are part of a complete or partial Western outfit, they may be read as a guide to character and status.

The utilitarian hat, meanwhile, is gradually becoming more acceptable, especially among men, whose relatively short hair and susceptibility to baldness make them vulnerable to extremes of climate. Knitted wool caps are still non-U in town for anyone over the age of eighteen; but there are now more respectable alternatives, some of which have begun to take on symbolic meanings of their own. The black fur hat that can be folded down to cover the ears on very cold days is associated with men of middle age and northern European origin or interests. There is also the floppy Irish tweed hat; widely advertised as becoming to all ages and sexes, it is in fact becoming to no one, but has the advantage that no type of precipitation can make it look worse than it already does. In the true country this hat is quite respectable; in town, however, its wearer appears to belong to a rural aristocracy of the species that is hardly distinguishable from the rural peasantry.

The flat wool cap which was in the past traditionally worn for golfing, shooting and many spectator sports is another possible utilitarian hat, and perhaps today the most popular one. In rural or suburban settings it may give a certain style and dash to the costume. The man who wears such a cap in the city, however, is automatically marked down one notch below the social status implied by the rest of his outfit; and he may even be suspected of owning a one-acre suburban estate that he has christened Tall Pines or The Snuggery.

Women who like to appear as tomboys or good sports may wear some type of male utilitarian hat, though not usually for purely utilitarian reasons. More often, when the weather is bad, they will shield their heads with scarves, and here they have a large vocabulary of expressive possibilities. The fabric of which the scarf is made can be related to outdoor temperatures, or it can be a class indicator—wool being considered aristocratic, chiffon *nouveau riche,* silk upper-middle class, cotton middle class or arty and synthetics working class. Another important consideration is the manner in which the scarf is tied, whether conventionally under the chin, exotically at the nape of the neck or on top of the head turban or charlady style. But most significant of all, probably, is the color and (if any) the pattern of the scarf, which, like color and pattern generally, convey a whole range of subtle and important personal messages.

VII
COLOR
AND PATTERN

Certain sorts of information about other people can be communicated in spite of a language barrier. We may not be able to understand Welsh or the thick Southern dialect of the Mississippi delta, but when we hear a conversation in these tongues we can tell at once whether the speakers are excited or bored, cheerful or miserable, confident or frightened. In the same way, some aspects of the language of clothes can be read by almost anyone.

The first and most important of these signs, and the one that makes the greatest and most immediate impact, is color. Merely looking at different colors, psychologists have discovered, alters our blood pressure, heartbeat and rate of respiration, just as hearing a harsh noise or a harmonious musical chord does. When somebody approaches from a distance the first thing we see is the hue of his clothes; the closer he comes, the more space this hue occupies in our visual field and the greater its effect on our nervous system. Loud, clashing colors, like loud noises or loud voices, may actually hurt our eyes or give us a headache; soft, harmonious hues, like music and soft voices, thrill or soothe us. Color in dress is also like tone of voice in speech in that it can completely alter the meaning of what is "said" by other aspects of the costume: style, fabric and trimmings. Just as the words, "Do you want to dance with me?" can be whispered shyly or flung as a challenge, so the effect of a white evening dress is very different from that of a scarlet one of identical fabric and pattern. In certain circumstances some hues, like some tones of voice, are beyond the bounds of polite discourse. A bride in a black wedding dress, or a stockbroker greeting his clients in a shocking-pink three-piece suit, would be like people screaming aloud.

Although color often indicates mood, it is not by any means an infallible guide. For one thing, convention may prescribe certain hues. The urban businessman must wear a navy blue, dark gray or (in certain regions) brown or tan suit, and can express his feelings only through his choice of shirt and tie, or tie alone; and even here the respectable possibilities may be very limited. Convention also alters the meaning of colors according to the place and time at which they are worn. Vermilion in the office is not the same as vermilion at a disco; and hot weather permits the wearing of pale hues that would make one look far more formal and fragile in midwinter.

There are other problems. Some people may avoid colors they like because of the belief or illusion that they are unbecoming, while others may wear colors they normally dislike for symbolic reasons: because they are members or fans of a certain football team, for instance. In addition, some fashionable types may select certain hues merely because they are "in" that year. There is an economic factor, too: unless they are rich or extravagant, most people do not own more than one or two coats, raincoats or bathrobes at a single time; the ones they have must be worn whether or not they match the current mood. A bright yellow winter coat, bought in a euphoric state of mind in October, may cover the blackest February depression; all it reveals is that at one time its wearer was happy or at least hopeful.

It must also be remembered that mood, unlike age, status or political views, can vary during the course of a day. The man who comes to work in a peaceful blue shirt and tie may by lunchtime have met with frustrations that make him wish he were wearing the yellow and black of an angry wasp; or he may have had a telephone call from his mistress which, if words had that power, would have turned his tie as well as his face crimson. It is also true, however, that the sort of experiences you are dressed for are often attracted to you naturally. At a party, the young woman in mouse-gray is as difficult to see as a mouse, while the ones in brilliant reds and pinks and oranges draw suitors just as a highly colored flower does insects—and are sometimes as readily pollinated.

Finally it should be noted that the effect of any color in dress is modified by the colors that accompany it. In general, therefore, the following remarks should be taken as applying mainly to costumes composed entirely or almost entirely of a single hue.

BLACK, WHITE AND GRAY

Three of the most common and important colors in costume —black, white and gray—are not technically colors at all, but representations of the absence or presence of light. All of them, especially the first two, are heavily weighted with conventional meanings—one of which, unfortunately, is a racial one. That we should now think and speak of "Whites" and "Blacks" is an historical error. The actual skin color of most Britons and Americans, as anyone can observe, is a pinkish tan, fading to dun in age or illness; flushing to rose as a result of high blood pressure or alcoholism—or temporarily as a result of exertion, anger or embarrassment. It is the dubious achievement of these pinkish-tan persons to have designated themselves the "White" race, and to have affixed the term "Black" to people whose skin is some shade of brown or gold. The result of this semantic sleight of hand has been to associate pinkish tan skin with virtue and cleanliness, and brown or golden skin with evil, dirt and danger.

WHITE: PURITY, INNOCENCE AND STATUS

In classical times, long before the "White" race was invented, white was the color of fair-weather clouds and the

When it is made of expensive and delicate materials an all-white costume can convey both refinement and high status. Queen Elizabeth, now the Queen Mother, with President Lebrun of France at a Paris garden party in 1938. Note especially the effulgent halolike hat, which symbolically transforms her into an English saint.

snow-topped mountains where the gods dwelt. It was sacred to Zeus, the king of the gods: white horses drew his chariot, and white animals were sacrificed to him by white-robed priests. In the Christian church, white is the color of heavenly joy and purity, and is associated with Easter and the Resurrection. In Christian art, God the Father, like Zeus, usually wears a long white robe.

In secular life white has always stood for purity and innocence. Logically, all-white outfits are most frequently worn by babies and very young children. They often become fashionable for unmarried young women, and sometimes (as in the early nineteenth century) for women of all ages. Innocent heroines in fiction customarily wear white on their first appearance, especially when—like Hardy's Tess or Henry James's Daisy Miller—they are destined for a tragic end. Because it is so easily soiled physically as well as symbolically, white has always been popular with those who wish to demonstrate wealth and status through the conspicuous consumption of laundry soap or conspicuous freedom from manual labor. It is traditionally worn by participants in the high-status sports of tennis and polo, especially in professional competition.

Perhaps because it soils easily, or perhaps because of its long association with infancy and early childhood, all-white clothing has often suggested delicacy, and even physical infirmity or weakness, especially when the material is fragile. Invalids in fiction and on stage—as well as in real life— often wear such clothes, and even today the woman who wishes to look especially innocent and dainty may wear an all-white costume. The man who imitates her, however, has usually been considered eccentric and dandified.

MARITAL, MEDICAL AND COLONIAL WHITE

Today certain social roles and professions seem to us to require white garments. In some cases, this necessity is of recent date: the traditional white wedding dress, for instance, is only about fifty years old. Before the 1920s a bride usually wore a new evening gown in whatever color suited her: it might be white, but it might just as well be pink, yellow, blue or green. After the wedding it became her best party dress. Today most young women are married in a special all-white costume of antique cut and fabric which is generally assumed to be a symbol of innocence and purity, and which will be worn only once in a lifetime. White is considered unsuitable for second marriages, or for brides who are evidently pregnant, though in the latter case the rule is sometimes broken. A cynic might wonder why this expensive and archaic garment should have become fashionable just at the time when changes in social mores and the availability of birth control had made it much less likely than before that a bride was a pure virgin. Prudence Glynn, an erudite and witty commentator on British costume, has suggested that either the modern bride "wants one marvellous, escapist, romantic moment in an otherwise drab life," or perhaps, "by wearing archaic dress she is stating her unconscious belief that the ceremony itself is archaic." It is also possible that the function of the white wedding dress and veil is magical: that by putting it on the bride cancels out her previous experiences, so that she may enter marriage emotionally and symbolically if not physically intact.

Before the twentieth century, cleanliness and godliness were not necessarily associated with health, and medical men, wishing to appear serious and competent, dressed in dark, sober clothes. The discovery of germs and hygiene, and the transformation of medicine from an uncertain art into an uncertain science, changed all that. The doctor was no longer a kind of skilled artisan who might relieve your aches and pains, but would never be asked to dinner in the best houses; he was now a godlike authority figure, an arbiter of life and death. This deified being gradually adopted a pristine white raiment, which today is the standard choice of members of the medical profession. Since any suggestion of their own weakness or illness is to be avoided, doctors and nurses wear garments of sturdy materials, starched as stiff as a board. Patients are also traditionally dressed in white; but their outfits are of a very different texture. When you enter a hospital, or go for a physical checkup, your own clothes are removed and replaced with a pale, shapeless, flimsy gar-

Limp, fragile white clothing often suggests invalidism. The loose, pale gown, now too large for the shrunken form of its wearer, resembles a shroud. Together with her hollow cheeks and bright eyes, it instantly tells her long-lost suitor that she is dying of consumption. Too Late, *1858 by William L. Windus.*

ment that fastens ineffectively up the back with strings or snaps like an infant's gown. You are thus simultaneously deprived of your chosen sartorial identity (in the language of clothes, struck dumb) and transformed into a half-naked, helpless, inarticulate creature that cannot even dress itself. (In some chic hospitals and examining rooms, the traditional infantine garment is very pale blue, suggesting trust and docility as well as helpless innocence, and perhaps therefore implying a slightly older baby.)

Stiffness and starch were also the mark of the traditional outfit of the Englishman in the tropics—though not that of the Englishwoman, which was usually made of flimsy, fragile muslin, satin and lace, as befitted her presumed delicacy and helplessness. What may be called British Colonial white, though seldom worn today, is familiar to all of us through films and cartoons. The white dress and hat of the female, the white shirt, trousers or shorts and topee of the male, were practical in a hot, sunny climate. But the British insistence upon the spotlessness and freedom from wrinkles of these garments also made them a portable sign of status, and symbolically transformed military occupation and commercial exploitation into justice and virtue, even into self-sacrifice. One of the most famous—and most ambiguous—cases of British Colonial white in fiction occurs in Conrad's *Lord Jim.* Jim (who is a lord only in the scornful designation of his peers) has deserted a sinking ship with a cargo of eight hundred native pilgrims. He always wears spotless white, which graphically expresses his incurable idealism and his identification with the romantic traditions of the British Empire. It is also a sign of false innocence shading into ignorance both of himself and of his world, and reminds us that one of the few negative associations of whiteness is with cowardice.

BLACK: GLOOM, GUILT AND SOPHISTICATION

Black, the reverse of white, is the color of night and darkness. For thousands of years it has stood for sorrow, sin and death. It is of course the traditional hue of mourning, and in classical mythology Death himself appears in sable robes. Its other ancient connection is with religious or secular asceticism, with the symbolic denial of the sensual life: monks and misers, priests and scholars frequently wear black. Like white, it is associated with the supernatural, but with the powers of darkness rather than those of light. The Furies, the three avenging goddesses of Greek drama, always dress in black, and so do witches, warlocks and other practitioners of the Black Arts. And, just as white suggests innocence, black suggests sophistication—which, after all, often consists in the knowledge or experience of the darker side of life: of evil, unhappiness and death.

Long, unkempt hair and beard, a simple black robe and sandals are the traditional costume of the religious ascetic or wandering holy man. Except for his hat, this Aquarian Age hermit could have been encountered on a rainy country lane a thousand years ago, rather than on a Connecticut road. Photograph by Don Snyder.

Sinister though some of these associations may be, the wearing of black clothing has been fashionable in many times and places since the fourteenth century. Anne Hollander, in *Seeing Through Clothes,* has traced the history of this fashion with considerable wit and erudition. As she remarks, the wearing of all-black or nearly all-black costume can have many meanings. When everyone else is in bright or pale colors, the entrance of a man or woman in black can have tremendous dramatic impact. Depending on the situation and the style of the costume, the newcomer may seem holy, evil, dangerous, melancholy, grief-stricken or any combination of these. Hamlet's "customary suit of solemn black" gives him an air of gloomy elegance and desperation that makes the rest of the Danish court appear false, ignorant, shallow or naïve. Novelists have often played with these confrontations and ambiguities, both in popular fiction (the black robes of the wicked monks and beautiful, dangerous Dark Ladies in Gothic romances) and in serious literature: in Hawthorne's *The Scarlet Letter,* for instance, both the adulterous minister Arthur Dimmesdale and the vengeful wronged husband Roger Chillingworth wear black.

Any new style that makes its wearers look dramatic is bound to be taken up, and the wearing of black has been no exception. By the late sixteenth century black clothing had become the fashion for both sexes at the Spanish court, though now it was modified by the addition of a white collar or ruff. From this time on, formal black costume for men was usually accompanied by a show of white at the neck and/or wrists—perhaps suggesting that though they might be somber or even dangerous, they were noble and pure underneath; and also, of course, that they were not wearing black to hide dirt. Women achieved the same effect with white coifs, veils and caps, even when they did not wear a white collar or neckerchief.

Since the styles of politically and economically dominant nations tend to become universal, it is not surprising that Spanish black soon became fashionable in Holland and Italy, and also in England, where by the end of the century Elizabeth's courtiers, and often the queen herself, wore it. When everyone adopts a mode, however, it soon ceases to be unique and exciting and becomes first conventionally fashionable, then merely respectable and finally drab. Such was the fate of Spanish black. By the middle of the seventeenth century it was old-fashioned, and suggested age, sober professionalism and religious piety: Puritan divines and their families wore it, and prosperous, pious merchants.

For the next hundred years or more, black with white accents was respectable rather than fashionable and daring. It
was not until the Romantic revolution that it regained some
of its original startling effect.

During the second half of the nineteenth century, as
Anne Hollander has pointed out, there were two sorts of
black clothing, "the conventionally sober, self-denying
black and the dramatic, isolating, and distinguishing black."
Servants, clerks, lawyers, doctors, clergymen and the elderly
wore sober black; the rich and fashionable wore dramatic
black. What distinguished the two was the richness of the
materials and the elaboration of the design—plus, of course,
the appearance and manner of the wearer:

> . . . "emotional" black could be of fragile velvet, superfine
> wool, or silk gauze, and intricately cut and trimmed, some-
> times with black glitter. Null black was economical and hard-
> wearing and did not show stains, and looked it.

In real life (as Ms. Hollander suggests) and also in fiction,
these categories could become blurred. The poor girl in her
simple black dress, like Lizzie Hallam in Dickens's *Our Mutual Friend,* might be presented or present herself as a dramatic heroine; while respectable dull elderly ladies might
spend large sums on jet, black satin and veiling.

MOURNING BLACK

The Victorian fashion for deep and elaborate mourning put
many Britons and Americans into black for years, and
helped to make it the most respectable and dignified hue for
female dress among those past middle age. In America one
was expected to wear black for a year after the death of
parents or children, and six months for grandparents or sib-
lings; even tiny children were put into black frocks. A
widow or widower was supposed to mourn visibly for two
years, and might—like Queen Victoria—choose to do so
permanently. For men, whose everyday clothes were somber

Nineteenth-century mourning costume was heavy and elaborate. Even small children wore all-black clothes for a year after the death of a parent or sibling, and a respectable widow kept her weeds for two years and sometimes for life. Mourning fashions, Harper's Bazar, *New York, 1895.*

in hue, mourning apparel did not demand much alteration of wardrobe; but for women it was a complex and expensive adjustment. Since Victorian families were large, and the death rate high, it must sometimes have seemed hardly worth bothering to order or make colored clothes—especially since there were many possible styles and degrees of mourning: it could be drab and melancholy, elegant and dramatic, or even sexually exciting.

Today formal mourning is only observed for heads of state, and very few men wear formal black and white except at society weddings and balls. Male evening dress has largely become the costume of officials and functionaries, principally waiters in expensive restaurants. On stage, however, as Anne Hollander has remarked, "The diabolic character of black male evening clothes retained its flavor well into the twentieth century. . . . It is the proper dress of the magician, of Dracula—even in the morning. In the first half of the twentieth century it was the popularly conceived costume of sexual villainy, as the daytime version (black frock coat and striped pants) was the popularly conceived costume of financial and political villainy."

BUSINESS, BOHEMIAN AND BRANDO BLACK

One of the longest-lasting styles of this century is what has been called Modern Bohemian Black. The basic garment for women is a black turtleneck sweater paired with a full black or colored skirt. This outfit, photographed in 1948 by Sid Grossman, looks completely contemporary today.

For men the contemporary equivalent of nineteenth-century black and white is the very dark gray suit, plain white shirt and narrow black tie—an outfit which, like its predecessor, can be drab or elegant, but today is seldom dramatic. Rather it suggests seriousness, steadiness, formality and self-restraint. Women in business or the professions also sometimes wear a black suit and white blouse. Wardrobe consultants suggest this combination to create an effect of authority and dominance; it is definitely not recommended for arousing either trust or affection. The elegant "little black dress" that first became popular in the 1950s is still seen, especially on well-to-do urban women past the age of thirty. It is usually worn with colorful accessories and one or two pieces of expensive jewelry, and is the contemporary equivalent of the respectable black satin or broadcloth of the Victorian matron.

Dramatic black appears today, too. Occasionally it is seen in a conventional setting, as when a teenage girl outwits or browbeats her parents into letting her wear a slinky, inky dress to a dance, upstaging her flower-hued classmates. But the most significant examples of the romantic all-black costume in this century have originated outside of bourgeois society. Of these, one of the most long-lasting has been what Anne Hollander calls Modern Bohemian Black. In this style, the essential garment for both sexes is a black turtleneck sweater. It is often accompanied by black trousers, and for women by a black skirt and black stockings or tights. Modern Bohemian men usually wear their hair longer than the current fashion, and often have beards. For Modern Bohemian women long straight hair is common, though not essential; what is important, however, is that there be no sign of visits to the hairdresser. Modern Bohemian Black originated in Paris after World War II and soon became the standard costume of beatnik intellectuals, artists and students. With the addition of denim, it is still being worn today.

Related to Bohemian Black is the style that Anne Hollander calls Dancer's Black, which features black leotards, tights, ballet shoes and (for women) dance skirts. As she notes, it was made popular in America by Martha Graham. Currently it seems to be worn by professional and amateur dancers of many schools (ballet, modern, ethnic, tap and musical comedy), occasionally with the substitution of colored garments for black (deep, rich tones of plum, blue and green are preferred). This costume appears to indicate a sensitive, serious outlook on life and a consuming devotion to one's art, and is sometimes worn not only by dancers but by female actors, musicians, painters and poets who wish to convey the same message. A modified version of Bohemian or Dancer's Black, which paired black sweater and tights with a dirndl skirt made of striped denim mattress ticking, was introduced as far back as 1943 by the brilliant American designer Claire McCardell. With variations in the color and length of the skirt, this outfit has been worn by artistic and intellectual women for almost forty years.

A more threatening type of all-black costume, which also dates from the 1940s, is what might be called Motorcycle Gang Black. This look, favored by working-class teenagers (in Britain they were known as Rockers) and popularized by Marlon Brando's early film, *The Wild One* (1953), drew heavily on the styles of the Italian fascists and the Nazi SS, although this connection was seldom publicly acknowledged. It included black leather jackets and boots, black trousers or jeans, black T-shirts or sweaters and huge dark goggles. The jackets and jeans tended to be complicated with shiny zippers and snaps and studs, and often also with printed insignia in Day-Glo hues. The total effect of the costume was to give its wearer the look of a giant insect from a science-fiction movie—an effect much increased today by the mandatory wearing of plastic helmets that resemble the heads of monstrous ants.

GRAY: MODESTY AND MYSTERY

Gray, which is neither black nor white but a combination of these two opposites, is an ambiguous, indefinite color. It suggests fog, mist, smoke and twilight—conditions that blur

Black clothes can evoke the powers of darkness as well as those of light. In his loose, soft black robe and open sandals the ascetic is vulnerable and nonthreatening; the tight, hard-surfaced, armorlike leather garments of Motorcycle Gang Black suggest aggression and violence—especially when, as here, they are decorated with Nazi insignia. San Francisco, 1967. Photograph by Ken Heyman.

shapes and colors. An all-gray costume can indicate a modest, retiring individual, someone who prefers not to be noticed, or someone who whether they wish it or not merges with their background, as Lily Briscoe in Virginia Woolf's *To the Lighthouse* does when a livelier, prettier girl enters the room. "She faded . . ." the narrator reports, "became more inconspicuous than ever, in her little grey dress."

Gray clothes can also suggest that one is mysterious, ambiguous, puzzling. After Mrs. Ramsey's death Lily Briscoe, trying to remember her, imagines her in gray, as ghostly and silent. This is appropriate, since ghosts, when they do not appear in sheets or shrouds, often wear an all-gray version of their former clothes, like the Elvira of Noel Coward's play *Blithe Spirit.* (This fashion in supernatural wear may owe something to the fact that for many years photographs, by means of which we commonly see the dead, were printed in black and white—or rather, most often, in tones of gray.)

Among living persons, much depends on the shade of gray that is worn. A dark shade, as in the famous "gray flannel suit" of the 1950s conformist businessman, may suggest conventionality rather than shyness: a dimming of individuality for professional rather than psychological reasons. As gray moves toward black it usually becomes stronger and more dominant, and may also take on some of the negative meanings of black. As gray moves toward white it becomes more innocent, and begins to suggest a refined charm or charming refinement, subtlety and sensitivity. A very pale gray suggests a wearer whose innocence is tinged with knowledge of the world, possibly with sadness or regret. In George Eliot's *Middlemarch,* when Dorothea visits Rome on her honeymoon, her growing disillusion with her husband, as well as her essential innocence and virtue, is expressed in this way. When Will Ladislaw meets her in the Vatican, she is described as

clad in Quakerish gray drapery; her long cloak, fastened at the neck, was thrown backwards from her arms, and one beautiful ungloved hand pillowed her cheek, pushing somewhat backwards the white beaver bonnet which made a sort of halo to her face.

Gray is the color of mystery and ambiguity, of transitional states between good and evil, or life and death. Now that most people are no longer buried in white shrouds, the ghost often appears in an all-gray version of his or her own clothes. Leonora Corbett, Clifton Webb and Peggy Wood in Noel Coward's Blithe Spirit *(1941).*

In gray and white, with a white halo, Dorothea is a kind of secular saint; Ladislaw's artist friend, who wants to paint her, says that he would dress her as a nun. In Victorian England, gray and white were the colors of half mourning. Dorothea's costume thus suggests both loss and chastity, and adds weight to the implication that her marriage is physically as well as emotionally a failure.

RED: LOVE AND ANGER

Red, above all, is the color of blood. Traditionally it stands for strength, vitality and heat—and for sudden danger, as with a red light. Physiologically, the sight of this color causes a rise in blood pressure, respiration rate and heartbeat, preparing us to take sudden physical action. If the reaction is intense, as in rage, we may literally "see red" as blood rushes to our brain; waving a red cloth at a bull presumably has the same effect. Sexual passion, too, displays a red flag: in both men and women, when aroused, the pertinent parts flush. It is no wonder therefore that bright scarlet and crimson garments have traditionally been associated both with aggression and with desire. The red coats of soldiers and fox-hunters, the red dresses worn by "scarlet women" in history and literature, are obvious examples. In the theater an all-red outfit on a woman is an accepted sign of flaming sexuality. In Tennessee Williams's *A Streetcar Named Desire* (1947), Blanche Dubois appears first in a deceptively innocent outfit that matches her name: "She is daintily dressed in a white suit with a fluffy bodice, necklace and earrings of pearl, white gloves and hat." In private, however, she wears a red kimono, referred to in the stage directions as a "scarlet satin robe"—thus revealing that she is really impure, in fact a nymphomaniac.

Whether aggression or desire is dominant seems to depend both on the shade of red worn and on the situation. In general, reds that shade slightly toward purple and/or black appear to be related most directly to sex. The glowing, velvety crimson of the damask rose is often associated with active passion; a darkened crimson seems to suggest a capacity for passion that, though deep and strong, is currently satisfied or dormant. A red that shades toward orange, on the other hand, seems to tend more often toward aggression. As Goethe writes in his *Theory of Colours,*

> The active side is here in its highest energy, and it is not to be wondered at that impetuous, robust, uneducated men should be especially pleased with this colour. Among savage nations the inclination for it has been universally remarked.

Children, as Goethe points out, are fond of vermilion; though he made this observation in 1810, it can still be confirmed in any elementary-school classroom. When the amount of red in a costume is slight, however, it may be difficult to guess its meaning: a bright-red tie may indicate physical energy and a lively interest in life, or it may be the sign of political radicalism.

Lighter shades of red, from rose to the faintest shrimp-pink, appear to be related to the affections. A deep rose is the traditional color of romantic love, both sexual and emotional. As more and more white (purity, innocence) is added, the sensual content diminishes and finally disappears. Pink is most often worn, in our society, by older women and preadolescent girls, both of whom are supposed to feel strong affection, but not passion. The older or younger the woman, the paler the shade of pink thought suitable for her —as a look at advertisements and the racks of clothing stores will show. Bright red, conventionally, is restricted to women in their sexual prime, and believed to be very unbecoming (i.e., unsuitable) to those beyond it. It is not, on the other hand, thought unbecoming to older men, though the man over fifty who wears a scarlet shirt is, like his younger peers, issuing a claim to high sexual or aggressive potential.

YELLOW: YOUTH, HOPE AND CHEER

Bright yellow, the color of the sun, increases blood pressure, respiration rate and heartbeat just as red does—though the effect is less consistently maintained. It is associated with light, cheerfulness, youth and hope. Appropriately, the ubiquitous buttons and stickers that have recently commanded us to SMILE and to HAVE A GOOD DAY are usually of this color. (In popular speech, to be "yellow" is to be cowardly, perhaps because of the fact that when we are frightened the blood often drains from our face, leaving it more yellowish-tan or yellowish-brown than before. This meaning of the word, however, does not transfer itself to clothes.)

Yellow is a common color for children's clothes, especially those of infants and toddlers, and it keeps its popularity through adolescence. With increasing age it becomes less common, though paler shades (perhaps representing a modified youth and hopefulness) continue to be worn by adults, usually as part of a multicolored outfit. The man or woman in a light-yellow shirt or dress is assumed to be an optimist and an extrovert—or at least to be feeling fairly cheerful and outgoing at the moment. Grown persons who wear entire costumes of brilliant butter- or margarine-yellow, on the other hand (unless they are on a holiday or at the country club and sometimes even then), are judged to be a little silly or immature. Far more popular, for adults, are the darkened yellows: gold, which by association suggests wealth and material prosperity; gamboge, saffron and curry, in which an infusion of solid, earthy brown counteracts the impression of naïve enthusiasm.

In certain occupations bright yellow clothing is worn for utilitarian reasons. The yellow slickers, trousers and sou'wester hats of fishermen and fire fighters make them more visible to one another in darkness, mist, smoke and fog; the foul-weather uniforms of police officers, for the same reason, are often of this hue. As well as having a practical value, they project a sense of energy and hopefulness that might well be useful in a crisis situation.

BLUE: HARMONY, HONESTY AND FAITH

Blue, the color of the sky and of faraway mountains, is associated with distance; as Goethe remarks in his *Theory of Colours,* "a blue surface seems to retire from us. . . . But as we readily follow an agreeable object that flies from us, so we love to contemplate blue, not because it advances to us, but because it draws us after it." Psychologically, blue has a calming effect, reducing blood pressure, respiration rate and heartbeat; it has traditionally been associated with harmony, serenity and rest. In the Middle Ages blue was the color of the true lover and the faithful servant, and it retains some of this meaning. It has always been a popular color for work clothes: the medieval peasant or apprentice often wore a tunic and hose of much the same shade as today's denim jeans and shirts. Blue also stood for faith in the religious sense, and by extension for humility and devotion; in religious art it is associated with the Virgin Mary, the handmaiden of God. Politically, in Britain, it implies conservative opinions, a loyal acceptance of the status quo. As Britannus explains in Shaw's *Caesar and Cleopatra* (1898): "Blue is the color worn by all Britons of good standing. In war we stain our bodies blue; so that though our enemies may strip us of our clothes and our lives, they cannot strip us of our respectability."

Today, in both Britain and America, blue is the most common color in clothing. Any holiday crowd, viewed at a distance, resolves itself into a speckled pattern of white, tan and all shades of blue from powder to navy, with occasional accents of red, brown or black. When the crowd is made up mostly of young people blue is even more dominant, because of the ubiquitousness of denim in this age group. By itself, however, the blueness of jeans should not be construed as indicating harmony, honesty, humility or any of the other qualities associated with the color. Those who customarily accompany their jeans with a blue sweater or shirt, however, may be taken as declaring that they are reasonably straightforward, hard working and content with a modest lot in life.

Mixing white with blue, as with red, moderates the energy of the message. Light blue suggests reverence rather than an intensity of religious faith; ease rather than deep relaxation; reliable effort rather than hard physical labor; for the conservative businessman or woman it is the traditional alternative to the white shirt or blouse. Like pink, it is a popular color for little girls and older women, though in both cases it implies a somewhat quieter and more retiring nature than pink does.

As blue moves toward black, it becomes more serious. Navy blue is black without its darker implications of death and sin, yet retaining its air of solemn importance, and even some, though by no means all, of its sophistication. At the same time, it still carries the favorable connotations of blue, declaring its wearer to be at least to some extent well-balanced, hard working and trustworthy. It is therefore, quite understandably, much favored by working people in all sorts of occupations, from the investment banker to the service-station attendant.

Gray, which mutes and subdues the meaning of all hues, has the same effect on blue. The hue of peace, harmony and relaxation, mixed with greater and greater amounts of gray, implies successively resignation, melancholy and finally depression. Persons who are "blue" or "have the blues" in the vernacular sense seldom wear the primary color, but very often appear in shades of bluish gray and in combinations of blue and gray.

PRIMARY RESPECTABILITY
AND SECONDARY RAFFISHNESS

The secondary colors, orange, green and purple, are less popular for clothing than the primaries, especially in conservative periods. Individually, and even more when combined, they suggest the unusual, the original, the peculiar: an orange-green-purple print fabric seems jazzier and more exotic than the same design in red, yellow and blue. In America, orange is often used for safety garments because of its high visibility (greater even than that of yellow). Traffic policemen, bicyclists at night and hunters in the woods wear garments of a brilliant, near-phosphorescent orange. Partly as a result, perhaps, this color has come to suggest danger and a call for attention. The addition of pink or white to orange softens the message, though not completely. Members of the Hare Krishna sect dancing and chanting on a city street in their light-orange robes are certainly demanding attention—and, if you are trying to get somewhere in a hurry, or are the parent of a susceptible teenager, can represent a real hazard. In ordinary life, to wear an orange dress or suit, or even one of bright peach, apricot or salmon-pink, is to demand to be noticed. (In smaller helpings—a sash or a scarf, for instance—these colors may seem merely lively.)

GREEN: OUTLAWS, FAIRIES AND IRISHMEN

Green, of course, is the hue of grass, trees and all growing things—of the country as opposed to the city. A red light halts us and alerts us to danger—or, in certain urban areas, to a dangerous kind of sex. Green releases us into the freedom of the wilderness and the forest. It is worn, most typically, by the outlaw Robin Hood (originally, according to some scholars, Robin Wood) and his band of Merry Men.

Because it is the color of vegetation, green has ancient and powerful connections with fertility and growth. It is the hue traditionally associated with magic and the supernatural. The fairies of Britain usually dress in green, and sometimes have green eyes, green hair and even green skin—like the Green Man of folklore and the Green Knight of medieval legend, both of whom may derive from pagan natural gods. To wear green often implies a connection with the powers of nature or the life force. In Virginia Woolf's *To the Lighthouse,* Mrs. Ramsey, who is presented as a kind of secular nature goddess, wears a green shawl with which she covers the boar's skull that stands in the book for Death.

During the ascendancy of magic and of freedom from urban restraints in the late sixties and early seventies, green was nearly as popular as blue among radicals; the most favored shades were forest green, pea green and especially olive (which mixed green with an earthy "natural" brown). Today they are less common, and if other signs in the costume do not contradict them, may be taken as suggesting love of the outdoors, and an interest in gardening and/or natural foods, alternative energy sources, ecological action and backpacking.

The other important association of green is with Hibernian origin or nationality; often with Republican, anti-British sympathies. At one time, in Ireland, to show even a scrap of green cloth was a serious, even a fatal, political act, for the authorities were, as the old song says, "hanging men and women for the wearing of the green." Even today some of these associations survive. In Northern Ireland, the preference of the supporters of Independence for green can be noted on television. Below the border, too, the purchase and display of bright green ties, scarves and sweaters—and of subtly greenish tweed suits—is in some sense a political statement, which does not lose its force when the Irishman or Irishwoman travels or lives abroad. For those of Irish ancestry, rather than Irish nationality, the wearing of the green is less serious; nevertheless, it is customary for them to appear in some green garment on Saint Patrick's Day. Since few people buy clothes that can be worn only once a year, anybody who owns a dress, shirt or sweater of a particularly vivid green is quite likely to have an Irish name or an Irish ancestor.

PURPLE: ROYALTY AND VULGARITY

Purple originally was the most expensive color for cloth, since the dye for it came from a rare kind of shellfish. As a result, in many societies—notably that of ancient Byzantium—the hue was reserved for royalty. "To wear the purple" came to mean to be of noble blood, and even today the coronation robes of the English royal family are of deep purple velvet. The invention of aniline dyes in the nineteenth century made the royal color more widely available, and for a time women of all ranks luxuriated in clothes of dazzling magenta, plum and orchid—as well as flame red and electric blue. By the end of the century, however, these intense chemical colors had begun to fall out of favor: they were now called harsh and unflattering, and were associated with pretentiousness and vulgarity. This was especially true of the purple and purple-red shades. When the heroine of E. M. Forster's *A Room with a View* becomes engaged to the wrong man, her mistake expresses itself in the language of clothes. Lucy's "new cerise dress has been a failure, and makes her look tawdry and wan," it is reported, and her own mother compares her to a flamingo. As the fiancée of the rich, snobbish, chilly highbrow Cecil Vise, Lucy is (as his name implies) caught in a vise. Attempting to please him, she suppresses her own natural interests and sympathies, and as a result looks tawdry and wan figuratively as well as literally.

After World War II bright purples and red-purples enjoyed something of a revival. Today they are again in disfavor, and wardrobe consultants refer to them as "lower-middle-class." The more subdued shades of purple, however, remain fashionable, and something of the original aura of special status still clings to them. Plum and heather tones suggest wealth and elegance, and are favored for party wear. When purple is mixed with white it marks an aristocracy of the mind and soul rather than one of wealth and power; it seems to imply special refinement, artistic or emotional sensitivity. The man in the lavender shirt, the woman in the lilac hostess gown, appear to have (or to claim) finer perceptions and more refined tastes than their peers in blue or pink. The contemporary designation of lavender as a gay indicator draws in part on these associations. When purple is mixed with gray the impression of sensitivity is both increased and made more ambiguous. Dim, muted mauves and violets are the colors of dreams and visions, of illusions and enchantments.

BROWN: STABILITY, ECONOMY, FRATERNITY

Brown, though technically a mixture of orange and black, is best considered as a color in its own right. It is associated with the earth and with nature—but nature in its dormant state: autumn and winter rather than spring or summer. It is the color of plowed earth, of the fields in winter and of weathered or finished wood: it suggests security, stability, strength. In both America and Britain it is the most popular color for country—or county—clothes; wardrobe engineers also recommend it for businessmen and women working outside of the major cities who want to inspire friendliness and trust in their bosses, employees and customers.

As a dyestuff, brown has always been inexpensive and easily obtained. A light brown is the natural hue of unbleached cotton, linen and wool, and also of hides; and substances that will dye cloth or leather a deeper brown are common. Drab, grayed browns are also the colors that show dirt least, and in a prelaundromat age when soap was expensive and water for washing had to be hauled from a well or the town pump, then heated over a fire, this was an important recommendation. These subdued natural hues were also favored by religious asceticism and Puritan morality, which distrusted brightly colored garments, considering them the occasion of pride and lust—both sinful in themselves and the cause of sin in others. Brown and tan therefore became the colors of piety, poverty, economy and modest ambitions.

Medium and dark browns are quiet, reassuring, solid; they suggest reliability and hard work. They often also imply a lack of social pretensions, which may of course be combined with high social status—the latter being indicated by the fabric and cut of the costume. A yellowish-brown is the ideal color for camouflage; it has always been favored by woodsmen and by those hunters who are in no danger of being shot by clumsy companions. It is therefore associated with woodland occupations and recreations: hunting, fishing, lumbering, camping, hiking and the like. The shade of greenish brown known as olive or khaki has in this century become the standard color for battle dress. Today, even in civilian clothing, it has a military look, and suggests practical, aggressive action. No doubt for this reason, it is seldom used in party wear.

Red-brown, on the other hand, is popular for both work and play. It is both warm and stable, combining the energy and heat of red with the steadiness of brown. According to the wardrobe engineers, it is one of the few colors that are effective both professionally and sexually, and for both men and women. It is also very popular in architecture; in America barns are traditionally painted this color, just as houses (especially farmhouses) are traditionally painted white. Semiotically speaking, the choice is appropriate. Both barn and farmhouse are the scene of physical work and sexual activity: the storage and consumption of food, procreation and the raising of young; but the barn is secular, the house—center of a spiritually legitimized family life—sacred.

Very light brown—tan or beige—is the most neutral of all colors, the least communicative. It is not by chance that the classic stage and screen detective appears in a tan trench coat. The spy also may wear tan, though there are apt to be glimpses of sinister black or mysterious gray beneath it. In itself, tan is neither cheerful nor sad, neither active nor passive. People who prefer to conceal their emotions, or must do so for professional reasons, often wear outfits that are largely or entirely tan or beige, sometimes with the addition of a conventional gray. The lighter these colors, however, the more likely it is that they have also been chosen to demonstrate status through Conspicuous Consumption.

COLOR AND CONFORMITY

The mood of a crowd, as well as that of an individual, can often be read in the colors of clothing. In the office of a large corporation, or at a professional convention, there is usually a predominance of conventional gray, navy, beige, tan and white—suggesting a general attitude of seriousness, hard work, neutrality, propriety and status. The same group of people at a picnic are a mass of lively, relaxed blue, red and brown, with touches of yellow and green. In the evening, at a disco, they shimmer under the rotating lights in dramatic combinations of purple, crimson, orange, turquoise, gold, silver and black. The temper of political meetings and rallies, too, can be judged by their hue. Conservatives present a design of subdued or primary colors, notably tan and a patriotic red, white and navy; while a radical demonstration at a distance looks like a pair of embroidered jeans—basically denim blue, but speckled with all the colors of the rainbow.

Apart from the chameleon, man is the only animal who can change his skin to suit his background. Indeed, if he is to function successfully he must do so. The individual whose clothes do not fall within the recognized range of colors for a given situation attracts attention, usually (though not always) unfavorable attention. When a child puts its pet chameleon down on the earth and it does not turn brown, we know the creature is seriously ill. In the same way, men or women who begin to come to work in a conservative office wearing disco hues and a disco mood are regarded with anxiety and suspicion. If they do not blush a respectable beige, navy or gray within a reasonable length of time, their colleagues know that they will not be around for very long.

PATTERN AND DECORATION

From a utilitarian point of view there is no need for clothes to be decorated with trimming or embroidery, or to be made of patterned fabrics. Since these elaborations add needlessly to the cost of garments, they have always tended to confer status. As a rule, the more complex the design, and the more colors used, the greater the prestige of the garment. It is also true, however, that a plain-colored material shows spots more readily than a patterned one, and once weaving and machine-printing had made patterned fabrics relatively inexpensive their status somewhat declined. Today there is not much difference in prestige between patterned and plain, unless the design is handprinted. Clothes that have obviously been decorated after they were assembled (usually by embroidery or appliqué) continue to be excellent advertisements for Conspicuous Consumption. Most prestigious of all are those garments that combine large areas of pale, easily soiled plain fabric with elaborate hand decoration.

The possible number of patterns is infinite. Moreover,

Sports that are physically less strenuous and demand specialized skills, such as baseball, are often played in costumes with medium-sized stripes. The unusually wide spaces between the stripes of the traditional baseball uniform may represent the large portion of time during each game when the average player is inactive. Babe Ruth, c. 1927. Photograph by Nikolas Muray.

any conceivable pattern can be produced in an immense range of color combinations, and printed on or woven into a wide variety of fabrics. For the sake of convenience, we can distinguish between abstract patterns, which are simply pleasing (or displeasing) arrangements of line and color, and representational patterns, which portray objects or symbols; though in practice these categories merge into each other. It is also possible to speak of geometrical and nongeometrical patterns. Though any pattern that repeats itself along the length or breadth of fabric is technically regular, the repeat may be so widely spaced, or the design so loose and flowing, that the regularity is not visible in a single garment.

STRIPES

All obviously geometrical patterns, including stripes, checks and regularly spaced images of anything from aardvarks to zinnias, seem to be related to the wish to order the universe in some way. Stripes, for example, often seem to express organized effort, a desire or ability to "follow the line" laid out by oneself or others. By association, they may suggest dependability and rectitude. The kind of effort involved seems to depend on the width of the stripes. Very broad ones tend to suggest organized physical effort of the sort necessary to members of an athletic team; narrow stripes appear to have more to do with mental activity and intellectual order. Bookkeepers, accountants and clerks are traditionally pictured as wearing shirts or blouses patterned with the narrowest of black-and-white or navy-and-white stripes, imitating the ruled lines of a ledger, and suggesting attention and energy devoted to ordering detailed matters. In certain cases, not only the breadth of the stripes but their obviousness may be informative. The pin-striped suit of the traditional gambler differs from that of the banker or stockbroker not only in cut but in the much greater definition of the stripes. Both men are concerned with figuring the odds on a large investment, but the gambler may be seen to do so more openly and without any air of being above the profit motive.

Organized athletic activity often seems to express itself in stripes, which vary in size according to the nature of the sport. When constant exercise of physical strength is required, the stripes tend to be very wide. Rugby players, New York, 1974. Photograph by Tony Marshall.

The gambler's pin-striped suit, like that of the stockbroker, suggests the ruled columns of a ledger. Note also the dark shirt and white tie of his friend, which, by reversing the customary colors of the business costume, implies a reversal of conventional values. Allan Jones and Julie Oshins in a production of Guys and Dolls.

In the recent past two special kinds of striped clothing were instantly recognizable and were often imitated in fashion. One was the convict's bold black-and-white vertically striped shirt and pants, which iconographically suggested the parallel bars of a prison. Outside the walls this pattern often appeared in pajamas and nightgowns, which were sometimes sold in his-and-her sets—humorously implying that marriage is a sort of imprisonment. (At times this jailbird nightwear was even printed with large numbers like the original prison uniforms.)

Blue and white horizontal stripes have been associated with sailors and the sea for over a hundred years; perhaps they imitate the line of the horizon. The striped French sailor's jersey, discovered by tourists on the Riviera in the 1920s, soon became fashionable in both Britain and America. At first it had a stylish and European as well as a nautical air: it suggested first-class steamers and expensive yachts, Mediterranean or Caribbean cruises. It was soon so widely copied and readily available that it lost its association with wealth and elegance. Today, especially when worn with white canvas shorts or trousers, it still suggests boating, though now in vessels of a smaller and simpler sort.

PLAIDS AND CHECKS

Plaid patterns also imply ordered effort, though of a less formal and collective kind. Plaid and checked materials seem to be worn more often for individual sports such as tennis and golf; stripes for team sports such as baseball and rugby. (The striped costumes of jockeys may be explained by the fact that horse racing is a competition between two-unit teams of horse and rider in which cooperation is essential.) As with stripes, it is usually true that the smaller the plaid, the less strenuously physical the activity. Large-scale check materials are thought of as appropriate for occupations that demand large motor gestures, especially outdoors: farming, logging, construction work, hunting, hiking and camping. Smaller checks seem appropriate for white-collar jobs and such leisure activities as golf, fishing and sailing.

Simple plaids that combine white and one other color in equal quantities are often spoken of as "gingham checks" even when woven of silk, wool or synthetics. Most often they combine white with primary red or blue. They are commonly associated with simple, old-fashioned rural activities, and suggest hard work and thriftiness, possibly even a respectable poverty. Often they are associated with cooking and eating: books of down-home recipes tend to be covered in small-scale gingham checks, and kitchen and restaurant tables with large-scale ones.

Traditionally, especially on stage and in films, red- or blue-checked gingham is worn by rural and small-town people. When these materials appear on more sophisticated types, they may merely be expressing lively energy and/or a desire for a simpler life. In other cases, especially when the rest of the costume is formal or chic—as with an art director in a dark-gray Savile Row suit and pink gingham shirt—we may suspect a certain *fausse naïveté*.

There are other plaid patterns with special associations: the outsize red-and-black checks of loggers; the graph-paper squares favored by architects, engineers and draftsmen; and the faded madras check of the Preppie Look, which suggests individual sports pursued in a gentlemanly, not too violent or competitive, manner. Most distinctive of all, amounting almost to a separate language, is the tartan of the Scottish Highlanders. Like the Irishman's or Irishwoman's green, these plaids have an ancient political significance. They, too, were once prohibited by British law: in 1746 an act of Parliament made the wearing of tartans in Scotland a political offense; it was repealed in 1785 after much protest. Even today the display of clan tartans is often a political act. It is also highly informative: since each clan has its distinctive pattern or patterns, a knowledgeable person can identify the owner of a shawl or kilt as a descendant of one of well over a hundred ancient families. Or, less happily, he can note with disgust that some ignorant Yankee or Sassenach is promiscuously displaying a plaid to which he or she has no hereditary right. Today such unhappy encounters are especially the lot of members of the Stewart, Gordon and Wallace clans. Their ancestral tartans, which feature particularly agreeable combinations of colors, are

Plaids and checks usually imply hard work, and are often worn by people who take life seriously. Here a large-scaled plaid suit is combined with a T-shirt and ballet slippers in Dancer's Black to indicate both artistic and moral commitment (the plaid is black and gray in the original as well as in this picture). Barbara Deming, American author and political activist. San Francisco, 1953. Photograph by Imogen Cunningham.

now widely reproduced commercially and worn not only by non-Scots but by umbrellas, wastebaskets, suitcases and pet dogs.

DOTS AND FLOWERS

Just as straight lines suggest order and control, so curved lines suggest freedom and relaxation. Dotted patterns, in which circles are arranged in a rectangular grid, are interesting from the semiotic point of view because they combine the extremes of rectangularity and curvilinearity. The effect of this paradox, perhaps logically, seems to be humor. The broader the circles, the broader and more physical the humor. Large dots, of the sort that are traditional for clown costumes, suggest farce, pratfalls and practical jokes. Medium or coin-sized dots imply a mood of lively fun: patterns on this scale are often used for party dresses, playclothes, pajamas and children's wear. Somewhat smaller dots seem to be associated with a largely verbal humor, which can be either simple or worldly, depending on the colors used. Stage and TV comedians of both sexes favor such patterns; for male comics the dotted tie (often a bow tie) is almost an occupational badge. When the dots are very small, rectangularity predominates, and what is projected is either mere good humor or (especially when black and white are used) a sophisticated wit, satire and irony.

Representational patterns usually combine straight and curved lines in a grid pattern that may be obvious or hidden, depending on the design, thus combining a certain amount of freedom and individuality with a certain amount of conventional order. Most such patterns consist of small irregularly shaped images (a bat, a boat, a bouquet) repeated at regular intervals. These designs often seem to symbolize their wearer's ability or wish to control some group of objects, beings or concepts. Thus the sports fisherman may wear a shirt printed with trout or tuna, the elementary-school child one printed with the letters of the alphabet. Another possibility is that the objects depicted may represent the wearer. The young woman whose sweater is decorated with the image of a cute red bear may think of herself as warm, strong and cuddly; the college pennants on a teen-ager's jacket may announce that he (or his parents) think of him as college material. It is important to remember, though, that a pattern may not mean the same thing to its wearer as it does to the uninformed observer. The man in the fish-patterned shirt may have been born in February under the astrological sign of Pisces; the woman with Bruin on her bosom may be presenting herself not as a bear, but as a lover of wild animals, a person whose name is Baer or a graduate of Cornell University.

In women's clothes by far the most common represen-tational designs are botanical. Flower patterns, especially, seem to stand for feminity; and they come in as many varie-ties as the women who wear them. The blooms may be tiny and delicate or huge and bold, to suit a range of female charm from Little Nell to Carmen. They may be familiar or rare: roses for the classic beauty, hibiscus for the exotic siren. Daisies may suggest a simple country girl, orchids a hot-house sophisticate. Trees, ferns, grasses, fruit and vegetables offer further symbolic possibilities. (The frequency with which apples appear on maternity clothes, for instance, can hardly be accidental.) And all these plants can be depicted in many styles, from the botanically exact (sometimes with their Latin names appended) to the totally decorative and impressionistic. Observation suggests that practical, down-to-earth women with some experience as gardeners prefer real plants in their natural colors. Abstract blurs that never grew on land or sea are more apt to appear on the clothes of women who, either because of circumstances or because of inclination, are somewhat out of touch with the natural world.

Once upon a time, men as well as women wore clothes covered with floral designs. After about 1800, however, ex-cept for an occasional flowered waistcoat, botanical decora-tion was limited to the female sex for over a hundred and fifty years. The countercultural explosion of the 1960s, with its relaxation of the rules for male dress, made flowered shirts and ties permissible and even fashionable for all but the most conservative. Social commentators linked what was sometimes called "the peacock revolution" with the sexual revolution of the sixties, and celebrated man's new

Floral patterns appear to symbolize the many varieties of femininity. This lady has chosen a delicate, small-scale, stylized clover pattern that suggests both age (it derives ultimately from Renaissance or even ancient art) and formal elegance, and has echoed it in the trimming of her white hat which, like that of the Queen Mother, faintly suggests a halo. Photograph by Tony Marshall, 1975.

Large-scale flowers seem to imply a large-scale, generously physical female nature. This cheerful lady dancing in a Newark, New Jersey park in 1969 presents herself as a great big bunch of daisies. Note the difference in hair style, jewelry and accessories between her and the subject of the previous picture. Photograph by Ken Heyman.

freedom to express himself sartorially as well as emotionally. As it turned out, the reign of the peacock was brief. Where have all the flowers gone? To secondhand racks, almost every one. Today the only chance most men have to wear botanically patterned clothing is on holiday in southern resorts, where so-called Hawaiian shirts are sold. Here they can select the patterns that best express the female side of their natures, and appear in public as the dainty ingénue, tropical siren or warm-hearted Mom they would have been if only they had had the luck to be born female.

WORDS AND SLOGANS

The decoration of clothing with symbolic designs or representations of natural objects is almost as old as clothing itself. The printing of actual words and phrases upon them, however, is a relatively recent development. Today hats, scarves, jackets and especially T-shirts function as billboards, supplementing the language of clothing and allowing a TV-reared, semiarticulate generation to communicate with friends and make instant contact with strangers. Occasionally the printed message is simply a brand name, asserting status through Conspicuous Consumption. As a teenager once explained to me, "Adidas are the best T-shirts. . . . Well, they're pretty much like other T-shirts really, but they cost more, and they have the name on them." But there are many other possibilities. Clothes today can advertise favorite products or cultural tastes (VIRGINIA SLIMS, VIRGINIA WOOLF), political opinions, membership in real or imaginary organizations (HARVARD UNIVERSITY, OLYMPIC SCREWING TEAM), real or imaginary personality (GROUCH, UNEMPLOYED ARTIST, FOXY LADY, MALE CHAUVINIST PIG), sexual preference (GAY POWER, EAT ME) and current mood (I'M FLYING, BLUE MONDAY). Since legible clothing is often given away with goods or services, it is not hard to accumulate a large collection. Even if you like, uh, don't know how to put it, you can thus express the idea, impulse or enthusiasm of the moment: you can let it all hang out—literally as well as symbolically, for T-shirts usually must be worn over the jeans or skirt for their inscription to be seen in full.

VIII
MALE
AND FEMALE

A visitor from Mars contemplating a man in a frock coat and top hat and a woman in a crinoline might well have supposed that they belonged to different species.

—James Laver, *The Concise History of Costume and Fashion*

In the past sexual modesty was often proposed as the purpose of dress. The Bible tells us that this was the original reason for wearing clothes: Adam and Eve, once they realized that they were naked, "sewed fig leaves together, and made themselves aprons." Historically, however, shame seems to have played very little part in the development of costume. In ancient Egypt, Crete and Greece the naked body was not considered immodest; slaves and athletes habitually went without clothing, while people of high rank wore garments that were cut and draped so as to show a good deal when in motion.

Some modern writers believe that the deliberate concealment of certain parts of the body originated not as a way of discouraging sexual interest, but as a clever device for arousing it. According to this view, clothes are the physical equivalent of remarks like "I've got a secret"; they are a tease, a come-on. It is certainly true that parts of the human form considered sexually arousing are often covered in such a way as to exaggerate and draw attention to them. People done up in shiny colored wrappings and bows affect us just as a birthday present does: we're curious, turned on; we want to undo the package.

The naked unadorned body, by contrast, is not intrinsi-

Clothes that simultaneously conceal and reveal, and—like a half-opened gift—invite us to imagine what lies beneath, are traditionally erotic in their effect. Jean Harlow, American movie star. Photograph by Nikolas Muray.

The average naked human body, on the other hand, is not very exciting, as most visitors to nudist camps soon discover. Photograph by Elliott Erwitt, 1968.

cally very exciting, especially en masse. Ingres' *Le Bain turc (The Turkish Bath),* in which twenty plump nudes are crammed into a circular frame that repeats their generous curves, can seem—as Kenneth Clark says—"almost suffocating." Without the large figure in the foreground, he adds "the whole composition might have made us feel slightly seasick." Too much nakedness in real life can have the same effect. Many visitors to nudist camps report that the sight of all that uncovered flesh brings fatigue and a sense of being slightly unwell. Later, after one gets used to it as the ancients were, it seems merely banal. Even in isolation an unadorned human body is often less exciting than a clothed one, and the most stimulating costumes of all are those which simultaneously conceal and reveal, like a suggestively wrapped gift hinting at delights beneath.

Whether it was the first cause or not, from the earliest times one important function of clothing has been to promote erotic activity: to attract men and women to one another, thus ensuring the survival of the species. If maximum fertility is to be achieved, we must select members of the opposite sex rather than our own to make love to. One basic purpose of costume, therefore, is to distinguish men from women. In some periods this separation is absolute: what is properly worn by a man cannot be worn by a woman, and vice versa. As might be expected, at such times the birth rate is usually high. In other periods, such as our own, many items of clothing are sexually interchangeable, and the birth rate is lower. Even today, however, most garments are recognizably male or female—as anyone who has sorted rummage for a charity sale will recall.

PINK KITTENS AND BLUE SPACESHIPS

Sex-typing in dress begins at birth with the assignment of pale-pink layettes, toys, bedding and furniture to girl babies, and pale-blue ones to boy babies. Pink, in this culture, is associated with sentiment; blue with service. The implication is that the little girl's future concern will be the life of the affections; the boy's, earning a living. As they grow older, light blue becomes a popular color for girls' clothes—after all, women must work as well as weep—but pink is rare on boys: the emotional life is never quite manly.

In early childhood girls' and boys' clothes are often identical in cut and fabric, as if in recognition of the fact that their bodies are much alike. But the T-shirts, pull-on slacks and zip jackets intended for boys are usually made in darker colors (especially forest green, navy, red and brown) and printed with designs involving sports, transportation and cute wild animals. Girls' clothes are made in paler colors (especially pink, yellow and green) and decorated with flowers and cute domestic animals. The suggestion is that the boy will play vigorously and travel over long distances; the girl will stay home and nurture plants and small mammals. Alternatively, these designs may symbolize their wearers: the boy is a cuddly bear or a smiling tiger, the girl a flower or a kitten. There is also a tendency for boys' clothes to be fullest at the shoulders and girls' at the hips, anticipating their adult figures. Boys' and men's garments also emphasize the shoulders with horizontal stripes, epaulets or yokes of contrasting color. Girls' and women's garments emphasize the hips and rear through the strategic placement of gathers and trimmings.

Sex-typing in juvenile fashion: the little boy's clothes are of darker colors and heavier materials, and emphasize the shoulders with purely decorative epaulets; the little girl's are lighter and flimsier, and emphasize the bosom with ruffles. Jason and Melissa Shank, 1968.

In the iconography of childhood, girls are often pictured as flowers, usually in an indoor or garden setting. White Plains, New York, 1934.

Boys, on the other hand, are pictured as wild animals, and usually appear outdoors. Faraway, 1952, by Andrew Wyeth.

RECTANGULAR MEN AND ROUNDED WOMEN

Even for children dress-up clothing tends to be sex-typed in shape as well as in color and decoration. By adolescence most of what we wear incorporates traditional male or female indicators: among them, for men, the garment that fastens to the right and the classic jacket, shirt and tie; for women the garment that fastens to the left, ruffles and bows, high-heeled shoes and the skirt in all its forms.

Male clothing has always been designed to suggest physical and/or social dominance. Traditionally, the qualities that make a man attractive are size and muscular strength. In the past this preference was practical: most men were farmers, hunters or warriors, and the woman who attached herself to a big, strong man had a better chance of survival. Men's garments therefore tended to enlarge the body through the use of strong colors and bulky materials, and to emphasize angularity with rectangular shapes and sharp points. They suggested or called attention to well-developed leg, shoulder and arm muscles by means of tight hose, trousers and jackets; and they increased the width of shoulders and chest with padding.

The modern sack suit, on the other hand, though often dark and always rectangular in cut, suppresses or conceals all the features that are supposed to constitute male beauty: broad shoulders, slim waist and hips, flat stomach and well-muscled legs. But, as pointed out earlier, for a man who lacks these attributes the sack suit is flattering. If it is well cut it can hide a sunken chest or a small pot. And whether a man is athletically built or not, it diverts attention from his physical qualifications and focuses attention on his economic and social status. The sack suit is a middle-class indicator, and in a world in which class membership is a safer guarantee of prosperity than pure brawn, an expensive version may have considerable erotic charm, especially for women who are looking for husbands rather than lovers.

Female costume, during most of modern European history, was designed to suggest successful maternity. It emphasized rounded contours and rich, soft materials, and tended to center interest on the breasts and stomach. Energy, strength and health were regarded as attractive, and they were expressed through bright, glowing colors and full-cut gowns with strong, sweeping curves that often accommodated and flattered the pregnant woman. Such clothes can be seen in many paintings of the Renaissance and Baroque period, and (in a somewhat more refined form) in those of the Rococo.

ROMANTIC FRAILTY

In the early nineteenth century, however, a new feminine ideal appeared. Women were redefined as something between children and angels: weak, timid, innocent creatures of sensitive nerves and easily alarmed modesty who could only be truly safe and happy under the protection of some man. Physical slightness and fragility were admired, and what was now called "rude health" was considered coarse and lower-class. To be pale and delicate, to blush and faint readily and lie about on sofas was ladylike; strength and vigor were the characteristics of vulgar, red-cheeked, thick-waisted servants and factory girls. The more useless and helpless a woman looked, the higher her presumed social status, and the more elegant and beautiful she was perceived as being.

Early nineteenth-century fashions were designed to give a look of fragile immaturity. They emphasized weakness of both structure and substance through the use of pale colors and delicate, easily damaged materials. More ominously, these clothes ensured the charming ill-health of their wearers by putting them into thin-soled slippers and short-sleeved, low-necked dresses of semitransparent muslin. When worn in the drafty ballrooms and along the icy, muddy lanes of a British or North American winter, such clothes were almost a guarantee of the feverish colds and sore throats that are so common in the novels of Jane Austen and the Brontës; looking at portraits of the period, it seems no surprise that consumption was the most dreaded disease of the time.

In the early-Victorian period clothes were designed to make women look delicate and helpless. Limp, fragile materials, pale colors and drooping lines were fashionable.
Florence Nightingale and Her Sister Parthenope, *by W. White, c. 1836.*

The well-dressed Victorian woman carried an amazing weight of clothing. There might be (as in this picture) as many as nine layers of cloth under her dress, or even more: the five petticoats shown here were by no means the limit of possibility. Her dress, hat and cape added even more pounds to the total. (Note, however, that this advertisement, though it celebrates the modern woman's freedom from such burdens, still pictures her as hobbled by high-heeled shoes and addresses her as "baby.")

FASHIONABLE DEBILITY: THE CORSET

By the 1830s, female fashions offered somewhat more protection from the climate, but they continued to suggest—and to promote—physical frailty. Early-Victorian costume not only made women *look* weak and helpless, it made them weak and helpless. The main agent of this debility, as many writers have pointed out, was the corset, which at the time was thought of not as a mere fashion but as a medical necessity. Ladies' "frames," it was believed, were extremely delicate; their muscles could not hold them up without assistance. Like many such beliefs, this one was self-fulfilling. Well-brought-up little girls, from the best motives, were laced into juvenile versions of the corset as early as three or four. Gradually, but relentlessly, their stays were lengthened, stiffened and tightened. By the time they reached late adolescence they were wearing cages of heavy canvas reinforced with whalebone or steel, and their back muscles had often atrophied to the point where they could not sit or stand for long unsupported. The corset also deformed the internal organs and made it impossible to draw a deep breath. As a result the fashionably dressed lady blushed and fainted easily, suffered from lack of appetite and from digestive complaints, and felt weak and exhausted after any strenuous exertion. When she took off her corset her back soon began to ache; and sometimes she still could not breathe properly because her ribs had been permanently compressed inward.

Over this debilitating foundation garment the Victorian woman wore several layers of shifts and chemises, three or more petticoats, a hoop skirt or crinoline and a long dress that might contain twenty yards of heavy wool or silk and was often also boned in the bodice and trimmed with additional fabric, ribbon and beads. When she left the house she added a heavy woolen shawl and a large bonnet or hat decorated with feathers, flowers, ribbons and veiling. Altogether she might carry from ten to thirty pounds of clothing; a contemporary writer, feeling this to be a bit of a burden, suggested seven pounds as the minimum for a respectable woman. Yet even with all this weight on her back the Victorian lady was not protected from the climate, since fashion (especially evening fashion) often demanded that her neck, shoulders and chest be exposed.

In this costume it was difficult to move about or walk vigorously, and almost impossible to run. But then, ladies did not "walk," since in polite discourse they had no legs— rather they "glided" or "swept" across the floor like carpet sweepers—and they certainly did not run. In an emergency

In the second half of the nineteenth century female fashions reached extremes of elaborate discomfort from which only the lower strata of the working class were exempt. By Victorian standards, though not our own, this shepherdess's uncorseted figure, loose, simple dress and healthy look would be considered coarse and unattractive. The Hireling Shepherd, by William Holman Hunt, 1851.

the proper thing to do was to faint, relying on the protection of the nearest gentleman.

Even more important than the medical justification of the corset was its social justification. Women were considered the frailer sex not only physically but morally: their minds and their wills as well as their backs were weak. A lady might be pure and innocent, of course, but this purity and innocence could be preserved only by constant vigilance. Therefore she must not attend a university or follow a profession; she must not travel without a chaperone; she must not visit a man's rooms; and she must not see any play or read any book that might inflame her imagination—even Shakespeare was dangerous except in the expurgated version of Thomas Bowdler. Even thus guarded, the early-Victorian woman was in constant danger of becoming the victim of man's lust and her own weakness. She needed to be at once supported and confined, in a many-layered, heavily reinforced costume that would make undressing a difficult and lengthy process.

Although she was so heavily armored against a frontal assault, the mid-Victorian woman was often readily accessible in another direction, since she had no underpants in the modern sense. She might if she chose wear what were called "drawers"—loose, wide-legged undershorts made in two separate sections, joined only at the waist and otherwise completely open—but these conferred status rather than protection. Though this left the Victorian lady embarrassingly exposed in case of accidents, closed underpants were considered immodest because they imitated male garments. Victorian feminists later drew attention to this contradiction: Dr. Mary Walker, for instance, remarked that "If men were really what they profess to be they would not compel women to dress so that the facilities for vice would always be so easy."

These extremes of inconvenience and discomfort, it should be noted, were suffered mainly by ladies, especially those who were well-to-do, since it is a universal rule that when clothes are uncomfortable, high-status clothes will be more uncomfortable. Working women (except when they were on holiday) wore looser and simpler clothes and much looser corsets, and they carried far less weight of cloth.

THE LADY AS A LUXURY ITEM

Why did the early-Victorian woman put up with early-Victorian fashions? Partly, no doubt, because they were admired by men and described everywhere as beautiful, elegant and charming. But also, certainly, because she believed the current propaganda: she thought of the clothes that imprisoned and deformed her as medically necessary and morally respectable. Tight lacing was associated in the popular mind with virtue: a well-dressed woman whose stays were loose, however rich her costume, was probably a loose woman. A girl of relatively modest means, however, if her shoes and gloves were tight enough, her dress properly fragile and her corset laced so that she could scarcely breathe, might hope to be admired. She might even, if lucky, become the petted and indulged and confined wife of a man of means.

In a patriarchal society a helpless, foolish, pretty woman is the ultimate object of Conspicuous Consumption. Rich men chose to purchase and maintain such a woman as a sign of their own economic and sexual power. What she looks like physically is not important; she may be a plump odalisque, a proper Victorian lady, or a twentieth-century Dumb Blonde of the Petty Girl type (now a vanishing species). For maximum status gain, however, such a woman must be of no practical use. She must be unable to type, cook, clean, care for children, manage an estate or keep track of your investments—all these things must be done by paid employees. Ideally, the clothes this woman wears will identify her as a luxury item. The Dumb Blonde is supposed to be in bouncy good health and to have a Florida tan, but her tight satin sheath, spike heels and long, brittle, varnished nails—like the Victorian lady's corset and crinoline—make her prestigious uselessness obvious.

The costumes of the Victorian lady and the expense-account blonde are examples of the principle still in force, that clothes which make a woman's life difficult and handicap her in competition with men are always felt to be sexually attractive. This is true not only of tight, figure-revealing garments, but also of heavy, clumsy fashions such as platform shoes and the trailing skirt. As Thorstein Veblen

In a male-dominated culture the possession of a completely useless woman is a sign of high status. Traditionally, she displays the purchasing power of her husband or lover, and her own incapacity for productive work, by wearing extravagant, uncomfortable and inconvenient clothes. The Woman of Fashion, *by James Tissot, 1883–85.*

pointed out over a hundred years ago, "The substantial reason for our tenacious attachment to the skirt is just this: it is expensive and it hampers the wearer at every turn and incapacitates her for all useful exertion." The woman who chooses to wear such clothes announces to everyone that she is willing to be handicapped in life in relation to men; men reward her for this by finding both her and her clothes attractive.

AESTHETIC AND REFORM DRESS

In a highly patriarchal period such as the mid-nineteenth century, as James Laver has noted, the costumes of men and women tend to be clearly differentiated, and anyone who adopts the dress of the opposite sex in public is likely to be considered shocking or even disgusting. Mrs. Amelia Bloomer's campaign for the divided skirt in the 1850s was greeted with ridicule and social ostracism. Though she gave her name to a garment, she failed utterly. Thirty years later, when the first partially successful reforms in female clothing appeared, they were not imitations of masculine styles: instead they merely attempted to moderate the most inconvenient and painful aspects of feminine fashion.

The Aesthetic and Reform Dress of the 1880s followed contemporary styles, though dresses were cut looser and had fuller sleeves. To us these clothes look very Victorian; at the time, however, they were considered revolutionary and thought to resemble medieval or Renaissance costume. The Dress Reform Movement was also concerned with what women wore beneath their dresses. A few radicals advised the abandonment of the corset; most, however, merely thought it should be reshaped to provide the "necessary" support without too rigid a constriction of the waist. The introduction of "health underwear" of wool (Jaeger) or cotton (Aertex) gave women more protection from the climate (and from sudden assault). Only a minority, however, adopted reformed dress, and they were mostly middle-class intellectuals, socialists and bohemians—the same sort of people who now go on antinuclear demonstrations, eat health foods and write poetry.

The Aesthetic Dress of the 1880s, which was adopted mainly by radicals, intellectuals and artists, was a compromise between admiration for the costumes worn in medieval and Renaissance paintings and a natural wish to avoid ridicule by conforming in some degree to current fashion. Like most compromises, it did not fully satisfy either aim. Cartoon from Punch, 1880, by George Du Maurier.

THE SUPERFICIALLY LIBERATED WOMAN

The more conventional late-Victorian and Edwardian woman, though she was no longer supposed to be childish and frail, was far from liberated by modern standards. Though her appearance was queenly, like most queens of recent years her freedom was hedged round with duties and restrictions. She was often called "divine"—and, as is the custom with goddesses, stood on a pedestal, which is an inconvenient place to stand if you want to do anything other than be worshipped. If you move at all, you are in danger of falling off—of becoming, in the popular phrase of the time, a "fallen woman."

The first wave of feminism, as historians of costume have pointed out, did not liberate most women from the bulky and elaborate clothes of the period. Indeed in many ways the female fashions of the time were more oppressive than those of midcentury. The corset had previously ended at or just below the waist, accommodating the many pregnancies of the early-Victorian woman. Now advances in medical science had decreased infant mortality, and it was no longer necessary or fashionable to have many children. The late-Victorian corset lengthened to midthigh, severely restricting locomotion. Gradually it began to push the chest forward and the hips back, creating the S-bend figure with its low-slung monobosom and protruding monorump. Over the corset were worn a corset cover, a camisole, several petticoats, and dresses with trailing skirts and trains. All these garments were richly trimmed with lace, ruffles, tucks, ribbons and embroidery; they were in constant danger of being rumpled or soiled, often giving a literal meaning to the current euphemism "soiled dove."

The ordinary woman who held a job or emancipated opinions might wear, instead of a lace-trimmed gown, a more plainly cut wool or linen suit (the "tailor-made") with a shirtwaist, tie and straw boater that imitated those of men. But this imitation was superficial. Beneath her clothes her corset was as uncomfortable and confining as ever, and when she lifted her heavy floor-length skirt she showed a froth of delicate petticoats and lacy stockings. The message

In the 1890s, as women began to go out to work and to participate in sports, simpler and more masculine styles appeared. The emancipated or working woman might wear a shirt, tie, jacket and hat very much like that of her male contemporaries. Beneath this costume, however, she continued to wear a tight corset and layers of petticoats, suggesting graphically that her emancipation was as yet only superficial. Mr. and Mrs. I. N. Phelps Stokes, *by John Singer Sargent, 1897.*

of this costume was clear: the masculine efficiency or intellectual force were only external; underneath she was still a
member of the frailer sex. To wear such clothes, however,
did not necessarily mean acceptance of the status quo. Some
feminists wore them deliberately in order to confuse or dis-
arm their opponents: indeed, several of the leaders of the
Emancipation Movement were famous for their stylishness.
This stratagem was also used during the second wave of
women's liberation, by Gloria Steinem among others.

THE MODERN GIRL

In the early twentieth century substantial gains in dress
reform were achieved. Slowly, women began to liberate
themselves from the duty of acting as walking advertisements of their own helplessness and their male relatives'
wealth. (The struggle was an uphill one, however, and it is
by no means over.) There was also a gradual relaxation of
the corset and a rise in the skirt, which cleared the ground
by 1905, and by 1912 was above the ankle. Once women
could breathe a little more easily and had no trains to trip
over they were better able to take part in sports. Some,
though to our eyes still absurdly handicapped, joined in
professional competition. By the end of World War I
women's clothes had become relatively unconfining, but
they were still sex-typed, and by no means as comfortable
as those of men. Various counterrevolutionary efforts were
made—notably, the introduction of the hobble skirt in 1910
—but these were generally unsuccessful. As in all transitional periods, however, they provided a useful guide to the
political and social views of the women who wore them.

The clothes of the 1920s were thought at the time to
represent an extreme of freedom for women, and certainly
they were a relief to anyone old enough to have worn the
styles of twenty years earlier. For one thing, they drastically
reduced the time spent in washing, ironing and mending,
and also in simply getting dressed and undressed. The
woman who bobbed her waist-length hair, for instance,
saved several hours a week that had previously been em-

ployed in brushing it out, washing and drying it, braiding it at night and putting it up in a pompadour over pads of wire mesh and false hair every morning.

Twenties' dresses often had little-boy collars or ties, but these were no more than piquant additions to a recognizably feminine costume; they declared that their wearer was charmingly boyish, but not that she was a boy. The fulminations of contemporary critics against mannish women and womanish men seem exaggerated today. In photographs of the twenties men and women do look more alike; but this is because they both look more like children, and the difference between the sexes is less pronounced in childhood. Even in her Buster Brown or Peter Pan collar the flapper of the 1920s (like the Gibson Girl of a generation earlier in her mannish shirt and tie) is only male from the waist up. Below it, her skirt, silk stockings and pumps proclaim that basically she is a female.

WEARING THE PANTS

Reform of the bottom half of women's costume got seriously underway in the 1890s, when the introduction of the bicycle was followed by the introduction of the divided skirt

The first general acceptance of pants for women came with the introduction of the bicycle in the late 1890s. Though the divided skirt recommended for this popular new sport was in fact quite modest, it aroused much initial resistance. Bicycling for Ladies, 1896. Photograph by E. Alice Austen.

The revolution in informal wear for women and girls that began in the twenties became general in the thirties. This costume, unthinkable in 1920, could still be worn today. Lynn Hoffman, author and family therapist, 1939.

for female bicyclists. Though at first it was called unfeminine and even shocking, the divided skirt was in fact voluminously modest. Eventually it was generally accepted—possibly because no one could mistake it for masculine dress.

Real trousers took much longer to become standard female wear. It was not until the 1920s that women and girls began to wear slacks and even shorts for sports and lounging. The new style was greeted with disapproval and ridicule. Women were told that they looked very ugly in trousers, and that wanting to wear The Pants—in our culture, for centuries, the symbolic badge of male authority—was unnatural and sexually unattractive. Nevertheless the fashion spread, and by the mid-1930s a woman could go on a picnic, play tennis or dig in the garden in clothes that did not handicap her. This freedom, however, was limited to the private and informal side of life. Wearing slacks to the office or to a party was out of the question, and any female who appeared on a formal occasion in a trouser suit was assumed to be a bohemian eccentric and probably a lesbian. Most schools and colleges insisted on skirts for classes and in the library until the 1960s; and even today this custom occasionally survives. At the Frick Collection Library in New York women may not be admitted unless they are wearing skirts; a particularly ancient and unattractive skirt is kept at the desk for the use of readers ignorant of this rule.

The woman who wore slacks or shorts before 1960, too, was only outwardly liberated. Underneath her clothes she was more pinched and squeezed and trussed-up than she had been in the twenties. Her bra hauled her breasts up toward the shoulders and forced them into the currently fashionable shape, often with the help of wires or deceptive padding. The straps of this bra usually cut into the flesh, leaving sore red lines on her shoulders and around her body to match the sore red lines left lower down by her tight elastic girdle. Even slim women wore girdles, since the fashionable figure had almost no hips or derrière, and a bouncy rear end was thought vulgar. There was also no other decent way to hold up the obligatory stockings: unless your skirt was very full, any garter belt would show an embarrassing outline beneath it.

TO FREEDOM AND PARTWAY BACK

The fifties and early sixties were the years of the baby boom, togetherness and the feminine mystique; and, as usually happens in patriarchal periods, female and male clothes were sharply distinguished. The New Look Woman and the Man in the Gray Flannel Suit were almost as distinct in silhouette as their grandparents. Nevertheless it was in this period that trousers for women began to edge their way into respectability. At first they took rather peculiar and unbecoming forms. The popular "toreador" or "Capri" pants, for instance, came in odd, glaring colors and ended a tight, awkward six inches above the ankle as if they had shrunk in the wash. They were often worn under maternity or mock-maternity smocks, producing a costume that resembled that of a medieval page. It was accompanied by shoes as narrow and sharply pointed—and no doubt as uncomfortable—as those fashionable in the fourteenth and fifteenth centuries. This outfit was appropriate, since the harassed, untrained middle-class mother of the baby-boom years—unlike her own parents—had no servants, and was reduced to waiting hand and foot on her husband and too many children.

In the late 1960s trousers for women finally became elegant as well as respectable, and underwear vanished or mutated into harmless forms. Even before the second wave of women's liberation got underway, the long struggle for comfort and freedom in female dress seemed to have been won at last. The introduction of panty hose freed women from the ugly and often painful rubber and metal and plastic hardwear they had been using to hold up their stockings. It was again permissible to have curves below the waist as well as above; and millions of girdles went into the trash can, where they were soon joined by millions of padded and wired bras. During the 1970s pants suits and slacks were worn to work, to parties, to the theater, in elegant restaurants and on international planes, by women of all ages. They were usually accompanied by comfortable low-heeled shoes or boots. Fashion editors asserted, and women believed, that the bad old days were over forever.

In the last few years, however, there have been ominous signs of retrenchment, and a counterrevolutionary move-

In the late 1950s and early 1960s women began to wear pants on social occasions. At first these took strange forms: the so-called toreador pants stopped several inches above the ankle and were accompanied by brief tops and spike-heeled shoes of a sort no bullfighter would have faced a crowd in. Diane Johnson, American novelist, 1965.

ment seems to be gaining force. If one is pessimistic it is possible to see the sixties and seventies as merely a period of temporary victory. Indeed, the entire history of female fashion from 1910 to the present can be viewed as a series of more or less successful campaigns to force, flatter or bribe women back into uncomfortable and awkward styles, not only for purposes of Vicarious Ostentation and security of sexual ownership, but also and increasingly in order to handicap them in professional competition with men. The hobble skirt, the girdle, the top-heavy hats of the teens and the forties, the embarrassingly short dresses of the twenties and the sixties, all have aided this war effort. Today its most effective strategic devices are fashionable footwear and the demand for slimness.

THE SHOE AS A STRATEGIC WEAPON

Attempts to limit female mobility by hampering locomotion are ancient and almost universal. The foot-binding of upper-class Chinese girls and the Nigerian custom of loading women's legs with pounds of heavy brass wire are extreme examples, but all over the world similar stratagems have been employed to make sure that once you have caught a woman she cannot run away, and even if she stays around she cannot keep up with you. What seems odd is that all these devices have been perceived as beautiful, not only by men but by women. The lotus foot, which seems to us a deformity, was passionately admired in China for centuries, and today most people in Western society see nothing ugly in the severely compressed toes produced by modern footwear. The high-heeled, narrow-toed shoes that for most of this century have been an essential part of woman's costume are considered sexually attractive, partly because they make the legs look longer—an extended leg is the biological sign of sexual availability in several animal species—and because they produce what anthropologists call a "courtship strut." They also make standing for any length of time painful, walking exhausting and running impossible. The halting, tiptoe gait they produce is thought provocative—perhaps because it guarantees that no woman wearing them can out-

Tight skirts and high-heeled shoes make ordinary activity difficult and even hazardous. The career woman who wears these clothes is announcing to the world that she is willing to be handicapped in relation to men, and men reward her by finding both her and her clothes attractive. Photograph by Bill Cunningham from The New York Times, *1979.*

run a man who is chasing her. Worst of all, if they are worn continually from adolescence on, they deform the muscles of the feet and legs so that it becomes even more painful and difficult to walk in flat soles.

Literally as well as figuratively modern women's shoes are what keeps Samantha from running as fast as Sammy. As anyone who has worn them can testify, it is hard to concentrate on your job when your feet are killing you—especially if you are faint with hunger because you had only half a grapefruit and coffee for breakfast so as to stay a glamorous ten pounds below your natural healthy weight. For a while in the sixties and seventies it was not necessary to be handicapped in this way unless you chose to be. During the last few years, however, women have begun wearing tight high-heeled shoes again, even with pants; and the most fashionable styles are those that, like clogs and ankle-strap sandals, give least support to the feet and make walking most difficult.

The Annie Hall Look as worn by Diane Keaton. Her outsize jacket, shirt and hat give her a tomboy charm that is unthreatening to men because it is clear that she is only playing, and is not really big enough to wear their clothes.

COUNTERREVOLUTION AND AMBIGUITY

There have been other signs recently that all is not well with the independent woman. One is the gradual demotion of the pants suit for both daytime and evening wear. By now it has become a low-status indicator, especially when made of polyester, and is seldom seen in middle-class circumstances. It has been replaced by the "skirted suit" recommended as the proper costume for white-collar success, which must of course be worn with panty hose and heels. Another ominous sign is the narrowing of the skirt to the point where ordinary gestures like sitting on a low sofa or stepping over a puddle become difficult.

Prudence Glynn, a former fashion editor of the London *Times,* was one of the first to point out the internal contradictions of much post-feminist fashion. The platform shoes and clogs that became popular during the seventies, for instance, are usually made on a wide last which does not compress the foot; however, they produce a clumping, awkward gait and are not only hard to manage but dangerous, often leading to serious injury. As Prudence Glynn puts it,

The Annie Hall Look quickly became popular and was worn by women of all sizes and types, so that at times the streets of British and American cities seemed to be full of little girls dressed in their big brothers' clothes. Photograph by Sandra Weiner, 1979.

"By their height they cater to an instinct in women to be taller and thus of more consequence vis-à-vis men. By their construction, which makes walking extremely difficult, they cater to an instinct to remain vulnerable."

Another popular style of the time, known as the Annie Hall Look after the clothes worn by Diane Keaton in the film of the same name, was ambiguous in a more complex way. Essentially it involved the wearing of actual men's clothing: elegant three-piece suits, vests, shirts, ties and hats in pale colors—beige, off-white, tan and gray—often with a twenties look. Everything was worn very large and loose—collars open, shirts ballooning out, sleeves and trouser legs rolled up. These clothes were accompanied by huge handbags and kooky, childish costume jewelry: ceramic and wood and painted-tin ice cream cones and rainbows and Mickey Mice.

The wearing of men's clothes can mean many different things. In the thirties, sophisticated actresses such as Marlene Dietrich in top hat and tails and elegantly cut suits projected sophistication, power and a dangerous eroticism. The slacks and sweaters of the war period, and the jeans and pants outfits of the sixties and early seventies, were serious gestures toward sexual equality.

The Annie Hall style is a double message. It announces that its wearer is a good sport, a pal: not mysteriously and delicately female, but an easy-going, ready-for-anything tomboy type, almost like one of the guys. She will not demand to be protected from the rain or make a fuss about having to stand up at a football game. She probably enjoys active sports and is good at them (though not annoyingly, competitively good). Besides, you can see from her Snoopy pin that she has a sense of humor and is just a kid at heart.

At the same time, however, these clothes convey an ironic antifeminist message. Because they are worn several sizes too large, they suggest a child dressed up in her daddy's or older brother's things for fun, and imply "I'm only playing; I'm not really big enough to wear a man's pants, or do a man's job." This is a look of helpless cuteness, not one of authority; it invites the man to take charge, even when he is as incompetent himself as the characters played by Woody Allen.

IX
FASHION
AND SEX

A sweet disorder in the dress
Kindles in clothes a wantonness.

     —Robert Herrick

As well as telling us whether people are male or female, clothes can tell us whether or not they are interested in sex, and if so what sort of sex they are interested in. This information, of course, may be more or less disguised. Clothes worn on the job, for instance, are supposed to downplay rather than flaunt sexuality, and to conceal any specialized erotic tastes completely. In reality even the most sedate costume may contain erotic clues, but anyone who dresses for work as if he or she were about to go out on the town is likely to arouse unfriendly gossip or worse.

On social occasions, on the other hand, any relatively young person who is not dressed to attract will lose face. As a result, bright, "sexy" clothes are sometimes worn by people who want to be admired and even loved, but have little interest in getting it on with anyone. Occasionally certain details of costume suggest their true feelings: the cuffs of the raincoat are tightly buckled and the ends of the straps fastidiously tucked in; the crimson shirt open nearly to the waist reveals not only a gold chain but a plain, discouraging-looking white cotton undershirt or bra; the strings of the semitransparent gauze blouse or the laces of the fashionable soft suede shoes are tied in a hard double knot.

Antisexual clothes may also be imposed by an external

Nineteenth-century English missionaries, horrified by the nakedness and free eroticism of the South Sea Islanders, hastened to provide them with "decent"—i.e., antisexual—clothing.

authority. The Mother Hubbards supplied by missionaries to cover the nakedness of South Sea islanders are a classic example, and school uniforms even today—especially those of girls—often seem designed to discourage erotic interest. Prison dress may serve the same purpose. Frequently, as Rachel Kemper notes, the "elegantly turned-out prostitute, thrown in the slammer, is issued black oxfords with Cuban heels, ankle socks, plain cotton dresses, and underwear with bras laundered flat and useless." Other prisoners, both male and female, may undergo the same sort of humiliation.

As Herrick points out, looseness and disorder in dress are erotically appealing. Soft, flowing, warm-hued clothes traditionally suggest a warm, informal, affectionate personality, and the garment that is partially unfastened not only reveals more flesh but implies that total nakedness will be easily achieved. Excessive neatness, on the other hand, suggests an excessively well-controlled, possibly repressed personality. Tight, bundled-up or buttoned-up clothes (if not figure-revealing) are felt to contain a tight, erotically held-in person. Hard, crisp fabrics—gabardines, starched cottons and stiff synthetics—also seem to deny sensuality, and so do grayed, dull colors. When drab-colored clothes are both unusually tight and unusually neat, observers will suspect not only sexual disinterest but impotence or frigidity.

A positive attitude toward sex can also be obvious or subtle. The young and naïve may appear in skintight jeans and T-shirts bearing the message HAPPINESS IS A WARM PUSSY; older and more sophisticated persons will convey the same sort of message in less blatant ways. And those whose erotic interests are unusual or even forbidden will send out sartorial signals that are invisible except to those who know the code.

FABRIC, FUR AND SKIN

The most sensual aspect of a garment is the material of which it is made. To some extent, fabric always stands for the skin of the person beneath it: if it is strikingly slick or woolly, rough or smooth, thick or thin, we unconsciously attribute these characteristics to its wearer. The man in the heavy, coarse wool pants and shirt, for instance, is assumed to be "thick-skinned" in the colloquial sense of the term: emotionally tough and perhaps callous. The man in the light-weight shantung suit is assumed to be "thin-skinned": sensitive, possibly touchy.

One of the oldest sartorial messages is the wearing of animal skins. Primitive hunters dressed in the hides of the beasts they had killed in order to take on the magical nature of the bear, the wolf or the tiger. Even today men and women in animal pelts are not only conspicuously consuming, they are also presenting themselves as animals. How seriously this claim is to be taken depends on the species of skin. To wear leather is not usually to assert that one is a cow, a calf or a bull, though occasionally the latter meaning may cling to a pair of chaps or a fringed jacket. More often, cowhide merely suggests the idea of sensual contact with the skin of the wearer; depending on the way the hide has been treated, it may present this skin as slick and tough like a motorcyclist's black leather jacket, or as soft and fuzzy like a suede dress. Less common hides may have more complex meanings. A deerskin jacket or vest, for instance, might suggest a wilderness romance, while one of alligator, snake or lizard might

Pornographic magazines for masochists are full of good-looking women in black leather clothing and boots, and any outfit of this material, even when well covered up and stylishly cut, has these overtones. Honor Blackman, judo expert and one of the stars of the British TV series The Avengers.

During the twenties and thirties stylish women appeared even on very warm days wearing the skins of foxes, complete with head, legs and tail. They might be wound round the neck, or draped casually over the shoulder like a hunter's trophy. Appropriately enough, one of the most fashionable female names of the time was Diana. London, 1934.

predict an expensive, somewhat cold-blooded and muddy encounter. Reptilian shoes and handbags, however, may convey nothing more chilling than excess wealth.

VENUS IN FURS

Fur is more likely than leather to turn its wearer into an animal symbolically. Sometimes the message is simple: the Russian in his bearskin hat and overcoat is a Russian bear; the girl going to her first dance in a new mouton coat is a lamb going to market. At other times it is unlikely that the fur-clad one wants to be credited with the characteristics of a particular beast. The self-centered viciousness of the mink, the obsessive industriousness of the beaver, the noisy maternal ardor of the seal are not necessarily to be expected from women (or men) clothed in their hides—though cases of such mimicry certainly exist. For one thing, most purchasers of fur coats are unfamiliar with the behavior of the beasts from which they come: all they want to say is "I am a very expensive animal."

The personality of some fur-bearing animals, however, is so well established in popular tradition that it cannot help but form part of the sartorial message. The timidity and philoprogenitiveness of the rabbit tends to transfer itself to those who wear coats made of rabbit fur, even when it is dyed brown or black and called "coney." Women who wear such coats are often expected to be bunnies in something like the *Playboy* sense: to be slightly (though charmingly) silly, sexually eager and apt to have a great many children (or, given current medical advances, a great many pregnancies).

The fox, on the other hand, is in popular tradition wily, courageous and independent, and the woman who wears its pelt is assumed to share some of these qualities—to be a "foxy lady." This fur became popular during the 1920s, when foxlike qualities were beginning to seem attractive in a female; it was in 1925, for instance, that David Garnett's witty novel *Lady into Fox* became an international best seller. The current use of the term "fox" for an attractive woman also dates from this era. A few years later there was a vogue for cloth coats topped with huge fox collars that concealed most of the face: in them the Depression woman looked out on a dog-eat-dog world from a mask of fur like a hunted but clever and resourceful animal.

Two particular uses of fur in women's costume deserve special mention: One is the practice, common in the 1930s and 1940s, of wearing round the neck one or more animal skins (usually fox, sometimes mink) complete with legs, tail and head—with the sharp little teeth bared, the glass eyes beady. It is not clear whether the fox or mink represented the animal nature of the woman who wore it, or whether it was a kind of trophy representing the man or men she had captured, hung round her neck in the primitive manner, as in some portraits of Diana the Huntress.

Another very symbolic fur piece was the muff, which became fashionable in the early nineteenth century and remained popular until World War II. At first muffs were made of swansdown or of expensive furs such as sable, bearskin and chinchilla. After swans had become a protected species, and all furs were expensive, the muff was more likely to be of lamb, sealskin or mink. As is clear from the ancient vulgar meaning of the word "muff," the woman who carried one was carrying a visible symbol of her private parts, which she represented as furry, soft, delicate and warm. On a cold day a favored man might be invited to place his hand in his companion's muff, encouraging him to hope for a similar but less symbolic opportunity in the future.

To wear fur may imply that beneath your civilized exterior you are a wild animal. As the ancient vulgar meaning of the word suggests, the fur muff, *or* boa, *is a particularly pointed symbol. Portrait of Sonia, 1890, by Henri Fantin-Latour.*

THE DECORATED BODY: TANNING AND TATTOOING

In addition to wearing the skins of animals, men and women can alter their own hides to increase (or decrease) their sexual charm. First, they may change the color of their skin, bleaching or darkening it to suit current standards of beauty. For many centuries a tan was the sign of someone who worked out of doors; it therefore indicated lower-class status. Ladies and gentlemen had pale complexions; indeed, the whiter a lady's skin was, the more beautiful she was considered to be. As a result women and even men took pains to avoid exposure to sunshine: the Victorian bonnet and parasol, for example, were not only decorative and symbolic, they also served as sunshades.

By the early twentieth century, however, many low-status jobs involved working long hours indoors, with only two weeks' vacation each year. A deep overall tan implied that you had the time and money to lie in the sun. If you lived in the northern United States, Canada or Britain, it was especially prestigious during the winter months, since it suggested expensive southern travel. A tan was also considered erotic, partly because it suggested healthy outdoor exercise, which in this century has usually been a turn-on, and partly because of the British and North American folk belief that people with darker skins (Latins, Arabs, Blacks) are more highly sexed.

The sun tan as a fashion, according to social historians, was invented by Gabrielle Chanel in 1920, and the first fashionable tans were acquired on the French Riviera. Within a few years almost no romantic hero was without one. Heroines remained divinely fair for a while longer, but by the 1930s many of them, too, had a golden or even darker skin, like Nicole Diver in Fitzgerald's *Tender Is the Night* (1934), of whom it is reported that "her back, a ruddy, orange brown, set off by a string of creamy pearls, shone in the sun." In the southern United States and the British Colonies, however, sun tans never really caught on. When you have a hot climate, a large dark-skinned laboring population and a rural economy in which most physical work takes place out of doors, there is no status advantage to a browner skin.

When the Beautiful People of the twenties and thirties oiled themselves all over and lay scorching on the sands of Nice, Miami Beach or Santa Monica, they did not realize that in thirty or forty years they would be cracked and wrinkled and aged before their time like old turkeys, or that they were greatly increasing their chances of getting skin cancer. As these turkeys came home to roost in the sixties and seventies, very deep tans became less fashionable, and today a medium beige is the preferred color.

A more painful but potentially less harmful method of

altering the skin is by tattooing. Traditionally, this art is practiced mainly on working-class men, especially sailors; but a surprising number of women—even on occasion aristocratic ones—turn out on close acquaintance to have a rose or butterfly engraved in some private spot. Besides the initial pain, the main disadvantage of tattooing is that it blurs with time, so that the design begins to look like a colored ink drawing held under a faucet. It is also difficult to remove if you enter another stratum of society or break up with the person whose name, surrounded by hearts and flowers, is inscribed upon your body. Small visible tattoos on a middle-class person suggest a wild and adventurous past, and often service in the Navy or Merchant Marine; many men and women, according to my research, find them sexually stimulating. Larger and more elaborate designs, especially those Japanese-style tattoos that cover most of the chest or back and contain many interlocked figures, are less popular: one of my informants remarked that it was like making love to an Oriental rug.

PAINT AND POWDER

The easiest way to decorate your skin is with cosmetics. In previous centuries it was not uncommon for men as well as women to use them discreetly; today only females are supposed to paint themselves, though the late Earl Mountbatten was observed to have used rouge and a blue rinse. More conventional men may smear their skins with greases or astringents, or choose to smell like leopards or old leather; or rather, like an idealized realization of these smells, as anybody will realize who has ever been in a stable or the cat house at the zoo. To counteract the suspicion of effeminacy, male cosmetics are always sold in a very macho manner, as Robert Brain has noted:

> [Manufacturers] tend to appeal to the warrior, the he-man, in selling cosmetics to men; scents and creams and aftershaves are advertised by boxers, footballers and cricketers. Men are told that the products will make them feel bold, brash, rugged, commanding, vigorous, brisk and stimulating.

This boldness, brashness and so forth is artificial in every sense. As has often been pointed out, cosmetics and perfumes and soaps actually cover up or wash away the natural odors of the human body that once served as sexual signals. We are being conditioned to reject the very smells that once turned us on, and to demand that human beings exude a vegetable or chemical odor.

Female make-up is conventionally thought of as a means of disguising age and imperfections. In fact, it only does this partially; its main effect is to create the appearance of erotic arousal: the wide eyes, the swollen, reddened lips, the flushing of the skin. Make-up has also been used to give the illusion that a face conforms to the current ideal. As a result, a large majority of twenties women appeared to have pouting, bee-stung mouths. When fashions matured during the Depression and World War II women showed their sophisticated skepticism by narrowing their eyes and permanently arching their eyebrows. In the sixties, when the world began to change again, eyes grew unnaturally large and round with surprise, an effect increased by the dark shadows and long sticky lashes that surrounded them. As fashions became more freaky, lips turned pale brown and then pale pink or white, finally disappearing almost entirely; for a while women were simply all eyes, like the pathetic children in sidewalk art shows. Under the influence of the back-to-nature and women's liberation movements of the seventies many women abandoned make-up altogether. Today it seems to be making a comeback, though it is still scorned by some of the young and by almost all serious feminists.

THE HAIRY APE AND THE PLASTIC DOLL

One of the most common signs of an active sexuality has always been the display of hair. Among men, though the hair style is primarily a political and social indicator (as suggested earlier), it often has a secondary erotic meaning. Monks and priests have traditionally shaved off most of their hair or cropped it short as a sign of celibacy and self-

An excess of hair, both on the head and on the body, suggests animality; some women, and a few men, claim to find it highly erotic in the opposite sex. Photograph by Don Snyder.

restraint. Perhaps that is why a shiny bare scalp has seldom been found erotically attractive, even though we are told by scientists that male baldness is associated with a good supply of male hormones. Luxuriantly fuzzy or silky beards, and loose Byronic curls, on the other hand, are often associated in the popular mind with a passionate nature. The deliberate exposure of male body hair (especially on the chest) is also considered a sign of sexual vigor, though not all women (or men) are attracted by the Hairy Ape type.

In most societies the fact that adult females have hair on their bodies is taken for granted and even appreciated. In Britain and North America, however, such growth has traditionally been strongly disapproved, and rigorously disposed of by shaving, waxing and electrolysis. (Even pubic hair has been seen as undesirable: John Ruskin, the Victorian art historian, is said to have been repelled to the point of impotence when, on his wedding night, he discovered that his wife was not as smooth as a marble statue.) To contemporary feminists this attitude is a form of patriarchal oppression, part of the male demand that women transform themselves into painted plastic dolls. Supporters of ecological action, organic gardening and herbal medicine are also very likely to view body hair as a natural crop. Today, therefore, it is not uncommon to see women whose underarms and legs show a flourishing growth. By checking the rest of their getup it is possible to classify them as either (a) foreigners; (b) serious feminists; or (c) supporters of the counterculture. Ladies with stubbly armpits and prickly legs, on the other hand, if not in the process of transformation into one of the above roles, are considered simply careless and untidy.

RAPUNZEL AND CO.

Long hair has always been an important, indeed a legendary attribute of femininity. It is a characteristic of fairy-tale heroines, including Rapunzel, whose locks were so long and so thick that the witch and the prince could climb them like a gym rope. Long, luxuriant hair is the traditional mark of

Long, thick, loose hair is a traditional sign of female sexuality, and it has been celebrated as such by artists of every time and place. In the mid-nineteenth century rippling waves like these were especially admired. Portrait of Jo (La Belle Irlandaise), *1866, by Gustave Courbet.*

the sexual woman in most countries and times. In Christian art, for example, Mary Magdalene is usually shown with hair down to her feet.

In the European tradition long, loose hair has almost always been associated with youth, and often with virginity —real or presumed. As a child a girl wore her hair down, sometimes in braids. When she reached adulthood or was married she would put it up according to local custom. She might braid it into a crown as in many peasant communities; she might cover it with a wimple or a lace cap, erect it into a powdered eighteenth-century fantasy, or puff it out into an Edwardian pompadour. She would seldom, however, cut it off. In the privacy of the marital (or extramarital) bedroom the cap would come off, the rolls be unwound, and what the Victorians called "woman's crowning glory" would be released for the delight of man.

The fashion for short hair in women dates from the 1920s, though there were brief instances of it earlier. In the beginning it meant freedom and independence, often including erotic freedom and independence, and for a while the old rule was reversed: a girl who bobbed her hair was more rather than less likely to be sexually available. By the 1940s, though, traditional meanings had been reestablished, and the glamour girl had at least shoulder-length hair, while the conservative college student, career woman or house-wife wore hers in a close, stiff permanent wave. Only artistic and bohemian women had really long hair, and they tended to twist it into a chignon or tie it back in a ponytail.

In the sixties and early seventies, however, young women began to wear their hair long again, now usually parted in the middle. Fashion demanded that it be straight; if it was not so naturally the curls could be ironed out by a friend or (with more difficulty) by their owner. Such a hairdo was compatible with—even an inducement to—the loss of virginity and marriage, just as it had been in past centuries, but it was not acceptable on the job market. My long-haired students, when it came time for them to gradu-ate and look for jobs, were often in great conflict as a result. To cut their hair (or even to put it up) seemed to them a sign that they had sold out to the Establishment, just as it was for their male contemporaries, and there was often the addi-tional problem that their boyfriends liked their hair long.

Today waist-length manes are uncommon except among the young, but longer-than-average hair, in every age group, has its traditional meaning: romantic ideas, emo-tional warmth and often sexual readiness. A sudden and drastic haircut implies rejection of these qualities, and con-temporary women are therefore often under pressure from their husbands or lovers to stay away from the hairdresser. At the same time they experience pressure in the opposite direction from current or potential employers, setting up the classical conflict between Love and Duty.

BLONDES, BRUNETTES AND REDHEADS

Tradition has always associated hair color and texture with personality, especially in women, without any apparent jus-tification—although the effect of being treated from early childhood according to a stereotype cannot be under-estimated. Blondes, we have been told, are preferred by gentlemen and (perhaps as a result) have more fun; brunettes are more deeply emotional; redheads are fiery and passionate. Definite colors indicate a forceful personality; drab, muted colors (ash blonde, mouse brown) a more retiring one. Straight-haired persons are serious, sometimes solemn; curly-haired persons are lively, possibly frivolous.

For centuries rippling golden hair (neither too straight nor too curly) was thought to be the most desirable for women. Roman ladies in both classical and Renaissance times bleached and dyed and crimped to achieve it, and it was a conventional attribute of the princesses in fairy tales. In the nineteenth century, however, when a deeply emotional nature was highly valued in women, most of the beauties in popular art had long, dark-brown hair. In fiction too there was a preference for brunettes. Blondes were apt to be portrayed as "light-headed"—naïve, frivolous or worse. In George Eliot's *Middlemarch,* for instance, noble, self-sacrificing, dark-haired Dorothea is contrasted with the shallow, selfish, pale-blonde Rosamond. Red hair, in the popular imagination, indicated passion and a quick temper; it was a disadvantage for a man and a serious misfortune for a woman. The best-known redhead in Victorian literature is "sandy-haired" Becky Sharp, the ambitious, unscrupulous antiheroine of Thackeray's *Vanity Fair* (1847–48). This prejudice continued into the twentieth century. The eponymous heroine of L. M. Montgomery's *Anne of Green Gables* (1908), a tremendously popular children's book that is still widely read today, declares that "nothing could be as bad as red hair." She therefore tries to dye hers black, but succeeds only in turning it green; the implication is that nothing can disguise a redheaded nature.

In this century red or yellow locks are no longer a disadvantage, but the traditional associations remain. Blondes are more often the heroines of comedy or melodrama, brunettes of mystery and tragedy. Curls suggest humor, and a redhead is expected to be tempestuous. What is new is the existence of options. Technical advances in coloring, curling and straightening make it possible for anyone who has the time and the money to change her hair as she would a hat. If she chooses, a woman can be in turn a bubble-headed blonde, a sleek, sophisticated brunette and a way-out redhead; or she can maintain permanently whatever color and texture suits her personality. As a result, the stereotypes have been reinforced, and even if you do not alter your hair you are likely to be judged by it and dealt with accordingly.

Men have the same freedom of choice, but they exercise it less often. It is no longer necessary to be dark as well as tall and handsome to be a hero, and male personality is not thought to change dramatically with hair color as it does with hair length. Very light blond or red-gold hair (especially if curly) is a handicap for men professionally, however; since these colors occur most often in small children, they suggest immaturity and impulsiveness.

SEXUAL SIGNALS: THE OLD HANDBAG

Today, as in the past, certain details of costume convey a direct sexual message. Bright-red clothing, the exposure of more than the usual amount of flesh and the wearing of revealingly tight garments are universally recognized signs. A simple, sometimes crude statement is made by the shirt unbuttoned to the waist, the extra-short miniskirt, the thin sweater that shows the nipples and the bulge in the trousers which, as Mae West put it, indicates that a man is glad to see you. At times there have been other accepted indications of sexuality. In the mid-nineteenth century, for instance, the woman who wore her bonnet well forward, blocking out her view of the world on both sides, was assumed to be modest and shy; one who wore her bonnet pushed toward the back of her head was assumed to be "fast"—that is, immodest and perhaps wanton. More recently, in the 1950s, a well-bred woman wore gloves—usually short white cotton ones —whenever she might expect to be introduced to strangers. If she forgot or misplaced them and had to touch the hand of a strange man with her own bare hand, she was aware of having made—inadvertently or not—a sexual gesture.

The most universally recognized sexual indicator in women, however, is the purse or handbag. Freudians may have been the first to state the connection directly, but the use of the term "purse" for the female pudenda dates from the early seventeenth century. The common phrase "old bag" for an unattractive, aging woman is about a hundred years old, and may be subliminally responsible for the female readiness to discard even a slightly worn purse. As a result, secondhand shops are full of old bags, often expensive leather ones, which, though perfectly functional and in good condition, have been rejected by their owners.

Sex is not all that is communicated by the handbag, of course. Its contents, for instance, may represent the contents of the mind, or serve as both a portable identity kit and a repair kit. At the same time, however, the bag conveys erotic information, if only in the eyes of the beholder. According to my male informants, a tightly snapped, zipped and buckled purse suggests a woman who guards her physical and emotional privacy closely, one whom it will be difficult to get to know in either the common or the Biblical sense. An open-topped tote bag suggests an open, trusting nature: someone who is emotionally and sexually more accessible. A handbag may also be small or large (I contain multitudes?), stiff or soft and brightly colored or dark. It may have many compartments, suggesting an organized mind or a woman who plays many roles in life; or it may consist of only one compartment in which everything is jumbled together. The handbag may also be extremely "feminine"—soft, flowered and fragile-looking—or it may resemble a man's brief case. The executive woman who carries both a handbag and a brief case appears to have two contradictory sexual identities; perhaps for this reason, wardrobe consultants strongly advise against the practice.

PHALLIC CLOTHING

Psychologists say that the walking stick or rolled umbrella is a male symbol when it appears in dreams; and in waking life men can often be seen using these symbolic objects to poke and prod or to signal for taxis in a way that bears out this interpretation. Walking sticks or canes are now rare except among men who really need them, but the umbrella remains popular. As might be expected, the male version tends to be large and heavy, and to gain prestige from a capacity for instant deployment. A shabby, small or—worst of all—ill-functioning umbrella is a source of shame that often seems excessive unless some erotic meaning is presumed. Of course, when the umbrella is actually unfolded it assumes a less phallic shape—which may be why upper-class British males often keep theirs tightly rolled even in a heavy drizzle.

When women put on men's clothes they usually take on considerable dignity, and sometimes great elegance and sophistication. Marlene Dietrich in 1933. Photograph from the Larry Carr Collection.

The male hat too has been considered a sexual symbol. As James Laver points out, periods of male dominance have coincided with high hats for men, among them the tall-crowned hat of the Puritans and the top hat of the Victorians. "With the advent of the New Woman in the 1880's," he remarks, "many men adopted the boater, which might be thought of as a very much truncated top hat. And towards the end of the century men began to wear, so to speak, the very symbol of their bashed-in authority: the trilby hat." If this theory is correct, the recent growth tendency of the cowboy hat may be significant.

Other details of male clothing have had a recognized sexual—and social—meaning. In the nineteenth century the amount of shirt front showing indicated a man's position on the scale from virtue to vice: the more linen that was exposed, the more unreliable he was. A discreet, buttoned-up look distinguished the proper gentleman or respectable tradesman or clerk, on whose honor a lady or even a poor working girl could depend. The somewhat undependable sporting chap showed more shirtfront; the downright cad who would take advantage of any erotic opportunity displayed even more, and often wore too much jewelry. Today excess jewelry on either sex is a lower-middle-class or *nouveau-riche* indicator, but it also still has overtones of sensual laxity.

A man's tie may also be sexually symbolic, especially if it is brightly colored or in some way unusual. James Laver remarks that the tieless Catholic priest is "symbolically castrated," while the old-fashioned British Evangelical clergyman always wore a white tie, "as if to indicate that he was potent but pure." Following Laver's lead, it might be proposed that the narrow woven cord or leather thong ties often favored by elderly American men suggest a withering or drying-up of the passions. Another possible clue is the kerchief worn in the outside breast pocket of the suit by well-dressed men. According to a journalist of my acquaintance, a casually burgeoning paisley scarf, especially if red, announces "I can get it up"; neatly folded white linen implies temporary or permanent disinterest in sex, and should be interpreted by women as a flag of truce.

OUTER AND INNER SELVES

The information or misinformation we want our clothes to convey about status, age, occupation, opinions, mood and sexual tastes may make it hard for us to decide what to wear. What often happens in such cases is that the outer layer represents the external or public person and the inner one his or her private self. When both layers are visible the message, though contradictory, is easy to read. The woman in the sensible gray wool suit and the frilly pink blouse is a serious, hard-working mouse with a frivolous and feminine soul. If, on the other hand, she wears a curvy pink silk dressmaker suit over a plain mouse-gray sweater, we suspect her of being privately preoccupied or depressed no matter how charming and social her manner.

Many combinations of outer and inner message are possible. A costume may be childish without and adult within, like the bright ruffled apron over the severe dark dress which informs guests that a serious career woman is only playing at cooking. It may be casual and countrified without and citified within, like the tan cord suit of the architect which is worn with a business shirt and tie to reassure his clients that their buildings will not run over the cost estimate or fall down. Or it may be high-status without and low-status within—as with the elegant Italian suit of the rock star, beneath which a T-shirt printed with the image of a sweating beer can assures his fans that he is still at heart a tough, oversexed, working-class kid.

Even when the styles of the inner and outer layer are

the same, there may be a significant difference in color. Someone whose visible underlayer of clothing is red, for instance, may be telling us of the heat and passion beneath his or her subdued exterior. When a color combination is already conventional, however, its meaning is conventional rather than personal. The wearing of a white shirt with a dark suit does not mean that you are outwardly serious and inwardly honest and trustworthy, merely that this character type has always been considered desirable in business and the professions. The reverse outfit—the gambler's white suit and dark shirt—suggests someone whose character and motives are somewhat shady, whatever the lightness and charm of his manner.

INTIMATE APPAREL

Sometimes, of course, the inner layer of clothing is covered by the outer one, and only those who are lucky or privileged will ever see it. One of the most interesting moments in any incipient love affair—or in any public dressing room— comes when someone whom we find attractive takes off his or her clothes and reveals a new message written in underwear. Often, indeed, it is not until we see this private costume that we have a real clue as to its wearer's erotic identity.

Asexual underwear, both male and female, is immediately obvious. It is usually white, drab, unadorned and made of nonsensual materials such as broadcloth; often it is somewhat too loose. If clean and fresh, it may indicate virginity, permanent or temporary chastity or a mild embarrassment about physical matters. When such underwear has a grayed or yellow tinge, and an exhausted look about the elastic, it is not merely asexual but antisexual. It actively repels eroticism, and may be intended to do so; it implies dislike of one's own body, possibly of all bodies. Persons who persist in making advances to the owners of such garments are asking for trouble.

Attractive underwear is harder to describe, since it depends so much on personal taste. For example, both sexes

During the years when films were subject to censorship, actresses spent a lot of time in their slips. Though not in fact very revealing, this costume acted as a symbolic equivalent of nudity, and as a result the lacy satin slip became an erotic signal in real life. Elizabeth Taylor in Butterfield 8, *1960.*

are in disagreement about what makes a pair of male underpants erotic or even decent. About all that can be said is that middle- and upper-class men over fifty seem to prefer boxer shorts in white, blue or tan, plain or striped. They consider anything else low-status, even vulgar, and believe that jockey shorts are bad for their sperm count, which they have a horror of diminishing even if not ambitious for fatherhood. Conservative men under fifty prefer standard white jockey shorts. They consider boxer shorts old-fashioned and fuddy-duddy, and think brief or colored shorts vulgar. Less conservative men, if they have reasonably flat stomachs, may wear low-cut jockey shorts, also known as "briefs" or "slips," often white but sometimes brown, red, green or blue. For with-it types such briefs are now available in many brilliant colors and exotic patterns. There are also those who wear no underpants at all—a practice regarded by some women as thrilling, by others as disgusting.

Most women under fifty seem to like colorful—but not way-out—briefs, as long as a man has the figure for them. To others, however, sex is associated with some other sort of underwear (possibly what their fathers or their first or favorite lovers once wore), and anything else is a turn-off.

In the matter of undershirts, too, there is little consensus. Some dislike them on principle, others demand them. The sleeveless white singlet associated with laboring men is admired by those who think of sex as working class, or of the working class as sexy. Conventional white T-shirts have their fans, and so do colored ones. There are even people who heat up at the thought of fishnet or thermal underwear, which to most Britons or North Americans merely suggests Scandinavian origin or determined outdoorsmanship.

LINGERIE: PURE, ROMANTIC OR PASSIONATE?

Anyone who has walked through that section of a department store lately knows that when they buy lingerie, most women prefer white. If they choose another color, it is often for practical reasons: to avoid the appearance of a ghostly bra or slip under a semitransparent blouse or dress. They like lace and frills, but in moderate amounts: what they want in their private lives is to look innocent, fresh and pretty. Some lady jocks prefer underthings that are white but plain and tailored, free of all decoration. The erotic implication of such underwear (you cannot call it lingerie) is that sex is a body-contact sport, a way of getting a good workout. If their jock underwear is startlingly functional (running bras worn on a date, for instance) they may think of making love as a kind of competitive activity—one in which, as Kinsey and his followers have warned us, the man is apt to come in second.

Since lacy white lingerie is readily available and avoids the problem of matching colors, many women usually wear it, adding a black nightgown or a red bra or a flowered slip from time to time, often because some man has given it to them. If they do not like him very much, they wear it less often. Consciously or unconsciously they know that such gifts may be sexual messages as well as sexual tributes—hints that they might be more experimental or more aggressive or more demure in bed.

Tan, beige or ecru underwear makes both pale and dark skin look rosy, and is therefore flattering. Its meaning is elegant and refined; it is the choice of the woman of any age who feels too old or too experienced to wear white, and too much of a lady to wear black or any definite color. Often she likes to think of herself as cosmopolitan, possibly Parisian, since Frenchwomen are reputed to wear lacy tan or brown lingerie.

Pink and rose, with a good deal of lace, are favored by women who think of love as romance, and of themselves as romantic heroines. The way to their private parts is through their hearts, and the man who neglects to take this road, even long after the wedding night, is apt to be received with hurt looks and half-suppressed sighs—if not rejected with headaches and tears. When the woman who seldom wears a pink nightgown puts one on, she may be silently asking for, or magically invoking, a sentimental experience. Pink or rose-hued lingerie should not be confused with the sort called "peach" or "flesh," although it resembles no known fruit or human skin. Underwear of this color is a bad sign unless it is worn by a dark-skinned woman, since it makes a fair complexion look yellowish, flawed and grimy. The woman who wears it is either color-blind or visually insensitive. This is not of course a contraindication for making love, but on the other hand it is no recommendation, and should be taken seriously if you are considering setting up housekeeping together, even in a nonsexual relationship.

Black underwear, in the popular imagination, is always erotic. When tailored and discreet in cut, however, it may also indicate a practical nature, since black always looks fresh and does not show dirt easily. Such simple black underthings are often worn by thoughtful, intellectual women who take sex very seriously. Lacy and revealing black lingerie, on the other hand, is sophisticated, daring and occasionally wicked in its implications. Women who prefer it are more likely to become bored with partners, places and sexual positions; they are also less likely to sit up in bed exclaiming tearfully "Oh, this is awful! What am I doing?"

The rare woman who customarily wears red bras and slips and panties will not say this either, but she is apt to be a handful in other ways. Often she will be passionate, but she may also have a temper, and may actually enjoy jealous scenes and prefer the sound of doors slamming and plates crashing to the music of Mozart.

Though white, tan, pink, black and red (and the egregious flesh) are the most common colors for lingerie, others are frequently available. They are usually bought or worn to express a mood, however (receptive blue, dreamy violet, cheerful yellow, jazzy orange), rather than to give erotic information. One can also buy underthings in patterns, usually floral ones which, as in outerwear, represent a delicate or a blowsy feminity according to the size of the blooms. Another favorite design is the jungle print, which imitates the pelt of a leopard or, less often, a tiger. As the name implies, this design announces that its wearer is a carnivorous wild animal. Threatening as this sounds, research suggests that these nylon leopards and tigers are less dangerous than they look, and if properly handled may turn out to be pussy cats.

FASHIONS IN ANATOMY

Though the reproductive process has not altered much over the years, what men find attractive in women seems to change regularly. The psychologist J. C. Flügel was the first to propose a theory of "shifting erogenous zones," according to which first one and then another part of the female body is uncovered and found exciting. The feature chosen need not have any natural connection with sexuality: the mid-Victorians were thrilled by plump, white, sloping shoulders; in the 1900s there was tremendous agitation over a glimpse of a well-turned ankle; and in the 1930s the back was a focus of erotic attention.

Some of these fashions in anatomy seem merely arbitrary, the result, as Flügel suggests, of boredom and over-familiarity with other parts of the body. Others may have a practical explanation. The medieval focus on the rounded belly, for instance, was functional in a period of high mortality, when constant pregnancy was necessary to keep the population stable. In the twenties and thirties excitement over the female leg celebrated the fact that women had become more mobile and independent; and the exposure of the breasts under translucent or clinging tops in the early seventies was accompanied by a renewed interst in breast-feeding. Since fashions, like dreams, are often multiply determined, it may be significant that these see-through or semi-see-through clothes, which were worn occasionally by men as well as women, appeared concurrently with the fashion for intimate self-exposure—or semi-exposure—in encounter groups.

Sometimes the currently thrilling bit of anatomy is only exposed in impolite society. In respectable circumstances it is elaborately wrapped up, and often exaggerated in the process. During the late-Victorian period, for instance, interest centered on the rear end, which was exposed in the final gesture of the cancan and exaggerated by the bustle. After a period of eclipse, the rear came into favor again during World War II, when a back view of the film star Betty Grable in a bathing suit was the favorite pinup of enlisted men. It then vanished again from fashion and was replaced

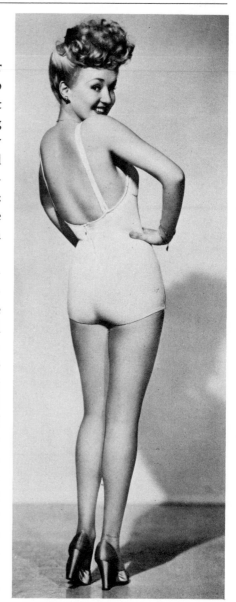

For fifty years, between about 1910 and 1960, the female behind was largely out of fashion and out of sight, neglected by designers and suppressed by tight girdles. During World War II, however, it reappeared briefly, as can be seen from this famous pinup photograph of the movie star Betty Grable. At the time this picture was considered very suggestive, even vulgar, though by current standards both Miss Grable's pose and her figure seem restrained.

The styles of the late 1950s were bunchy, boxy and often very unbecoming. As Richard Avedon's photograph suggests, these clothes demanded that women fit themselves into a kind of Happy Housewife uniform that suppressed both sexuality and individuality.

by the breasts and suppressed by the girdle for almost twenty years. In the 1970s, however, girdles became a sign of age or prudery; the buttocks reappeared as a focus of erotic interest while the bosom diminished. Today C-cup or larger breasts are regarded as a disadvantage, and Woolworth's sells both "minimizing bras" and "natural-line" elastic panties that allow for or create rear cleavage. Blue jeans for both men and women are cut so as to call attention to a rounded behind rather than compressing it into a flat unirear. What all this may mean is difficult to say. One very interesting writer on fashion, the anthropologist Robert Brain, has however remarked that in animal species the "swelling and coloration of the backside is particularly conspicuous in those species which have the most aggressive and quarrelsome males."

Not only different parts of the body, but different body types, go in and out of fashion. By modern standards the Edwardian beauty was disgustingly pale and fat; Twiggy, the ideal child-woman of the sixties, now looks to us like a victim of anorexia. The styles of most eras are designed to flatter the woman who conforms to the current ideal, and to allow the woman who falls a little short of the ideal to approximate it more closely. Anyone whose natural appearance is far off the mark, however, is likely to be positively uglified by fashion. The sophisticated, intricately cut and stiffened New Look clothes of the post–World War II period were becoming to tall, slim women, but they made short, plump ones look like barrage balloons. Today square shoulders and an athletic frame are in style, and the woman whose small stature and rounded figure would have made her a Victorian beauty has difficulty finding a dress that does not make her appear to be wearing football pads.

Occasionally a style develops that does not really flatter anyone. In the late 1950s women wore bunchy, boxy, square-cut or A-line jackets and dresses which, unlike the sculptured gowns of ten years earlier, did not seem to have an artistic and emotional life of their own yet refused to shape themselves to their wearers. Instead they enclosed us like ill-fitting cardboard costumes in a grade-school pageant. The only advantage of these clothes was that they made you look slightly pregnant whether you were or not, simplifying the life of baby-boom mothers. It was an appropriate outfit for the years of the Feminine Mystique, when all women were supposed to fit into the standard mold of Happy Housewife.

In *Seeing Through Clothes,* Anne Hollander points out that the human body as portrayed in painting and sculpture changes its shape to fit the fashions of the time; that "all nudes in art since modern fashion began are wearing the ghosts of absent clothes—sometimes highly visible ghosts." Photography, rather than liberating our perception of the body, has helped to tie it closer to fashion. Through a biased choice of models and poses it seems to offer scientific proof that we are—or ought to be—the right shape for contemporary clothes. When posing for photographs, late-Victorian nudes protruded their behinds like bustles; twenties' nudes adopted a debutante slouch and nudes of the forties tucked in their tummies and hips and stuck out their chests to produce the flat-bottomed, melon-breasted figure then considered most desirable.

Human anatomy does not always conform to current fashion; but then, fortunately, neither does erotic taste. As a result, women with flat bottoms and men with full beards, or whatever physical idiosyncrasy is out of favor at the moment, can usually find someone for whom they represent perfect beauty.

Theda Bara, the original vamp, photographed in 1917. Her hypnotic, kohl-rimmed stare was said to drive men to madness. The slippery, shiny material of her costume and her heavy, barbaric-looking jewelry are standard attributes of the exotic seductress, even today.

EROTIC STYLES: THE VAMP AND THE PEACOCK

In different eras different styles of self-presentation as well as different body types are considered sexy. Here there is more overlap, and it is probably true to say that few psychological types ever go completely out of erotic fashion. The heavy-eyed, fleshly sensuous vamp of the 1920s can still be seen at artistic events, draped in a contemporary version of her classic fringed silks and ropes of beads. The busty blonde of the 1950s in her towering platinum wig has become a country music star; the baby doll of the 1960s pouts and cuddles in the privacy of many bedrooms.

Though styles of erotic appeal persist, over the years some of them have altered their significance, since the language of dress, like the spoken language, contains terms whose meaning changes with time. The words "naughty" and "mischievous," which once indicated the blackest thoughts and deeds, now suggest endearingly childish misbehavior; and today heavy eye make-up is no longer the sign of the man-eating tigress but that of the flirtatious teenager. Similar evolutionary changes have occurred in the sartorial equivalent of forbidden words: the skintight sweater, the shirt open to the navel.

Sometimes a style persists but is worn by different sorts of people. In the 1900s, for instance, evening fashions for unmarried girls were sharply distinguished from fashions for matrons and spinsters. A "girl," who might be thirty, wore delicate fabrics and pale colors, often white. A woman wore heavier and richer materials, usually in more brilliant or darker shades, often black. The unmarried girl who appeared in an evening dress such as her mother might wear with perfect propriety—a low-cut, jet-trimmed, ruby-red or emerald-green satin, for instance—was considered either very fast or very badly brought up. Today the signals have been reversed. Well-bred girls go dancing in revealing costumes of neon red, orange and green. Their mothers, on the other hand, wear modestly cut party clothes in the same limited range of colors they favor for day: brown, tan, black, white and pale or navy blue. One possible reason for this change is that there has been a shift in sexual morality. Aristocratic Edwardians, though they paid lip service to virtue and demanded virginity before marriage, condoned a discreet promiscuity afterwards. Today well-born young women, like the female young of some Polynesian tribes, are tacitly allowed to sleep around and even live around a bit before marriage. After the wedding, however, they are expected to behave themselves or get out.

The fashionable male type also changes from one era to the next, though not all men change with it. Prudence Glynn suggests that male clothing promotes either "sexual allure or the territorial prerogative—the offer of the safe nest, [d]epending on the social climate." In 1900 territorial rights were dominant:

What those frock coats and morning coats and snug overcoats
said to women was that the men who wore them were . . . able
to provide a well-appointed nest in which the females and
young could be tucked up safely. Trespassers entered upon the
hearts and laurel shrubberies of these men at their peril.

The same message is presumably conveyed by the Man in
the Gray Flannel Suit of the 1950s and his more recent
avatars. In the 1920s, and again in the 1960s, fewer eggs
were being hatched, and women consequently felt less need
for nests. They therefore began to favor a more dashing and
colorful sort of fellow, causing a revolution in male dress
and grooming. But though there may be more or fewer pea-
cocks and nesting roosters around, both are fairly common,
and the woman who is looking out for either type can usually find it.

ALIENS, NOBS AND PROLES

The idea that people from other parts of the world are sexier
has a long history, and though there is no objective evidence
to support this belief, it has caused many pleasant surprises
for foreign visitors. Which foreigners are considered sexier
depends on the individual, and also to some extent on the
era. In the 1920s, many North American and British women
dreamed of being carried away by a sheik, often personified
as the film star Rudolph Valentino. Latin lovers of both
sexes were popular in the 1930s, and in the 1970s Asians,
especially those with an aura of mystical knowledge, made
a great many conquests. Since the supply of foreigners who
are in fashion at the time is usually not large enough to go
around, ordinary natives of Britain and North America
sometimes add to their sexual charm by wearing the appropriate exotic garments: in the 1970s Nehru shirts, ivory and
brass beads and sandals of water-buffalo hide. In the fantasies of some observers, such outfits implied, even promised,
exotic and holy erotic transports of the sort described in the
Kama Sutra.

Not everyone, of course, finds the currently popular
type attractive. Fortunately there is always a range of stereo-

types to choose from; indeed, a single foreign country may provide more than one. A woman can get herself up in a black Oriental silk kimono embroidered with gold dragons to look like the Dragon Lady; or she can wear a pink-flowered kimono and stick knitting needles through her hair to suggest that she will be as subservient and eager to please as a geisha. Sometimes there is a localization of erotic appeal nearer home, so that, for instance, the New Yorker or Londoner may wear rough northern hiking clothes to project a hearty outdoor sexuality, while the genuine woodsman or woodswoman assumes a dark, elegant suit to tell others that he or she prefers a sophisticated erotic experience.

Another common delusion is that members of the other classes are more highly sexed. Those who have not grown up among them often seem to believe that the rich and well-born are always at it, and feel erotic agitation at the sight of a sable coat or the label of an expensive tailor. Others think that the working class is more natural, more sensual and more passionate. This latter belief has often been reflected in fashion, and is probably responsible in part for the popularity of carpenters' overalls, auto mechanics' jump suits and fishermen's jerseys—just as it is for the thrill felt by some refined persons when they hear direct and ungrammatical speech on erotic topics. There are even people who feel that work clothes are more attractive when they are rumpled and stained, becoming the sartorial equivalent of dirty language.

Sometimes the thrill of the exotic and the thrill of the proletarian are combined, resulting in an outbreak of Greek fishermen's shirts, Italian policemen's capes, French sailor blouses and Argentine gaucho pants. A few years ago there was a fashion among women (and some men) for what might be called Hot-Climate Work Clothing: pale, baggy cheesecloth or homespun cotton pants fastened round the waist with a drawstring, together with layers of shirts and vests and jackets of the same materials. Worn alone, or with jeans, these clothes suggested hard labor in a practical and/ or humanitarian cause. More often, however, the peasant effect was canceled by elegant thin-strapped high-heeled sandals, thin pale scarves and glittery gold chains and ban-

Rudolph Valentino in The Sheik *(1921). His costume, though technically inauthentic, is a compendium of macho gear: sword, dagger, cartridge belt (but, oddly enough, no rifle), open-necked shirt, immense cape and high, chain-trimmed leather boots.*

gles. The resulting costume did not seem to indicate an interest in planting beans or baking bread, but rather a playful identification with the Near East. Though most of these clothes were made in India, the style was usually referred to as "the harem look." It suggested an acquiescent, nonliberated sexuality and, as in the 1920s, a welcoming attitude toward sheiks. It was especially popular in London, which at the time was being invaded by wealthy Arabs.

LOVE AND DEATH:
THE INVALID AND THE SPECTER

One of the most persistent specialized forms of erotic appeal is that which connects love and death, sometimes so closely that only what is damaged or dangerous can arouse the passions. In the Romantic period of the late eighteenth and early nineteenth century, the sexual instinct and the death wish were often intertwined. Not only were frailty and delicacy admired; for many Romantics actual illness was sexually exciting. The favored disease was pulmonary tuberculosis, the high fever of which brought a hectic flush to the cheeks and brightness to the eyes, mimicking sexual arousal; it was also believed to produce an unearthly and feverish sensuality in both sexes.

The thin white muslin dresses of the time encouraged respiratory infections and also imitated the invalid's nightgown—or, as some contemporary writers pointed out, the corpse's burial garments. The *Ladies' Monthly Museum* of June 1802 speaks of "the close, all white shroud-looking, ghostly chemise undress of the ladies, who seem to glide like spectres, with their shrouds wrapt tight about their forms." So provocative was this costume that the heroines of Gothic romance have ever since worn some version of it, usually in the form of a nightdress. Semiotically this is a very appropriate choice, since like the Gothic thriller it combines the erotic appeal of innocence and death.

For the Victorians death was so interesting that not only the dying but the bereaved were felt to be sexually charged. A widow, especially a young one, was assumed to be in a state of heightened emotionality that made it easy for her to be taken advantage of. Her supposed willingness to be "consoled"—to become a Merry Widow—was the subject of many low jokes. It may also have been one reason for the strict rules about mourning dress and behavior, which if not followed were a source of scandal and suspicion.

Even after life was over sexuality continued. Nineteenth-century literature and folklore is full of passionate ghosts who haunt their living lovers like Cathy in *Wuthering Heights* (1847), or arise from the tomb to clasp them in a clay-cold embrace as in the tales of Edgar Allan Poe. Often these wraiths wear the classic white shroud, sometimes stained with blood, creating an image that even today makes a long white gown patterned or trimmed with irregular splotches of red somewhat troubling.

DRACULA AND VAMPIRELLA

A more violent romantic revenant is the vampire, who returns from the grave not to haunt but to suck the blood of those he loves. The most famous of them, of course, is Dracula, the hero or villain of the novel of that name by Bram Stoker (1897). His continued popularity is deserved, for he combines the charms of the exotic, the aristocratic, illness, death and sexual ambiguity. He is a foreigner, a count and also a bisexual: though his favorite victims are innocent young women in nightdresses, he also preys upon young men. He characteristically wears full evening dress and a batlike black cape, and has rather long black hair. Dracula's attack is a symbolic rape, and if repeated destroys the rapee, who does not die but also turns into a vampire, one of "the undead." The legend thus gives dramatic expression to the nineteenth-century belief that illicit sexual love is not only debilitating but habit-forming, and literally a "fate worse than death."

More recently women's liberation, or some more sinister force, has produced Vampirella, a comic-book heroine whose costume is a kind of space-age female Dracula outfit, scanty and revealing. She has the traditional black hair, white face and unnaturally red lips, with the inspired addition of long red nails. So archetypically terrifying and thrilling are these figures that any black-haired, pale-complexioned man or woman who appears in all-black formal clothes projects a destructive eroticism, sometimes without conscious intention. Others, of course, may assume this costume as a deliberate sexual message. Today, for instance, the wearing of black leather garments is an accepted signal that you are "into" sadomasochism and interested in playing the part of master or slave either in harmless fantasy or dangerous reality.

THE WILDER SHORES OF LOVE

Several other minority sexual interests are well represented in costume. The nineteenth-century fascination with childhood, for example, has survived into the twentieth century. Respectable Victorians sentimentalized over the charms of children, especially little girls; less respectable ones, as Stephen Marcus informs us in *The Other Victorians,* went out and bought them. Today childishness in dress is out of fashion, but children are still the focus of sexual interest for a small and necessarily secretive minority, and there is a larger minority who like to imagine themselves or their lovers as children. Such interests are probably responsible for some of the more infantile fashions one sees, especially in nightwear. Even a naturally proper style, like the shepherdess or "Laura Ashley" Look still popular in Britain, occasionally plays on this interest. A recent addition to this costume is a lace-edged petticoat that is deliberately allowed to hang down several inches below the skirt; besides making consumption conspicuous, it imitates the half-conscious seductiveness of the little girl who doesn't know that her pretty white underwear is showing.

In the past only that minority of homosexuals who wanted to resemble members of the opposite sex were easily identifiable. Most straights therefore believed that all gay men wore markedly feminine styles and all gay women dressed in men's wear. Today, when they are out of the

Although women in male clothes usually look like gentlemen, men who wear women's clothes, unless they are genuine transsexuals, seem to imitate the most vulgar and unattractive sort of female dress, as if in a spirit of deliberate and hostile parody. Photograph by Coreen Simpson, 1980.

The male transsexual feels himself to be a woman in a man's body; he finds dressing in female costume psychologically satisfying rather than erotically thrilling, and usually prefers the sort of clothes a woman of his own age and social position would choose. From Attitude, *a book of gay paper dolls by Tom Tierney, 1979.*

closet, it is apparent that most homosexuals dress like everyone else, at least when in mixed society. Many gay men, in fact, have now adopted the "macho look," and to the casual observer seem more masculine than most heterosexuals. They wear work clothes (especially when not at work): plaid shirts, jeans, athletic shirts, coveralls and heavy work shoes; they also favor Western gear, particularly cowboy hats and boots. To complete the image, they often grow large bushy mustaches and exercise for hours in the gym to develop their muscles.

In order to facilitate an active and diverse erotic life, many gays employ a sartorial signal system. As Hal Fischer has pointed out, those who wish to play an active or masculine role wear a bunch of keys or a single earring or a bandanna in their back pocket on the left side; those who prefer to play a passive or feminine role wear one or more of these indicators on the right. If they are "into leather" (sadomasochism) the same signals apply, but the activities they invite are somewhat different.

There are of course some men, both homosexual and heterosexual, who deliberately dress in women's clothes. Peter Ackroyd has distinguished three types, each of which has a characteristic costume. First, there are the transsexuals, who feel themselves to be women in men's bodies. For them dressing as a woman is psychologically satisfying rather than exciting, and they usually wear the sort of clothes that a respectable woman of their own age and station would normally wear. Second, and far more common, are the transvestites, most of whom are heterosexual and often married. For them the wearing of female clothing is sexually thrilling, and the outfits they choose are often exaggeratedly female and erotic in an old-fashioned, unliberated way. To the keen observer, however, as Ackroyd points out, the transvestite does not really look feminine, since usually "he will, unconsciously or surreptitiously, leave clues to his male gender. . . . A transvestite never forgets—and never allows us to forget—that he is a man in women's clothes." Finally, there are the professionals or amateurs who dress in drag, and are usually homosexual. As Ackroyd says, the drag queen "parodies and mocks women." The typical drag costume is at best a clever caricature of media-stylized female appeal, and at worst a cruel travesty of female ugliness.

Lesbians, most of the time, are indistinguishable from other women, though since today they are usually strong feminists they tend to use little or no make-up and to favor pants and comfortable shoes. A few, however, have adopted extremely short haircuts and prefer to wear men's rather than women's shirts and jackets and coats. Though there are occasional female transsexuals, female transvestites are rare; as Ackroyd remarks, "male clothing has no 'erotic value' because of its ready availability for women within our culture." A male impersonator or "drag king" is almost unheard of today, though in the late-Victorian era, when women were still forbidden by custom to wear male dress, they were common on the stage. Interestingly enough, women who wear men's clothes usually dress like gentlemen, or even like aristocrats, whereas men who dress in women's clothes, unless they are transsexuals, seldom look like ladies.

Beyond these recognized minority styles of erotic appeal there are many more that have attracted only a very limited audience. Probably there is no garment ever worn that has not figured in the sexual life of someone, somewhere. In Britain today, for instance, there is a society devoted to the wearing of rubber rainwear of the sort associated with A. A. Milne's John, who as you may recall had

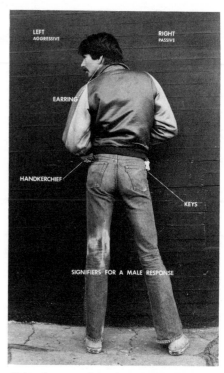

Urban homosexuals in America have evolved a dress code that informs possible sexual partners of their erotic preferences. Photograph from Gay Semiotics, *by Hal Fischer.*

Edible underwear, made in several fruit flavors and recommended by the manufacturer as "perfect for Pool and Spa Parties, Roadside Picnics, Quickie Lunches, TV Dinners, Bed-Time Snacks." The tie strings can also be eaten.

great big waterproof boots on, a great big waterproof hat, and a great big waterproof mackintosh. For those who are interested, great big waterproof jerseys, pants, gloves, capes and face masks are also available.

In the larger British and North American cities many other peculiar sorts of clothing designed to encourage a diversity of erotic experiences are for sale. For example, it is possible to buy edible underwear, marketed under the name of Candy's Bikini and Candypants and available in strawberry, raspberry, orange, lemon and lime; there is also a liquorice-flavored bra named Teacups. If clothes were words, these would be like talking with your mouth full.

Some readers of this book will feel a certain sticky discomfort at the thought of wearing such garments, or the others described here. They may recall Thoreau's advice that we should distrust any enterprise that requires new clothes. Indeed, whenever a new garment comes into our lives by purchase, gift or barter, it is worth asking what we, or its donor, intend this garment to say about us that cannot be said by the clothes we already own. A similar question might be asked about the clothes we throw away. But thinking seriously about what we wear is like thinking seriously about what we say: it can only be done occasionally or we should find ourselves tongue-tied, unable to get dressed at all.

More generally, the idea that even when we say nothing our clothes are talking noisily to everyone who sees us, telling them who we are, where we come from, what we like to do in bed and a dozen other intimate things, may be unsettling. To wear what "everyone else" is wearing is no solution to the problem, any more than it would be to say what everyone else is saying. We all know people who try to do this; but even if their imitation of "everyone" is successful, their clothes do not shut up; rather they broadcast without stopping the information that this is a timid and conventional man or woman, and possibly an untrustworthy one. We can lie in the language of dress, or try to tell the truth; but unless we are naked and bald it is impossible to be silent.

Source Notes

CHAPTER I: Clothing as a Sign System

PAGE:

10   "Always wear gloves . . .": Emily Post, *Etiquette* (1945), p. 459.

14   "The tendency of fat . . .": Emily Post, *Etiquette* (1922), p. 593.

16   "Identification with . . .": Ted Polhemus and Lynn Proctor, *Fashion & Anti-Fashion*, p. 20.

19   "Complete forgetfulness was needed . . .": Anthony Powell, *Faces in My Time*, p. 98.

19   "until quite recently . . .": James Laver, *Modesty in Dress*, p. 57.

20   "survived into modern times . . .": Laver, *Ibid.*, p. 63.

28   "Garments intended to deflect . . .": Rachel H. Kemper, *Costume*, p. 9.

29   "Paint, ornament, and rudimentary clothing . . .": Kemper, *Ibid.*

32   "they'd just as soon rest . . .": Enid Nemy, "New Yorkers, etc.," *New York Times,* July 23, 1980; Section 1, p. 20.

35   ". . . our attitude towards clothes . . .": J. C. Flügel, *The Psychology of Clothes*, pp. 20–21.

36   "refused to wear any clothes . . .": *New York Times,* January 11, 1981; Section 1, p. 6.

CHAPTER II: Youth and Age

PAGE:

37   Children's clothes: Phillis Cunnington and Anne Buck, *Children's Costume in England, 1300–1900*, pp. 122–24, 141–42.

CHAPTER III: Fashion and Time

PAGE:

60   "changes in fundamental modes . . .": George Bush and Perry London, "On the Disappearance of Knickers: Hypotheses for the Functional Analysis of the Psychology of Clothing," *Journal of Social Psychology,* Vol. 51 (May 1960), pp. 359–66.

64   "the more closely a woman's shoulders . . .": Madge Garland, *The Changing Form of Fashion*, p. 18.

65   "For the first fifty years . . .": Geoffrey Squire, *Dress and Society 1560–1970*, p. 153.

66   Beards and mustaches: Gerald Carson, *The Polite Americans*, p. 132.

68   ". . . the full beard is the most natural . . .": From *The Illustrated Book of Manners*, quoted in Richard Corson, *Fashions in Hair*, p. 135.

CHAPTER IV: Fashion and Place

PAGE:

85   The dress of Hasidic males: Solomon Poll, "The Hasidic Community," in Mary Ellen Roach and Joanne Bubolz

PAGE:

Eicher, eds., *Dress, Adornment, and the Social Order,* pp. 142–57.

95   "In the grand salon . . .": Tom Wolfe, Introduction to René Konig, *The Restless Image,* p. 15.

98   Black costume: Jack Schwartz, "Men's Clothing and the Negro," in Roach and Eicher, *op. cit.,* pp. 164–74.

99   "He was choked up tight . . .": "Honky-Tonk Bud," quoted in *The Life: The Lore and Folk Poetry of the Black Hustler,* Dennis Wepman, Ronald B. Newman, and Murray B. Binderman, eds., p. 62.

99   It takes money: Schwartz, *op. cit.,* p. 170.

CHAPTER V: Fashion and Status

PAGE:

115   "Man from the earliest times . . .": Lawrence Langner, *The Importance of Wearing Clothes,* p. 12.

116   "utter detestation . . .": Gerald Carson, *The Polite Americans,* pp. 12–13.

116   "It is . . . unfortunately . . .": Henrietta Ward, *Sensible Etiquette of the Best Society,* pp. 251–53.

118   "An honest heart . . .": Lillian Eichler, *Book of Etiquette,* Vol. II, p. 147.

118   "In real life . . .": Anne Hollander, *Seeing Through Clothes,* p. 443.

119   "were as proud of their girth . . .": Robert Brain, *The Decorated Body,* p. 99.

121   "In the world of good society . . .": Lillian Eichler, *op. cit.,* p. 154.

130   The costume of the upper-class British male: I am indebted to Roland Gant and Nigel Hollis for this information.

134   "shows the family out of doors . . .": Anne Hollander, *op. cit.,* pp. 38–39.

141   "uncoordinated, bandy-legged . . .": John Berger, *Looking,* p. 12.

142   In a movie, . . . an inch of ribbon, etc.: Dale McConathy with Diana Vreeland, *Hollywood Costume: Glamour! Glitter! Romance!,* p. 28.

143   "transforming rayon into silk . . .": Roland Barthes, "The Diseases of Costume," *Partisan Review* (October 1967).

143   The Hollywood producers, however: McConathy, *op. cit.,* pp. 117–19.

149   "the most English of sports . . .": Quentin Bell, *On Human Finery,* p. 43.

CHAPTER VI: Fashion and Opinion

PAGE:

169   "long hair connotes . . .": William Thourlby, *You Are What You Wear: The Key to Business Success,* pp. 107, 112.

174   "Beards are like sunglasses . . .": Thourlby, *Ibid.,* p. 112.

CHAPTER VII: Color and Pattern

PAGE:
186   "wants one marvellous . . .": Prudence Glynn, *In Fashion*, p. 91.
190   ". . . 'emotional' black . . .": Anne Hollander, *Seeing through Clothes*, pp. 377–80.
192   "The diabolic character . . .": *Ibid*., p. 376.
196   "The active side . . .": Johann Wolfgang von Goethe, *Theory of Colours*, para. 775.
198   "a blue surface . . .": *Ibid.,* paras. 780–81.

CHAPTER VIII: Male and Female

PAGE:
213   "almost suffocating.": Kenneth Clark, *The Nude*, p. 220.
214   Alternatively, these designs may symbolize their wearers: Jean Umiker-Sebeok, "Nature's Way? Visual Images of Childhood in American Culture," in *Semiotics of Culture,* ed. Irene Portis Winner and Jean Umiker-Sebeok, 1979.
221   "The substantial reason for . . .": Thorstein Veblen, *The Theory of the Leisure Class,* p. 172.
229   "By their height . . .": Prudence Glynn, *In Fashion,* p. 53.

CHAPTER IX: Fashion and Sex

PAGE:
231   "the elegantly turned-out prostitute . . .": Rachel H. Kemper, *Costume,* p. 12.
236   "[Manufacturers] tend to appeal . . .": Robert Brain, *The Decorated Body,* p. 45.
244   "With the advent of the New Woman . . .": James Laver, *Modesty in Dress,* p. 122.
244   "symbolically castrated . . .": *Ibid.,* p. 124.
251   "swelling and coloration. . .": Robert Brain, *op. cit.* p. 143.
252   "all nudes in art . . .": Anne Hollander, *Seeing Through Clothes,* pp. 85–86.
254   "What those frock coats . . .": Prudence Glynn, *In Fashion,* p. 132.
256   "the close, all white . . .": quoted in Elizabeth Ewing, *Dress and Undress,* p. 52.
259   Many gays employ a sartorial signal system: Hal Fischer, *Gay Semiotics,* 1977.
260   "he will, unconsciously . . .": Peter Ackroyd, *Dressing Up,* pp. 19–20.
260   "parodies and mocks . . .": *Ibid.,* p. 14.
260   "male clothing has no . . .": *Ibid.,* p. 41.

Selected Bibliography

Ackroyd, Peter. *Dressing Up: Transvestism and Drag: The History of an Obsession.* New York: Simon and Schuster, 1979.

Bell, Quentin. *On Human Finery.* New York, Schocken Books, 1976.

Berger, John. *Looking.* New York, Random House, 1979.

Brain, Robert. *The Decorated Body.* New York, Harper & Row, 1979.

Carson, Gerald. *The Polite Americans.* New York, Morrow, 1966.

Carter, Ernestine. *The Changing World of Fashion.* New York, Putnam's, 1977.

Clark, Kenneth. *The Nude: A Study in Ideal Form.* New York, Pantheon, 1956.

Cooper, Wendy. *Hair: Sex, Society, Symbolism.* New York, Stein and Day, 1971.

Corson, Richard. *Fashions in Hair.* New York, Hastings House, 1965.

Cunnington, C. Willet, and Cunnington, Phillis. *Handbook of English Costume in the Nineteenth Century.* Boston, Plays, Inc., 1970.

Cunnington, Phillis, and Buck, Anne. *Children's Costume in England, 1300–1900.* New York, Barnes & Noble, 1965.

Ewing, Elizabeth. *Dress and Undress: A History of Women's Underwear.* New York, Drama Book Specialists, 1978.

Fischer, Hal. *Gay Semiotics: A Photographic Study of Visual Coding Among Homosexual Men.* San Francisco, NFS Press, 1977.

Flügel, J. C. *The Psychology of Clothes.* New York, International Universities Press, 1966.

Garland, Madge. *The Changing Form of Fashion.* New York, Praeger, 1970.

Glynn, Prudence. *In Fashion: Dress in the Twentieth Century.* London and New York, Oxford University Press, 1978.

Goethe, Johann Wolfgang von. *Theory of Colours.* London, John Murray, 1840.

Green, Ruth M. *The Wearing of Costume.* London, Pitman, 1966.

Hesketh, Christian. *Tartans.* New York, Putnam, 1961.

Hollander, Anne. *Seeing Through Clothes.* New York, Viking, 1978.

Kemper, Rachel H. *Costume.* New York, Newsweek Books, 1977.

Konig, René. *À la Mode: On the Social Psychology of Fashion.* New York, Seabury Press, 1973.

Langner, Lawrence. *The Importance of Wearing Clothes.* New York, Hastings House, 1959.

Laver, James. *Clothes.* New York, Horizon Press, 1932.

———. *The Concise History of Costume and Fashion.* New York, Abrams, 1969.

———. *Costume.* New York, Hawthorne Books, 1963.

———. *Modesty in Dress.* Boston, Houghton Mifflin, 1969.

———. *Style in Costume.* London and New York, Oxford University Press, 1949.

———. *Taste and Fashion, from the French Revolution to the Present Day.* London, G. G. Harrap, 1945.

McConathy, Dale, with Vreeland, Diana. *Hollywood Costume: Glamour! Glitter! Romance!* New York, Abrams, 1976.

Molloy, John T. *Dress for Success.* New York, P. H. Wyden, 1975.

————. *The Woman's Dress for Success Book.* Chicago, Follet, 1977.

Pike, Martha V., and Armstrong, Janice Gray, eds. *A Time to Mourn: Expressions of Grief in Nineteenth-Century America.* Stony Brook, N. Y., The Museums at Stony Brook, 1980.

Polhemus, Ted, and Proctor, Lynn. *Fashion & Anti-Fashion: An Anthropology of Clothing and Adornment.* London, Thames and Hudson, 1978.

Roach, Mary Ellen, and Eicher, Joanne Bubolz, eds. *Dress, Adornment, and the Social Order.* New York, Wiley, 1965.

————. *The Visible Self: Perspectives on Dress.* Englewood Cliffs, N. J., Prentice Hall, 1973.

Rudofsky, Bernard. *Are Clothes Modern? An Essay on Contemporary Apparel.* Chicago, P. Theobald, 1947.

————. *The Unfashionable Human Body.* Garden City, N. Y., Doubleday, 1971.

Squire, Geoffrey. *Dress and Society 1560–1970.* New York, Viking, 1974.

Thourlby, William. *You Are What You Wear: The Key to Business Success.* Kansas City, Kansas, Sheed, Andrews, and McMeel, 1978.

Umiker-Sebeok, Jean. "Nature's Way? Visual Images of Childhood in American Culture," in *Semiotics of Culture,* ed. Irene Portis Winner and Jean Umiker-Sebeok, The Hague, 1979.

Veblen, Thorstein. *The Theory of the Leisure Class.* New York, Macmillan, 1912.

Wilcox, R. Turner. *The Mode in Costume.* New York, Scribners, 1958.

Yarwood, Doreen. *The Encyclopaedia of World Costume.* New York, Scribners, 1978.

Illustration Credits

When credit is not given, the illustration is either privately owned or the photographer is unknown.

Frontispiece. Drawing by W. Miller, © 1978, The New Yorker Magazine, Inc. May 22, 1978.

PAGE:

tion of the Costume Institute Library of the Metropolitan Museum of Art.

47   Photograph courtesy Teenform, Inc.

48   "My darling Imogen. I haven't seen you in fifty years!" Photograph by Donna Deitch of Imogen Cunningham and Mrs. Krassner, 1977.

49   Photograph by John Myers, 1975.

50   Still from *It Happened One Night,* 1934. Photograph © 1980 by Columbia Pictures Industries, Inc. Courtesy Columbia Pictures Corporation.

57   Photograph courtesy of The Theatre and Music Collection, Museum of the City of New York.

CHAPTER III: Fashion and Time

PAGE:

61   Mary Darly, *Comic Prints of Characters,* London, 1776. Courtesy of The Print Collection, Art, Prints and Photograph Division, The New York Public Library, Astor, Lenox and Tilden Foundations

63   Benjamin West, *The Hope Family of Sydenham, Kent.* 1802. The Museum of Fine Arts, Boston, Abbot Lawrence Fund.

64   Song sheet cover, "The Queen and Prince Albert's Polka." 1840. Photograph © BBC Hulton Picture Library, London.

67   Photograph by J. J. Mayall, 1861. © BBC Hulton Picture Library, London.

69   "The Cocroft children in the trees." Photograph by E. Alice Austen, 1886. The Staten Island Historical Society.

70   Charles Dana Gibson, *Sketches and Cartoons,* 1898.

71   Photograph by Barraud, 1888. The National Portrait Gallery, London.

72   Photograph by Frances Benjamin Johnston, 1904. Courtesy The Library of Congress, Washington, D.C.

74   Photograph © BBC Hulton Picture Library, London.

76   John Held, Jr. *Life* magazine cover, 1926. The Granger Collection.

77   Wide World Photos, Inc.

79   *Mother and Child, San Francisco,* 1952. Dorothea Lange. Photograph Collection, The Museum of Modern Art, New York. Reproduced by permission of The Oakland Museum.

82   Photograph by Frances Benjamin Johnston, 1909. The Library of Congress, Washington, D.C.

CHAPTER IV: Fashion and Place

PAGE:

85   Williamsburg, Brooklyn. Photograph by Bernard Hermann, 1975.

87   Photograph reproduced courtesy of the United Nations.

88   Anthony Van Dyck, *James Stuart, Duke of Richmond and Lennox.*

PAGE:

132.   Anthony Van Dyck, *James, Seventh Earl of Derby, His Lady and Child,* c. 1632–41. © The Frick Collection, New York.

137, 140   Photographs by Sir Benjamin Stone. Reproduced by permission of The Sir Benjamin Stone Collection, Birmingham Public Libraries, England.

142   Still from *Lady in the Dark,* 1944. Copyright © by Universal Pictures, A Division of Universal City Studios, Inc. Courtesy of MCA Publishing, A Division of MCA, Inc.

145   Brown Brothers.

151   Edward Hopper, magazine cover for *Hotel Management,* March 1925.

CHAPTER VI: Fashion and Opinion

PAGE:

155   Drawing by Jackson, May 31, 1950. Courtesy of *Punch.*

158   Photograph by Bill Owens, 1972. Magnum Photos, Inc.

160   Photograph by Michael Evans, 1981. Courtesy of The White House, Washington, D.C.

161   Photograph by Thomas Victor.

164   Photograph by Burk Uzzle. © 1967 Magnum Photos, Inc.

165   Nathaniel Elliot Worthington III, a poster. Reproduced courtesy Punch Posters.

167   Posy Simmonds, *Mrs. Weber's Diary* © 1979 by Posy Simmonds. Courtesy of Jonathan Cape Ltd.

169   Paul McCartney, Ringo Starr, George Harrison and John Lennon. The Granger Collection.

170   Ambrose Burnside. The Library of Congress, Washington, D.C.

171   Matthew Arnold. © The BBC Hulton Picture Library, London.

172   Major General Ulysses S. Grant. Etching from *Harper's Weekly,* 1863.

173   Charles Dickens. © The BBC Hulton Picture Library, London.

174   Walt Whitman. Photograph by Mathew Brady. The Library of Congress, Washington, D.C.

175   Benjamin Disraeli. © The BBC Hulton Picture Library, London.

180   Photograph of Larry Hagman © 1981, CBS, Inc. Reprinted by permission of CBS, Inc., Lippin & Grant and Larry Hagman.

CHAPTER VII: Color and Pattern

PAGE:

185   World Wide Photos, Inc.

186   William L. Windus, *Too Late,* 1858. The Tate Gallery, London.

188   Photograph by Don Snyder

191   *Harper's Bazar,* August 31, 1895. Photograph by Geoffrey Clements made possible by the cooperation of the Costume Institute Library of the Metropolitan Museum of Art.